EDW

'A judicious assessment of the character and reign of a king who remains to this day a controversial figure – the Bill Clinton of his times'

Anthony Pollard, *University of Teesside*

The reign of King Edward IV occupies a pivotal place in late medieval English history, marking the transition from a medieval to a renaissance monarchy. The personality of the young monarch was undoubtedly a factor in this transition, yet there has been much controversy over the king's character. Was Edward a vain and self-indulgent playboy, more interested in his own pleasures than the well-being of his kingdom, or was his life cut tragically short, thus preventing him from fully establishing the 'new monarchy' now more commonly associated with his son-in-law, Henry VII?

A central personality in both historical study and literary fame, Edward IV is as fascinating a character now as he was for William Shakespeare over four centuries ago. This book seeks to provide an easily accessible, chronological introduction to the king's life, character and kingship, as well as to the historiographical issues that surround them.

Drawing together both recent research and original sources, Hannes Kleineke has written a concise and accessible biography, which is an invaluable read for all those interested in fifteenth-century history.

Hannes Kleineke is a Senior Research Fellow at the History of Parliament, and joint winner of the Parliamentary History Prize 2006. He has published widely on the political and social history of late medieval England, especially the Yorkist period.

ROUTLEDGE HISTORICAL BIOGRAPHIES

SERIES EDITOR: ROBERT PEARCE

Routledge Historical Biographies provide engaging, readable and academically credible biographies written from an explicitly historical perspective. These concise and accessible accounts will bring important historical figures to life for students and general readers alike.

In the same series:

Bismarck by Edgar Feuchtwanger
Gladstone by Michael Partridge
Emmeline Pankhurst by Paula Bartley
Henry VII by Sean Cunningham
Hitler by Martyn Housden
Lenin by Christopher Read
Louis XIV by Richard Wilkinson
Mao by Michael Lynch
Martin Luther by Michael Mullet
Martin Luther King Jr by Peter J. Ling
Mary Queen of Scots by Retha M. Warnicke
Mussolini by Peter Neville
Nehru by Ben Zachariah
Trotsky by Ian Thatcher
Mary Tudor by Judith M. Richards

Forthcoming:

Henry VIII by Lucy Wooding
Neville Chamberlain by Nick Smart

EDWARD IV

Hannes Kleineke

Routledge
Taylor & Francis Group

LONDON AND NEW YORK

First published 2009
by Routledge
2 Park Square, Milton Park, Abingdon, Oxon, OX14 4RN

Simultaneously published in the USA and Canada
by Routledge
270 Madison Ave, New York, NY 10016

Routledge is an imprint of the Taylor & Francis Group, an informa business

© 2009 Hannes Kleineke

Typeset in Garamond by Saxon Graphics Ltd, Derby
Printed and bound in Great Britain by TJ International Ltd, Padstow, Cornwall

British Library Cataloguing in Publication Data
A catalogue record for this book is available from the British Library

Library of Congress Cataloging in Publication Data
Kleineke, Hannes.
   Edward IV / Hannes Kleineke.
   p. cm. — (Routledge historical biographies)

1. Edward IV, King of England, 1442–1483. 2. Great Britain–History–Edward IV, 1461–1483. 3. Great Britain–Kings and rulers–Biography. I. Title.
   DA258.K54 2008
   942.04′4092–dc22
   [B]
                                                                    2008009165

ISBN10: 0-415-36799-9 (hbk)
         0-415-36800-6 (pbk)

ISBN13: 978-0-415-36799-8 (hbk)
         978-0-415-36800-1 (pbk)

CONTENTS

List of Plates

PLATES (BETWEEN PAGES 86 AND 87)

GENEALOGIES

ACKNOWLEDGEMENTS

No book is written in isolation, and it is only fair to acknowledge those who have directly or indirectly influenced this present volume. I have at various times discussed aspects of Edward IV's life and career with other scholars. Rowena E. Archer, Caroline Barron, Michael Bennett, Jim Bolton, Clive Burgess, Paul Cavill, Sean Cunningham, Elizabeth Danbury, Peter Fleming, David Grummitt, Maria Hayward, Stephanie Hovland, Adrian Jobson, Jessica Lutkin, Jonathan Mackman, Stephen Mileson, Charles Moreton, Stephen O'Connor, Simon Payling, Amanda Richardson, Anne Sutton and Livia Visser-Fuchs have all played their part in shaping my thinking. Michael Hicks and Tony Pollard in particular have long been extremely generous in sharing their knowledge of the Yorkist age. Tony and Robert Pearce read the entire book in manuscript and made valuable comments. Throughout the process of writing this book, Linda Clark has been unfailingly supportive and tolerant of my frequent preoccupation with questions at best indirectly connected with our work for the History of Parliament trust. Of two other debts, one is perhaps more obvious than the other. How much this book owes to the work of the late Charles Ross will be readily apparent to many readers. James Ross, in his turn, has on frequent convivial occasions been a congenial and knowledgeable sparring partner, who could always be relied upon to challenge anything I might say. Needless to say, any errors that remain are my own.

I am indebted to Eve Setch, and particularly Lizzie Clifford, of Routledge for their encouragement and their hard work in seeing the volume through the press. Thanks are also due to many of my non-historian friends for their tolerant interest in the project. In particular, Andrew Parish ensured by weekly requests for progress reports that I kept my eye on the ball in the latter stages of the project. Finally, throughout the writing of this book my parents have remained interested and highly supportive. It is to them that it is dedicated.

London, February 2008

1. LANCASTER AND YORK

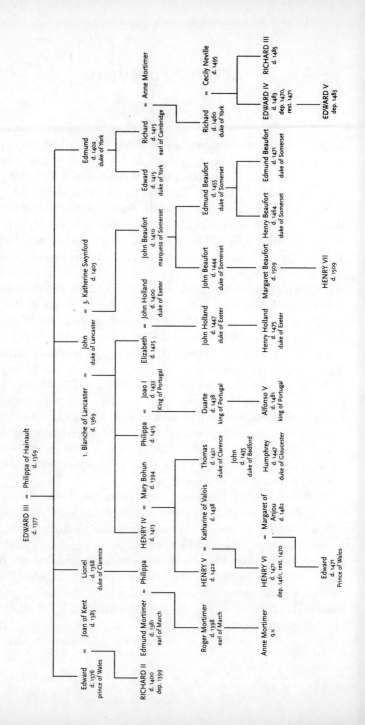

2. YORK AND NEVILLE

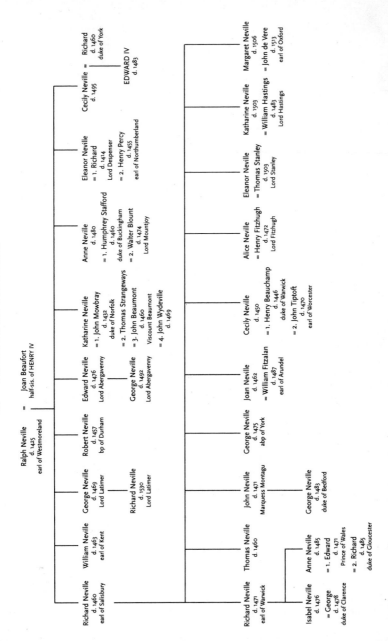

Ralph Neville = Joan Beaufort
d. 1425 half-sis. of HENRY IV
earl of Westmoreland

Richard Neville
d. 1460
earl of Salisbury

William Neville
d. 1463
earl of Kent

George Neville
d. 1469
Lord Latimer

Richard Neville
d. 1530
Lord Latimer

Robert Neville
d. 1457
bp of Durham

Edward Neville
d. 1476
Lord Abergavenny

George Neville
d. 1492
Lord Abergavenny

Katharine Neville
d. 1483
= 1. John Mowbray
d. 1432
duke of Norfolk
= 2. Thomas Strangeways
= 3. John Beaumont
d. 1460
Viscount Beaumont
= 4. John Wydeville
d. 1469

Anne Neville
d. 1480
= 1. Humphrey Stafford
d. 1460
duke of Buckingham
= 2. Walter Blount
d. 1474
Lord Mountjoy

Eleanor Neville
= 1. Richard
d. 1414
Lord Despenser
= 2. Henry Percy
d. 1455
earl of Northumberland

Cecily Neville = Richard
d. 1495   d. 1460
              duke of York

EDWARD IV
d. 1483

Thomas Neville
d. 1460

John Neville
d. 1471
Marquess Montagu

George Neville
d. 1483
duke of Bedford

Richard Neville
d. 1471
earl of Warwick

Isabel Neville
d. 1476
= George
d. 1478
duke of Clarence

Anne Neville
d. 1485
= 1. Edward
d. 1471
Prince of Wales
= 2. Richard
d. 1485
duke of Gloucester

George Neville
d. 1475
abp of York

Joan Neville
d. 1462
= William Fitzalan
d. 1487
earl of Arundel

Cecily Neville
d. 1450
= 1. Henry Beauchamp
d. 1446
duke of Warwick
= 2. John Tiptoft
d. 1470
earl of Worcester

Alice Neville
= Henry Fitzhugh
d. 1472
Lord Fitzhugh

Eleanor Neville
= Thomas Stanley
d. 1503
Lord Stanley

Katharine Neville
d. 1503
= William Hastings
d. 1483
Lord Hastings

Margaret Neville
d. 1506
= John de Vere
d. 1513
earl of Oxford

3. THE FAMILY OF EDWARD IV

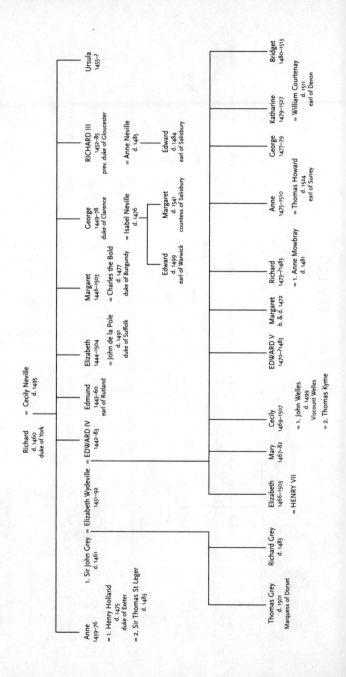

1

INTRODUCTION

EDWARD AND HIS HISTORIANS

The last kings of medieval England have, with few exceptions, found some difficulty in capturing the popular imagination. This has led at least one recent historian to describe several of them as 'enigmatic'.[1] Yet, to themselves and their contemporaries they did not represent an enigma; they are, to the casual modern observer (in Sellar and Yeatman's classic terms) quite simply not memorable. Pride of place among these 'unmemorable monarchs' must surely fall to Edward IV (1442–83): brother to Richard III whom William Shakespeare caricatured as the hunchback who murdered his nephews, and grandfather to Henry VIII, the overweight womaniser to whom he bequeathed many traits of his character, Edward himself is known to few. Mention of Edward's great edifice at St George's Chapel, Windsor, may elicit some glimmer of recognition, since successive royal weddings have popularised the building on national television, but the response to the king's name is most likely to be 'When was he, then?'. This is hardly a new state of affairs. The young Jane Austen recorded in her satirical *History of England* that Edward 'was famous only for his Beauty and his Courage, of which the Picture we have here given of him, and his undaunted Behaviour in marrying one Woman while he was engaged to another, are sufficient proofs'.[2] We may take some comfort from John Farman's pithy summary in his *Very*

Bloody History of Britain Without the Boring Bits, which judges that 'Edward, being the true heir to Richard II, became the new flavour of the month. He had a high old time in London; so much so, that he died in 1483 from sloth and over indulgence.'[3] At least, then, Edward was not boring. Nevertheless, recognition of his name was not helped by Shakespeare, who ignominiously split his reign between the third part of *King Henry VI* and the first acts of *Richard III*.

Historians, for their part, have taken some degree of interest in Edward IV, but their judgement has been, and remains, varied. The very range of different assessments has provided fertile ground for historiographical examination, such as the studies of Edward's reputation by Keith Dockray and, most recently, Michael Hicks, or similar work by Tony Pollard on Edward's queen, Elizabeth Wydeville.[4] Undeniably, the variety of judgements that have been passed on Edward's life and reign owe something to the complexity of the available source material, which is not only varied but scattered. The picture that emerges is thus, at the same time, varied in texture and in many facets contradictory. In some areas, a clear image of the king's character and actions seems to emerge; in others the picture is blurred and different sources contradict each other. As a result, for his contemporaries and his later historians alike, King Edward IV has presented something of a conundrum. Successive generations have found difficulty in reconciling their admiration for Edward's apparent success as a ruler with the flaws they detected all too clearly in his character and judgement.

The earliest accounts of Edward and his reign were penned within a short period of his death. In the summer of 1483 Dominic Mancini, an Italian visitor to England, probably sent there by the Archbishop of Vienne with a specific brief to produce a memorandum on the tense political situation, recorded what he heard about the king. He noted that Edward had 'ruled England with great renown', yet when he had first become king he had 'behaved for a while in all things too dissolutely' and, 'though not rapacious for other men's goods, he was yet so eager for money, that in pursuing it he acquired a reputation for avarice'.[5] While Mancini had no personal knowledge of Edward IV and his reign, a second contemporary account in the form of a continuation of the chronicle of Crowland Abbey in Lincolnshire, was apparently written by a senior clerical figure in the ranks of the Westminster bureaucracy who had met the king in person and witnessed many of the events he described. Although sympathetic to Edward, he was also candid about what he perceived as his principal shortcomings. He noted that Edward had been a 'most provident king', yet 'was thought to have indulged too intemperately his passions and desire for luxury' and had also in the final years of his reign 'exercised his office so haughtily ... that he appeared to be feared by all his subjects, while he himself feared no man'.[6]

Written from something more of a distance, but still based on first-hand narratives, were two accounts drawn up a generation later by the learned humanists Polydore Vergil, an Italian-born archdeacon of Wells, and Sir Thomas More. While neither of them had met the king, they had access to many who had served or at least known him. By their day, as More admitted, Edward's posthumous reputation had increased as a result of 'the cruelty, mischief and tempestuous world that followed', and this was reflected in the almost unequivocally positive judgement at which both More and Vergil arrived. There had, More maintained, never been 'any prince of this land attaining the crown by battle so heartily beloved by the substance of the people'. He had been

> a goodly personage and very princely to behold, of heart courageous, politic in counsel, in adversity nothing abashed, in prosperity rather joyful than proud, in peace just and merciful, in war sharp and fierce, in the field bold and hardy, and nevertheless no further than wisdom would, adventurous.

At his death in April 1483 he had left England

> in quiet and prosperous estate: no fear of outward enemies; no war in hand, nor none towards but such as no man looked for; the people towards the Prince, not in a constrained fear but in a willing and loving obedience; among themselves, the commons in good peace.[7]

It has rightly been noted that More's flattering assessment owed a great deal to his classical model, Tacitus's contrasting of the 'good' Augustus and the 'bad' Tiberius, which More sought to emulate in his comparison of Edward IV and Richard III even to the extent of partly paraphrasing Tacitus.[8] Nevertheless, Vergil's account agreed with him in many points. To Vergil, Edward had been

> of sharp wit, great courage, of exceptionally retentive memory touching those things which he had once learnt, diligent in conducting his business, prepared in times of trouble, stern and horrible to the enemy, bountiful to his friends and acquaintances, most fortunate in his wars. ... All internal division appeased, he left a most wealthy realm abounding in all things, which by reason of civil wars he had received almost utterly void as well of able men as of money.[9]

It Edward had a principal failing, both authors agreed, it was his abandonment 'to bodily lust' (Vergil), and 'fleshly wantonness', which had, however, diminished with age (More).[10]

Later Tudor chroniclers like Edward Hall, Raphael Holinshed and John Stow followed More's and Vergil's positive assessment of Edward's achievement, and through their chronicles it found its way into the plays of William Shakespeare, who did not, however, see fit to give Edward's name to one of his histories. It was not until the early eighteenth century that the French historian Paul de Rapin-Thoyras incorporated the rather more negative views of the biased Burgundian agent Philippe de Commynes into his altogether more critical account of the reign.[11] Equally critical was the assessment of the Scottish historian David Hume, who (although not as heavily influenced by Commynes as Rapin), in his 1761 *History of England*, declared Edward to have been 'of a temper well fitted to make his way through ... a scene of war, havoc and devastation', one of 'horror and bloodshed, savage matters, arbitrary executions, and treacherous, dishonourable conduct on all parties'. Edward, he wrote,

> was bold, active, enterprising; and his hardness of heart and severity of character rendered him impregnable to all those movements of compassion, which might relax his vigour in the prosecution of the most bloody revenge upon his enemies.

The Edward IV who emerged from the writings of Rapin and Hume was personally deeply flawed. He was lazy and debauched, intent primarily on his own comfort, avaricious and cruel, and spurred into energetic action only by an immediate crisis; in particular, Rapin-Thoyras deplored the king's 'Cruelty, Perjury and Incontinence',[12] while to Hume Edward's virtues were offset and negated by the flaws of his character. He had been more splendid and showy, than either prudent or virtuous; brave, though cruel; addicted to pleasure, though capable of activity in great emergencies; and less fitted to prevent ills by wise precautions, than to remedy them, after they took place, by vigour and enterprise.[13]

Hume's and Rapin's views were almost uncritically adopted by most of the medieval historians of the nineteenth century, primarily concerned with constitutional theories of parliamentary sovereignty, to which they saw all medieval history as a prologue. Above all, Bishop William Stubbs did much to blacken the king's character. He 'failed to discover any conspicuous merits' in it, and although he was prepared to allow Edward a reasonable level of education, personal courage and affability, a coherent foreign policy and some degree of willingness to enforce the law, he saw him as ultimately a fratricidal monster with a talent for extortion:

a man vicious far beyond anything that England had seen since the days of John; and more cruel and bloodthirsty than any king she had ever known. ... The death of Clarence was but the summing up and crowning act of an unparalleled list of judicial and extra-judicial cruelties which those of the next reign supplement but do not surpass.[14]

Something of a reassessment came only in the 1870s, when J.R. Green postulated that Edward had been the creator of a 'new monarchy'. Green believed that 'in his earliest years [Edward] showed little taste for the work of rule', but he maintained that in the second half of the reign the king 'was silently laying the foundations of an absolute rule. ... His pleasure-loving and self-indulgent temper needed the pressure of emergency, of actual danger, to flash out into action.' The resulting monarchy had been placed on sound foundations with the introduction of a new system of financial administration, but had above all sported the sinister features of an elaborate state-sponsored spy-system, the use of torture and direct royal interference with the administration of justice.[15]

It was, however, not until the early years of the twentieth century that the study of Edward and his reign was placed on what we might recognise as a modern footing – an extensive, even exhaustive, survey of the available sources, administrative as well as narrative, continental as well as English. Cora Scofield's two-volume study of the reign, first published in 1923, remains unmatched in its detail, and if subsequent writers have challenged some of her conclusions, they have nevertheless been forced to acknowledge her immense achievement. Building on Scofield's work, and studying the administrative records for the reign in ever greater detail, historians such as J.R. Lander, A.R. Myers and Bertram Wilkinson took Green's judgement a step further. To them, Edward had been a strong king who had rescued England from the turmoil of civil war, and had restored the institutions of government, in the process laying the foundations for the Tudor state. Their flattering view was qualified by K.B. McFarlane, who laid at least some of the blame for the ongoing civil war at Edward's door, for his failure 'to establish any presumption that order, justice and the rights of property would be maintained'.[16] Also rather more critical was Charles Ross, who in 1974, almost half a century after Scofield, produced a shorter, but nonetheless comprehensive, narrative of Edward's career and reign, which alongside the earlier work remains the standard account of the subject. To Ross, Edward's excessive self-belief was his fatal flaw, and was principally to blame for the downfall of his dynasty in the immediate aftermath of his death.[17]

The lasting value of the work of Scofield and Ross can hardly be better illustrated than by the lengths to which more recent authors have had to go to lend their accounts of the king a sheen of greater originality. Jonathan Hughes's effort to read Edward and his reign through the prism of alchemical and astrological belief, and to contextualise it within the Arthurian mythology of his day, is a useful attempt to ground a fifteenth-century monarch in the thought-world of his contemporaries. It does, however, suffer from a lack of concrete evidence for Edward's own beliefs and thoughts, and is not helped by over-readings of the evidence, such as the suggestion that the waspish Philippe de Commynes's complaints about Edward's increased effeminacy towards the end of his reign reflect the king's bisexual tendencies.[18] A similarly selective overemphasis is found in the work of a long line of apologists of Richard III who have pored endlessly over any available shred of evidence, however flimsy, biased or unreliable, of Edward's illegitimate birth or of a legal obstacle to his marriage to Elizabeth Wydeville, in an attempt to justify their hero's seizure of the throne. Thus, most recently Michael Jones, seeking to establish that Richard's title to the throne had credibility at least in his own mind, has once again dredged up the tale of the French archer (first fortuitously identified by no less a schemer than Louis XI of France) who claimed to have fathered Edward (the Duke of York being conveniently absent on campaign).[19] Perhaps rather more helpful is the extensive work that has been done over the past half century on the world in which Edward lived, the culture of his court, his book-collecting and his chivalric attitudes.[20] Our understanding of the king has also been considerably enhanced by a series of biographical studies, many of them of book-length, of a number of the key figures who surrounded him: his father and younger brothers, his queen, the 'Kingmaker' Earl of Warwick, and more recently even his short-lived eldest son and heir.[21]

Nevertheless, valid questions over Edward IV's place in English history remain, and in 1995, perhaps not surprisingly in an age when popular political debate seemed obsessed with the private morals of public figures, Keith Dockray succinctly summed the question up as 'Edward IV – playboy or politician?'[22] As yet, no answer has met with universal agreement, and Edward's place in English history remains as controversial as ever. Seen through the eyes of Christine Carpenter's 'new constitutionalism', Edward is once more the model monarch: after an uncertain start, he evolved to become

> one of the greatest of English kings. Taking the throne in an almost impossible situation, that remained acute for a decade, he was able to rescue the monarchy and landed society from what can best be described as a shambles and leave his dynasty securely settled on the throne.[23]

For almost three months, it is tempting to add. Nevertheless, Carpenter's overall positive assessment of Edward's achievement is at least in part shared by Michael Hicks, whose recent survey of the evolution of Edward's reputation followed on from the author's book-length biographical studies of the principal actors of the Yorkist age: Edward's two brothers, his mentor Warwick, his son and heir, and latterly also his younger brother's wife, Warwick's daughter. Hicks's balanced discussion finds Edward a king who 'insisted on his dignity and respect', an effective ruler who was willing and able to delegate responsibilities where appropriate; but also a human being driven by emotion, 'inconsistent, unscrupulous and not altogether honest', lacking in foresight and understanding of other men's motives. 'If not himself a great king,' Hicks concludes, 'Edward was mightily effective and paved the way for more authoritative government in the future. A good king, nevertheless he could do better.'[24] Others, however, continue to be rather more critical. In Anthony Pollard's view, Edward's undeniable successes on the battlefield and his domestic achievements in stabilising the crown's finances were outweighed by his misjudgements, his lack of consistency and sustained interest in the rule of his realm, and his failure to comprehend the consequences of his actions. By over-promoting some members of his family and relying on often mutually antagonistic factions for the rule of the regions, he created inherent instability which laid the foundations of his dynasty's downfall. Ultimately, Pollard concludes, Edward's 'vision did not stretch beyond his origins. His rule remained as it had begun, that of a faction victorious in two civil wars.'[25] Perhaps the severest of Edward's current critics is Colin Richmond. To his mind, Edward was guilty of 'a failure at critical junctions of his reign to safeguard the long term interests of his dynasty'. Although he acknowledges that it was 'this heavy eating, heavy drinking, heavy whoring king' who – at least temporarily – brought the civil wars to an end, even this achievement was wrecked within months of his death. This, to Richmond, was manifestly the result of 'a major failure of [Edward's] kingship: It has to be an under-mighty king, prone to what K.B. McFarlane called a "want of consistency", who finds it expedient to kill one brother and let the other do exactly as he pleases.'[26]

WRITING EDWARD'S BIOGRAPHY

It is not the purpose of this volume to offer a radical re-interpretation of the life and reign of Edward IV, or to present any major new discoveries about the reign: the sources are well-known, and – failing a revolutionary new discovery – have been extensively pored over by generations of scholars. Rather, it is intended to provide a pen-portrait of the first Yorkist king for a broad readership beyond the ranks of those specialising in the history of England in the fifteenth century. In doing so, it not only draws on the original sources of the reign, but is, of course, also heavily indebted to the authors that have gone before and have done so much to illuminate the king's life, not least Charles Ross and Cora Scofield. Unlike their works, this book is unselfconsciously a biography, rather than a history of a reign. Events that did not directly involve

Edward IV have thus at times been summarised in brief. The reader seeking to know more about them is referred to the literature indicated in the notes and list of further reading.

In writing the biography of a king there is naturally some temptation to reduce it to little more than an account of the principal events of the reign. Such a focus is not entirely without justification in what is, inherently, a political biography. Medieval monarchy was deeply personal, and a king's involvement in the politics of his reign was deeper than that of most, if not all, modern statesmen. Yet it is imperative that the biographer should not lose sight of the private identity of his subject, the man behind the monarch, the real being behind the ruler. In this respect, as in many others, the student of fifteenth-century England does well to follow the lead given by the pioneer of fifteenth-century history, K.B. McFarlane. He took a deep interest in medieval Englishmen as individuals, an approach summarised by the editor of his unpublished writings as seeking 'some glimpse, however, fleeting, of thinking, living individuals, apprehended dimly, but not romanticized and above all not to be patronized.'[27]

Yet, the sources present obvious difficulties. Medieval kings did not, as far as we know, keep diaries or journals in which they recorded their thoughts and attitudes. The administrative records of the kings' government, which alone have come down to us in any substantial numbers, are more suited to the writing of a history of the reign than a personal account of the monarch. Furthermore, the long runs of Exchequer, Chancery and plea rolls aside, the available documents are often fragmented survivals, which may by chance reflect accurately the attitudes of the age, but may just as likely not do so at all. Again, we may turn to McFarlane: 'Few of us', he wrote, 'would care to be judged posthumously by the evidence of our note-books alone.'[28] Sources for the reign are not in short supply, but they are complex. Compared with other rulers, Edward IV is badly served by narrative sources. There are nevertheless a number of useful accounts of the reign, several of them compiled by men with detailed insight into events, and even personal acquaintance with the king. Among the best informed of contemporary chroniclers were the two fifteenth-century continuators of the chronicle of the Lincolnshire abbey of Crowland. The first of these (continuing the narrative to 1470) identifies himself as a prior of the abbey; the identity of his successor continues to be a matter of debate, but historians are in general agreement that he possessed privileged information and probably held a post in the ranks of the Westminster administration.[29] Personally acquainted with Edward IV were two Burgundians, Jean de Wavrin and Philippe de Commynes. Wavrin, seigneur de Forestel, between the 1440s and 1470s assembled materials for a history of England. Much of what he gathered was derived from the historical works available to him, but, particularly for the reign of Edward IV, he also incorporated original insights, some undoubtedly gained during a visit to England in 1468, others from his extensive contacts at the Burgundian court. Commynes, who spent a large part of his career in the service of Louis XI of France, became acquainted with Edward during the king's exile in the low countries in 1470–71, and also encountered him on other occasions. Nevertheless, his often critical account is unquestionably coloured by his service to Edward's great adversary, the king of France.[30]

The city of London was central to many of the dramatic events of the reign, and the chronicles compiled there are consequently of considerable interest. One of the most vivid accounts of events in London, as well as further afield, is provided by the Great Chronicle of London, an account compiled in the early sixteenth century by the London alderman Robert Fabyan, who as a young man had lived through Edward's reign in the capital. Among the sources used by Fabyan was a now lost compilation, the so-called 'Main City Chronicle', used by a number of chroniclers working in London in the second half of the fifteenth century. Among the more notable of the works these men produced is a chronicle previously ascribed to the authorship of the London skinner William Gregory, which has important information on the first decade of Edward's reign. London was, however, not alone in maintaining a communal record of historical events.[31] Chronicles were also kept in other cities and towns, and provide important information on what occurred away from the political and commercial hub of the capital. Notable examples of such provincial accounts include *The Maire of Bristowe is Kalendar*, a list of town officials in which the town clerk Robert Ricard began to enter notes on local and national events from the 1440s, the Coventry Annals, and the chronicle of Exeter preserved in the annals compiled in the sixteenth century by the antiquarian John Hooker.[32]

Among the narratives most closely contemporary to the events described were those contained in a variety of letters written by a range of authors and addressed to a variety of recipients. Some of these news-letters were commissioned and circulated on the king's own orders, including accounts of the northern risings of 1469–70 and of Edward's invasion and restoration in 1470–71, which were circulating on the European continent not long after the event.[33] Others were written by private individuals, ranging from the king's own relatives, his sister the Duchess of Burgundy, and his cousin the Bishop of Exeter, to a range of lesser men. Some of this correspondence can seem deceptively first-hand, disguising the fact that its authors often based their reports on second-hand information. This is, for instance, true of the regular reports sent home by various Italian diplomats, who were usually based in the Low Countries or in France and relied on the news that was brought to them from beyond the Channel. By comparison, other news passed on by letter, such as the correspondence of the Paston, Stonor and Plumpton families, or the report sent to the citizens of Cologne by the merchant Gerhard von Wesel, who witnessed Edward's recovery of his kingdom in 1471 from the London Steelyard, contain mostly first-hand information, their reliability being qualified above all by the limits to the informa-tion available to the letter-writer in question, and the degree to which they had to rely on hearsay.[34]

The narrative sources aside, Edward IV's reign presents considerable archival problems to the modern historian. An individual's personal archive lies naturally at the heart of any biography, and in the case of a king this personal archive is to a large extent synonymous with the records of government. Yet, as a result both of administrative reform during the reign and of archival reorganisation by later generations, the government records of Edward IV's reign are less complete and in many instances more scattered than those of previous monarchs. Thus, the abandonment of the cumbersome traditional practices of administering royal finance through the exchequer in favour of the treasury of the king's chamber, which has left few records, means that for large parts of the reign only fragmentary records of royal expenditure can be found. Equally, where for earlier reigns the business of the king's council can be documented through a series of signed bills and warrants recording both the business before the council and the identity of the councillors attend-ing to it, any similar material from the reign of Edward IV is dispersed or lost.

THE BACKDROP TO THE REIGN: THE LANCASTRIAN USURPATION AND THE DUAL MONARCHY, 1399–1449

The political instability that formed the backdrop of much of the life and reign of King Edward IV had its roots in events that had taken place more than four decades before his birth. On 29 September 1399 Henry Bolingbroke, Duke of Lancaster, had deposed King Richard II and usurped the throne, thereby for the first time since the civil wars of the mid-twelfth century breaking the legitimate royal succession, which since 1189 had passed uninterrupted from father to son, or at least grandson, in the direct male line. In subsequent years, Bolingbroke, now King Henry IV, and his son, Henry V, had secured their line on the throne, and in contemporary eyes the house of Lancaster's rule had received divine vindication by Henry V's victories on the battlefields of France, the greatest being that at Agincourt in 1415. It was as a result of these victories that in 1420 King Charles VI of France had been forced to agree in the Treaty of Troyes that the crown of France, to which English kings since Edward III had laid claim, should after his death descend to Henry V and his heirs.

So secure was Lancastrian rule in England by 1422 that on Henry V's sudden death on 31 August his 9-month-old son, Henry VI, succeeded to the throne unchallenged. Naturally, an infant king could not be expected to rule himself, so arrangements were put in place which provided for a form of conciliar government under the leadership of the king's uncles John, Duke of Bedford, and Humphrey, Duke of Gloucester. Even before the provisions for the government of England during the young king's minority had been put in place, Charles VI of France also died on 21 October 1422, and under the terms of the Treaty of Troyes Henry VI thus lawfully also became King of France. Yet, here his succession was not undisputed: the agreement at Troyes had disinherited Charles VI's adult son, the dauphin, who as Charles VII became the focus for the many members of the French nobility who were disinclined to accept the terms of the agreement. The defence of the young king's French realm soon became the principal preoccupation of the council in England. Under the leadership of the Duke of Bedford as regent of France the early years of Henry's reign saw a number of notable victories that continued the successes of Henry V. It was, however, not long before

English fortunes began to decline, and one by one the English-held towns of France fell to Charles VII. As the English position in France deteriorated, the lords of the council began to squabble over the conduct of the war. Their task was not made any easier by a shortage of ready funds. Henry V's conquests had already stretched England's resources to the limit, and in the absence of an adult king it proved impossible to raise sums comparable to those which the dead monarch had been able to levy using his personal authority. The Duke of Bedford's death in 1435 deprived the English in France of their undisputed leader, and signalled the beginning of the end of the dual monarchy. In 1437 Henry VI, still aged only 15, was formally declared an adult, but it soon became clear that he was the antithesis of his martially minded father.

There has been some debate over the extent – if any – to which Henry VI played an active part in the politics of his reign. Assessments have ranged from a suggestion that the king's fitful and often capricious influence accounted for the inconsistencies that characterised his government during the 1440s, to a summary dismissal of any suggestion that Henry actively determined policies and the argument that England was ruled by a succession of leading ministers who used the royal household as their power base.[35] Whatever the truth of the matter, it would seem from what little is known of Henry and his opinions that a policy of a negotiated peace with France was not out of keeping with the monarch's own wishes. Such a policy had, indeed, been advocated even during the king's minority by some members of the council, most notably by Henry's half-uncle, Cardinal Beaufort, the wealthiest prelate in England, on whose loans to the crown much of English campaigning in France became increasingly dependent. The policy of a negotiated settlement had, however, brought the cardinal into conflict with the main exponent of a policy of continued conquest, the protector, Humphrey of Gloucester. In the short term it was the peace party which carried the day. The indictment of Gloucester's second wife, Eleanor Cobham, for witchcraft in 1441 allowed for the duke to be sidelined, and negotiations with the French led to Henry VI's marriage in 1445 to a French princess, Margaret of Anjou, in return for a prolonged truce, which was accompanied by a secret commitment to surrender the county of Maine to the French king. The royal household was in no doubt that the latter part of the agreement needed to be kept secret. Not only was it certain to be highly unpopular in the country as a whole, but it would also give the Duke of

Gloucester an opportunity to present himself as the champion of Henry V's legacy in opposition to Henry VI's ministers and courtiers. It was evidently decided that the duke needed to be silenced more effectively. Consequently, on 18 February 1447, when Gloucester arrived at Bury St Edmunds to attend parliament, he was met by a group of lords who placed him under arrest and denied his request to see the king. Within five days, the duke was dead, probably from shock or a stroke. Nevertheless, fingers of suspicion rapidly began to point at the King's chief minister, William de la Pole, marquess of Suffolk, and the court, but nothing could be proven.

Yet Gloucester's death, whether by natural causes or otherwise, had constitutional implications. Now aged 25 and married for more than a year Henry VI was still childless; his uncle had been his next male heir, and consequently heir presumptive to the crown of England, should the king die without offspring. Gloucester's childless death left Henry VI the sole surviving descendant in the direct male line of Henry IV, and raised the question who would succeed to the throne, should he fail to produce an heir. There were a number of possible candidates, but none with as unambiguous a claim as that of the king's uncle and last surviving brother of the great Henry V. Should the Lancastrian claim prevail, and the crown pass down in the line of the male descendants of John of Gaunt, the best-placed candidate might have been Edmund Beaufort, Duke of Somerset, Gaunt's grandson by his third wife Katharine Swynford. Yet although Gaunt's children by Katharine Swynford, originally born out of wedlock, had been legitimised by an act of parliament in 1397, in 1407 Henry IV had explicitly debarred them from the succession to the crown.

Were a claim through the female line to be permitted, there were two possible Lancastrian candidates, Alfonso V, King of Portugal, and Henry Holland, Duke of Exeter, the grandsons of John of Gaunt's two daughters by his first wife, Blanche of Lancaster. Yet the possibility that the crown could descend in the female line called into question the very claim of the house of Lancaster to have been Richard II's rightful heirs. Whereas King Richard had been the son of Edward III's eldest son, Edward, the Black Prince, Henry IV was descended from King Edward's *third* son, John of Gaunt, Duke of Lancaster. The Lancastrian claim depended on the exclusion from the succession of the offspring of Philippa, the sole child of Edward's *second* son, Lionel, Duke of Clarence, on the grounds of her gender. If it were admitted that the crown could descend through a female line, the claim to Richard II's inheritance fell to Philippa's descendants, and in 1447 to Richard, Duke of York, son of Philippa's granddaughter Anne Mortimer. Richard's claim was further strengthened by the fact that on his father's side he was the grandson in an unbroken male line of Edward III's fourth son, Edmund, Duke of York. He was thus undeniably heir male to both Richard II and Henry VI if both inheritance through the female line and the claims of the Beauforts were disallowed.[36]

THE LOSS OF FRANCE AND CADE'S REBELLION

The early 1440s had seen a shift of political power from the council of Henry VI's minority to the royal household, in whose ranks William de la Pole, Earl of Suffolk (subsequently created Marquess and Duke of Suffolk) became increasingly prominent. It was he who had taken the lead in the negotiations leading to the king's Angevin marriage, and who had agreed to the surrender of Maine. It had, however, proved impossible to honour the latter commitment, and in March 1448 the French took the county and its capital, Le Mans, by force. In May Edmund Beaufort, Duke of Somerset, took up post in Rouen as the new lieutenant-general of France. Yet, whereas the French had made good use of the years of truce and had recent experience of the conquest of Maine, the English pursuit of the war had been fitful, and few effective provisions for the defence of Henry VI's remaining possessions in France had been made. Barely a year after Somerset's arrival the war was renewed, and the military situation in Normandy rapidly went from bad to worse. Even a detailed report of the military crisis provided by Somerset failed to shock parliament into agreeing to the urgently required taxation, and one by one the fortified Norman towns fell to Charles VII. On 4 November 1449 Rouen surrendered, and on Christmas day Harfleur fell. Somerset retreated to Caen, the second city of Normandy, but surrendered on 1 July 1450. Almost simultaneously the sieges of the remaining English strongholds in the duchy came to an equally ignominious end. The duchy of Normandy, which Henry V had formally acquired by the Treaty of Troyes, was lost, and thousands of the defeated English combatants with their dependants flooded back into England.[37]

Already popular feeling ran high, and panic began to spread among Henry VI's ministers. In the autumn and winter of 1449 a number of them resigned, and in January 1450 the Duke of Suffolk was impeached of treason and exiled, only to be intercepted and murdered on 2 May on his way to the continent. Worse was to follow. In June, while parliament still deliberated at Leicester, news arrived that Kent was in open revolt. This notoriously volatile county had been a hotbed of rebellion in the Peasants' Revolt of 1381, and it once again produced a rebel leader, a man calling himself Jack Cade, but – more threateningly – also adopting the pseudonym of John Mortimer, evoking memories not only of Edward II's downfall at the hands of Roger Mortimer, Earl of March, but also of subsequent opposition to the Lancastrian dynasty by Earl Roger's descendants, who were themselves in line to the throne by the marriage of a fourteenth-century Earl of March to Edward III's granddaughter. The rebels of 1450 were sufficiently organised to produce a manifesto of grievances, headed by the complaint that access to the king was monopolised by corrupt and evil counsellors who had separated Henry VI from his 'true' magnates and natural councillors, the four dukes (foremost among them the king's kinsman Richard, Duke of York), other than the Duke of Somerset who was blamed for the surrender of Rouen, and the other earls and barons of England. On 3 July Cade's men entered the city of London, began to plunder it, and beheaded the unpopular treasurer, James Fiennes, Lord Say and Sele, and his son-in-law, William Crowmer, a former sheriff of Kent. Cade set up his headquarters in Southwark, but was denied access to London by the citizens, who on 5 July succeeded in shutting the gateway at the entrance to the bridge. An offer of a general pardon persuaded many of the rebels to desert their leader, and on 9 July Cade departed, accompanied only by a small group of supporters. On 12 July he was apprehended at Heathfield in Sussex and died on his way back to London of the wounds sustained during his arrest.[38]

THE DUKE OF YORK'S OPPOSITION

The grievances voiced in Cade's manifesto had resonated beyond the ranks of his immediate followers. A new parliament summoned to meet at Westminster in November proved, if anything, as hostile to the royal household and its part in the loss of Normandy as that of November 1449 had been, and the popular cause was now also adopted by some of the most powerful lords in the realm. Perhaps the greatest of the magnates who had watched the deterioration of the military situation in France with dismay was the king's kinsman, Richard, Duke of York. The wealthiest magnate of his day, York had served as Henry VI's lieutenant-general of France from 1436 to 1437, and again from 1441 to 1445. York had invested his own resources in the defence of the king's French dominions, and had experienced the same increasing difficulties as many others in securing payment from the Exchequer of the wages of war owing to him and his soldiers. To the duke, the fault for the disaster in France lay squarely with the lords about the king who were monopolising and mis-allocating the available resources. The replacement of Suffolk as the king's chief adviser by the Duke of Somerset, the man whom he (not entirely without justification) blamed for the loss of Normandy, was unacceptable to York. We cannot be certain whether it was the news of military catastrophe in Normandy or the invocation of his name by Cade's rebels that caused York to leave Ireland, where he had been serving as the king's lieutenant since June 1449, but in early September 1450 he landed at Beaumaris in northern Wales and made for London. At least some at court were in no doubt that the landing represented a direct threat to their position; a group of lords was dispatched to intercept and arrest the duke, but he evaded them, reached London with a following some 4,000 strong, and gained admission to the king to protest at his treatment. Although Henry VI reassured York of his continued confidence in him, he denied him the leading role in the council that he sought.

It has rightly been pointed out that it would be simplistic to ascribe Richard of York's assumption of the leadership of the opposition to Henry VI's ministers to a single motive, be it justifiable grievances or naked ambition.[39] Nevertheless, there can be little doubt that over the course of the 1440s the duke had suffered a series of slights at the government's hands, some perhaps more calculated than others, which profoundly shaped his attitude towards Henry VI's advisers. York had spent much of his younger adulthood in the defence of the king's French realm, and on the Duke of Bedford's death had succeeded him as Henry VI's lieutenant-general there. He had liberally employed his own resources in the pursuit of the war, and on his dismissal from office in 1446 was owed the vast sum of over £38,000 by the crown. Yet he could reasonably feel that his authority as lieutenant-general had been undermined by the appointment in 1443 of John Beaufort, Earl of Somerset, as governor of Gascony, with the command of a field army and equipped with wide-ranging powers concerning the conduct of his campaign.[40] At the same time, Somerset's claims for cash to pay his soldiers were given preference over the claims of other creditors, including those of the Duke of York. Further cause for discontent was the flood of new dukedoms created by Henry VI between 1443 and 1446, which York could reasonably regard as diminishing his own rank. Not since Richard II's creation of his 'duketti' in 1397 had there been such a flood of new additions to the highest rank of the peerage, normally jealously reserved for the king's immediate family. Thus, at the death of the Duke of Bedford in 1435 there had been just three dukes in England: Gloucester, the 'son, brother and uncle of kings'; John Mowbray, Duke of Norfolk; and York himself, whose title derived from his descent from Edward III's fourth son, Edmund of Langley, Duke of York. Now, in August 1443 John Beaufort was created Duke of Somerset; his brother Edmund had been elevated to the rank of Marquess of Dorset two months earlier. The following year saw the elevation of John Holland, Earl of Huntingdon, to the dukedom of Exeter, and that of Humphrey, Earl of Stafford, to the dukedom of Buckingham, while William de la Pole was advanced from Earl to Marquess of Suffolk. In April 1445 Henry Beauchamp, Earl of Warwick, was made a duke, and in the summer of 1448 the elevation of the marquesses of Suffolk and Dorset to ducal rank completed the reorganisation of the higher ranks of the nobility. Although the patents of creation explicitly preserved the precedence of the royal dukes of Gloucester and York, Duke Richard could not fail to perceive the advancement of lords of the Lancastrian bloodline like Holland, Stafford and the Beauforts as a threat to his own position.[41]

As the lords and their retinues began to arrive for parliament in the final days of October, the atmosphere in London was tense. Throughout the late summer and early autumn the remnants of Somerset's defeated Norman army had been entering the city, there had been some open rioting, and to keep some semblance of control the mayor and aldermen placed iron chains across the major streets. Order was eventually restored by the efforts of the Dukes of York and Norfolk and the Earl of Devon, who – as the only magnates not implicated in the failure in France – could command some respect among the crowds.

Meanwhile, the Commons in parliament proved resistant to demands for fresh grants of money. Taxation, they maintained, should be provided in a national emergency for the defence of the king's realms. By contrast, the routine costs of the king's household ought to be met from the king's own resources, principally the revenues of the crown estates. If these were insufficient because the king had been too liberal in granting them away to his servants, the answer was not for the community of the realm to provide additional funds, it was for the king's imprudent grants of lands to be revoked. In April 1451 parliament consequently passed an act cancelling all crown grants made before Lady Day (25 March) 1451. In most other areas, however, the king was able to resist the Commons' demands. Calls for the banishment of a number of the king's courtiers, including the Duke of Somerset, were curtly denied. At this point, the debate acquired a new dimension, when the question of the succession was raised by the Bristowian MP Thomas Young, one of York's legal councillors. Ever since the death of Duke Humphrey in 1447 the question of who would be king in the event of Henry VI's death had lurked beneath the surface of political debate, but had never been openly posed, let alone answered. After four years of marriage, the king remained childless. Young now openly proposed in parliament that York should be recognised as heir presumptive, and seems to have found some support in the ranks of the Commons to whom York was preferable to a Beaufort or a de la Pole. There was, however, no support for such a measure among the lords, nor was the king prepared to be dictated to on dynastic issues such as this. Young's demand, which may have had at least York's tacit support, was summarily dismissed and its champion confined in the Tower. Parliament was dissolved at the end of May 1451.[42]

The measures that parliament had taken for the reform of the government and the king's household, and the reordering of royal patronage were being undone by the end of the year. Many of the lands and fees resumed by the crown were being returned to their former holders, and Somerset's influence over the king was as entrenched as ever. York, by contrast, found himself increasingly isolated. Among the lords, only the Duke of Norfolk and the Earl of Devon were prepared to make common cause with him, and – far from being motivated by high-minded considerations for the welfare of the realm – both had personal reasons for opposition to the court. Devon was embroiled in a long-running quarrel with the newly ennobled William, Lord Bonville, and the latter's supporter at court, James Butler, Earl of Wiltshire. Norfolk for his part, wished to assert his authority in his native East Anglia, where even after the Duke of Suffolk's fall some of the former minister's associates still held considerable sway.

By the end of 1451 York had decided on another attempt to remove the Duke of Somerset's influence at court. Although, as before, he was still lacking the support of the vast majority of the lords, he could at least count on two West Country peers, the Earl of Devon and his ally Lord Cobham, who were prepared to take up arms to settle their grievance against their court-supported rivals Bonville and Wiltshire. More problematic was the rallying of the popular support which, while parliament was in session, had been given voice in the House of Commons. With parliament in abeyance, York resorted to the device of a popular manifesto, pledging his loyalty to the king and demanding the removal of Somerset, on whom he placed the blame for the failings of the government and the disastrous conduct of the French war. At the same time, he proceeded to raise armed men throughout his estates. In all of this, York seems to have been genuine in merely seeking recognition as Henry VI's heir, rather than to supplant him, and by implication to remove Somerset as the king's chief councillor. Already, however, some of his supporters were developing other ideas: in eastern England there was open talk of Henry's imminent deposition.[43]

The king's response to York's open sabre-rattling (his resolve stiffened by the lords around him, led by the Dukes of Somerset and Buckingham) was to summon him to appear before the council at Coventry, but at the same time to assemble his own force strengthened by county levies to confront the duke, if necessary. When York refused to go to Coventry and instead prepared to march south on London, the royal army also turned south. Henry once more appealed to York to submit, while at the same time ordering the city of London to deny the duke access. York was consequently forced to pass the capital by, and led his army to his own Kentish estates at Dartford. On 1 March 1452 the royal army drew up on Blackheath. York arrayed his men on nearby Brent Heath outside Dartford, and anchored seven armed ships in the Thames estuary. At the same time, frantic last-ditch attempts to prevent open bloodshed continued. Intermediaries, including Bishop Waynflete of Winchester, Bishop Bourgchier of Ely and York's brother-in-law and nephew, the Earls of Salisbury and Warwick, went to and fro between the camps. On 2 March they eventually succeeded in brokering an understanding by which the king agreed to hear York's complaints against Somerset, who was to be confined to the Tower pending a formal inquiry. Yet when York and his supporters Devon and Cobham entered the king's tent, they found Somerset by Henry VI's side, and it was York who was placed under arrest, taken back to London and confined in his house at Baynard's castle until 10 March, when he was forced to take a solemn oath at St Paul's never to rebel against his sovereign again. Devon and Cobham were likewise arrested.

York seemed to be further from the reins of power than ever before. Yet within 18 months an unexpected sequence of events reversed the political situation in his favour. While York was sidelined from the government, the military situation in English Gascony deteriorated dramatically. The energetic activity of the renowned John Talbot, Earl of Shrewsbury, the 'English Achilles', had allowed the English to recapture the city of Bordeaux, which had fallen to Charles VII in June 1451, but this sudden reversal merely spurred the French into greater activity. Grimly aware of the imminent threat posed by the French king's extensive preparations for an assault on the remaining English holdings in France, parliament had met at Reading in March 1453 and had agreed unusually generous grants of money.[44]

THE FALL OF GASCONY, THE KING'S ILLNESS AND YORK'S FIRST PROTECTORATE, 1453–5

Even as an army to reinforce the Earl of Shrewsbury was being raised in England, news arrived that disaster had struck on 17 July 1453 at Castillon. The English had been roundly defeated, and Shrewsbury and his eldest son killed. In subsequent weeks the English hold on Gascony collapsed. On 19 October 1453, Bordeaux capitulated. Of the French possessions that Henry VI had inherited from his father, now only the fortified port of Calais and its small hinterland, the Pale, remained in English hands. It is hard to overstate the impact of the news in England. The shame of the defeat turned public opinion against the king's ministers, if anything even more dramatically than the loss of Normandy had done three years earlier. But even more damaging was the impact on the king himself. Around the beginning of August 1453 Henry VI fell ill.

The nature and cause of this illness have been a matter of some debate among scholars, but as far as the limited evidence allows us to tell, it manifested itself as a complete mental and physical collapse, which left the king essentially prostrate and unresponsive.

The king's council was faced with an immediate dilemma. It was impossible to know when the king would recover, or indeed whether he would recover at all. The pragmatic solution would be to return to the arrangements of Henry's minority, but there was a problem over who should assume leadership in the council. During the minority this role had naturally devolved on his uncles, the dukes of Bedford and Gloucester, whose position as the king's next heirs presumptive was unquestionable, but in 1453 the dynastic situation was less clear. The queen's pregnancy gave hope of a solution to the question of the succession, but until an heir should reach years of discretion, he could not assume the role of protector. After the birth of Henry VI's son, Prince Edward, the formidable Queen Margaret proposed that she should rule on her son's behalf, but England, unlike France, had no tradition of female regencies, and the prospect of a council dominated by the pushy Frenchwoman held little attraction for the English nobility. Scarcely more palatable to many about the king, above all to the Duke of Somerset, was the Duke of York, but it soon became clear that York's nearness of blood to the king made it impossible to exclude him from the council at a time of national and dynastic crisis.

The great council which assembled at Westminster in November 1453 was notable not only for the heavily armed retinues which accompanied the attending lords to London, but also for the open attack on the Duke of Somerset's conduct of the French war led by John Mowbray, Duke of Norfolk, which dominated the session. As a result of the charges brought by Norfolk, Somerset was committed to the Tower, pending a formal trial for treason. The road should now have been clear for York to assume the regency as protector during the king's continued illness, but the queen's mistrust of the duke continued to cause political stalemate. Only in February 1454 would the council agree that Duke Richard should re-open parliament as the king's lieutenant, but it failed signally to reach a decision about the longer-term arrangements for the government of the realm during Henry's incapacity.

In the event, matters were brought to a head by the sudden death in March 1454 of the experienced chancellor, Cardinal Archbishop John

Kemp, who had played a pivotal role both in the administration and in the king's council for the previous four years. The appointment of a new chancellor, as well as the nomination of a new primate, were matters of central importance that the council was reluctant to address without consulting the king, yet a delegation of peers sent to see Henry was – in spite of its best efforts – unable to elicit any response from him. By the end of March the council had agreed that York should be made protector with powers similar to those accorded to the king's uncles in 1422. Although these powers were clearly limited under the terms of the Act of Parliament establishing the protectorate, the extent to which York intended to reform the government was apparent from the start. On 2 April one of York's principal supporters among the nobility, his brother-in-law Richard Neville, Earl of Salisbury, formally assumed the office of chancellor in full parliament. This was nothing if not an unusual step. Since the 1370s the chancellorship had effectively been the sole preserve of prelates, who had often served an administrative apprenticeship as keepers of the privy seal or as the monarchs' secretaries. Not since the tenure of Michael de la Pole, Earl of Suffolk, in the mid-1380s had the office been granted to a lay magnate.

Richard of York's protectorate did not resolve the political crisis at a stroke. If anything, a series of events during the months of his ascendancy caused England's troubles to deepen. Somerset had been captain of Calais (after the fall of Gascony the last remaining English possession in France), and York's attempts to assume the captaincy and remove his rival's lieutenants were in the first instance frustrated by the garrison's open mutiny over its unpaid wages. By the time the question of the soldiers' pay had been settled, York's protectorate had come to an end.

Even more damagingly, many of the regions of England were in upheaval. The violent feuding of the aristocracy and gentry in Wales and the north of England necessitated the protector's personal intervention and prevented him from taking personal charge of disturbances elsewhere, in Derbyshire and the south-west. In the north, separate disputes between the two great houses of Percy and Neville on the one hand, and the young and violent Henry Holland, Duke of Exeter, and the elderly chamberlain of the royal household, Ralph, Lord Cromwell, on the other had become interwoven. York's appointment to the protectorship with Neville backing gave these previously private quarrels a wider political dimension. Moreover, the unstable Henry Holland clearly believed that his blood links to the house of Lancaster gave him a better claim than York to rule during the king's incapacity, and in the spring of 1454 he orchestrated what seemed like a major rising in the north, openly staking his claim to rule and distributing the livery of the royal duchy of Lancaster. The rebellion, such as it was, rapidly crumbled before the approaching protector, and by November the duke and two of the leading Percy troublemakers had been placed under arrest.

The need to deal with the problems of Calais, Wales and the north had absorbed much of York's attention and energy, and had left him little time to concentrate on any reform of the government that he might have intended, when in December 1454 King Henry VI suddenly began to show signs of recovery. He recognised his son for the first time, and once more appeared to understand what was being said to him. He had no recollection of what had passed during the months of his illness, and learnt for the first time of Archbishop Kemp's death. Nevertheless, in early 1455 he was able to resume the reins of government. York's protectorate was at an end, and so was his ascendancy.

Henry lost little time in releasing Somerset from the Tower, declaring him innocent of the charges against him and restoring him to the captaincy of Calais. This was not to be Henry's only unwise decision. Like Somerset, the Duke of Exeter was also released, and in March the Earl of Salisbury was dismissed from the chancellorship and replaced by Thomas Bourgchier, Archbishop of Canterbury. Although Bourgchier was connected to York and his Neville allies through the marriage of York's sister to the new chancellor's brother, Henry, Viscount Bourgchier, taken together, the recovered king's measures signalled a clear intention of returning to the status quo before his illness, and undid much of what York and the Nevilles had achieved during the protectorate.

Early in March, York, Salisbury and Warwick absented themselves from the court, and it was probably about this time that they resolved to impose their will on the king by force. Certainly, the court was also preparing for a showdown. On 21 April a great council was summoned to meet at Leicester a month later. The declared purpose of the council was to provide for the king's threatened safety (a statement which York and the Nevilles could reasonably take to be directed against them), and to this end some armaments were ordered for Henry VI's own entourage, while summons for military contingents were sent to various towns and lords. York and the Nevilles had also rallied their armed retainers, and moved south to intercept Henry before they could reach Leicester.

The two armies encountered each other at St Albans on 22 May. Some last-ditch attempts at a negotiated settlement failed and in a short but violent fight in the marketplace and streets of the town, Somerset, Henry Percy, Earl of Northumberland, and Lord Clifford were killed. York took charge of the king and removed him to the abbey, before escorting him back to London on the following day. Two days later, on Whitsunday, a formal crown-wearing was staged at St Paul's cathedral, the king receiving his crown from York's hands. The principal offices of state, previously held by Somerset and his associates, were redistributed among the victors: York became constable of England, Warwick captain of Calais, while York's brother-in-law, Viscount Bourgchier, was made treasurer. However, to give the new government a broad base, other officers like the chancellor, Archbishop Bourgchier, and the keeper of the privy seal, Thomas Lisieux, remained in post. To legitimise what had been done, a parliament was summoned to Westminster.[45] Ostensibly, its purpose was to bring about a reconciliation between the lords, and steps to this end included the issue of a general pardon to all who had taken up arms on York's side against the king, and a formal enrolment of a declaration of loyalty to Henry VI by York and his allies.

During the summer of 1455, however, when parliament was in recess, Henry, whose recovery had been at best partial, fell ill once more. Although it is possible that his ailment on this occasion was not as serious as the one that had afflicted him two years earlier, it appears that he was once again unable to rule himself, if indeed he had ever fully recovered his powers. On 12 November York, as the king's lieutenant, re-opened parliament, and in subsequent days the Commons pressed the lords to agree to a renewed appointment of the Duke of York as protector. For some weeks the lords resisted, but under the impression of fresh violence in the south-west on 17 November they agreed to a new protectorate.

If at this time York had intended a more sweeping reform of the abuses identified in preceding years, it was the question of the reordering of royal patronage over which he foundered. In autumn the parliament had agreed a fresh act of resumption, but it was rendered largely ineffective by sweeping exemptions and the grant to the not wholly incapacitated king of the power to make further exceptions at his discretion. In the face of the opposition of the king and most of the lords to effective resumption of crown grants, York resigned his protectorship on 25 February 1456.

For two years after the end of the protectorate an uneasy truce prevailed. It was less of a peace than an absence of open war between the rival factions. The court now looked to the redoubtable Queen Margaret for leadership while Henry VI's son was under age, and it was the queen who took the lead in regrouping her supporters. In the first instance, York continued to be charged with tasks such as the opening and closing of parliament as the king's lieutenant, and was recognised as Henry's chief councillor, but his influence in the government rapidly diminished as that of the queen and her supporters grew. In April 1457 the Earl of Devon and those associated with him in the violence of the autumn of 1455 were pardoned; the earl's son and heir was married to one of the queen's ladies, Marie of Maine. In October 1456 Archbishop Bourgchier was replaced as chancellor by Bishop Waynflete of Winchester and Viscount Bourgchier was stripped of the treasurership in favour of the young Earl of Shrewsbury. The privy seal was entrusted to Queen Margaret's own chancellor, Laurence Booth.

There was to be one last effort at a reconciliation between the increasingly entrenched rival camps of lords, and for the last time Henry VI played a significant part in his own right. In March 1458 a great council met in London, and the agreement it brokered was given public expression on 25 March 1458, the feast of the Annunciation of the Virgin Mary, when a 'Love-day' (a formal ceremony of reconciliation) was held at St Paul's cathedral. Henry VI walked in procession wearing his crown, preceded by Salisbury and the young Duke of Somerset, side by side, and followed by York leading Queen Margaret by the hand.

In the event, this ritual reconciliation achieved nothing, as it failed to find a way of reconciling the rival interests. No answer was found to the principal question of who should guide, if not control, the king, who even when not completely incapacitated, had shown himself barely able to rule without direction. Henry had shown himself on more than one occasion unwilling to work with the Duke of York, whose position – in dynastic terms, but even more so in terms of wealth and influence – made him impossible to discount. Instead the king preferred to support the rival interest of his own Beaufort kinsmen. Other feuding lords aligned themselves with these two camps: the Nevilles and Bonvilles with York, the Percys and Courtenays with the Beauforts. A further obstacle to a lasting settlement was the formidable Queen Margaret, deeply suspicious of any challenges to her husband's rule, which her infant son was one day to inherit, who increasingly took over the leadership of a narrow party of Lancastrian loyalists around the king. In the summer of 1459 the settlement broke down completely.[46]

2

THE MAKING OF A KING

CHILDHOOD AND EDUCATION

The future Edward IV was born on 28 April 1442 at Rouen in Normandy, where his father, Richard, Duke of York, was serving as King Henry VI's lieutenant of France.

It was not the mother's first pregnancy, nor was the boy the ducal couple's first surviving child: an earlier son, Henry, had died in infancy, while a daughter, Anne, was by now 3 years old. Yet, provided that he lived, the boy had great expectations. Duke Richard was the greatest English landowner of his day, and his vast estates would in time come to his legitimate male heir. As was customary at the time, the boy was baptised on the same day, either in the chapel of Rouen castle or, according to another version of events, in the cathedral itself. Thomas, Lord Scales, and Elizabeth, titular Lady Say, the wife of the Duke of York's retainer Sir John Montgomery, acted as godparents.[1]

Considerable importance has of late been attached to the manner of Edward's baptism, which – if indeed it did not take place in the cathedral – has been cited as evidence of contemporary doubts over the child's paternity. More than two and a half decades after the event, in 1469, there were indeed rumours that Edward had not been fathered by the Duke of York, but by a mere French archer. These, however, were allegations spread by the disgruntled Earl of Warwick with the collusion of the wily King Louis XI of France. The same, or similar, stories were apparently put about by Edward's younger brother, the Duke of Clarence, in the months of his final quarrel with the king in 1477–8,[2] and resurfaced once more in the early days of Richard III's coup d'état in 1483. Then it was asserted that Duchess Cecily herself had some years earlier, in a fit of pique at her eldest son's unsuitable choice of bride, volunteered to submit to a public inquiry to prove that he had been conceived in adultery, but within days these renewed allegations were dropped again and did not find their way into the declaration of Richard's royal title.[3]

In recent times, the story of Edward's supposed illegitimacy has been dredged up once more by apologists for Richard III anxious to demonstrate that Edward's youngest brother was convinced, at least in his own mind, of his legitimate right to the throne. It has been suggested that the duke and duchess could not have conceived the boy together, as they appear not to have been together in the same place at the appropriate period, but as Charles Ross, and more recently Michael Hicks, have rightly argued, none of the evidence for Edward's bastardy is conclusive, and it represents at best a possibility that the boy baptised at Rouen in April 1442 was not the Duke of York's son.[4] Then as now, the stories were put about by those who wanted to bastardise Edward for their own ends, in the same way as Henry VI's opponents had in the later 1450s sought to raise questions over the legitimacy of the Lancastrian Prince Edward.[5] Crucially, beyond the uncertain circumstances of his baptism there is no suggestion that the Duke of York ever regarded or treated Edward as anything other than his legitimate son and heir. Nor, crucially, did others who mattered: within four years of the boy's birth King Charles VII of France was prepared to consider him as a husband for one of his younger daughters. In 1460, when the Yorkist claim to the crown was being put forward, popular ballads were at pains to emphasise the boy's legitimate birth, in contrast with that of Henry VI's heir, Prince Edward, which in turn popular rumour began to call into question.[6]

Over subsequent years, the Duke and Duchess of York had a further nine children, five of whom survived into adulthood. Of these, Edward's next brother, Edmund, a year his junior, was closest to him: their proximity of age meant that they shared much of their early education. The Duke of York and his family returned from France in 1445, and remained in England for the next four years. It was perhaps when the duke took up the post of lieutenant of Ireland in the summer of 1449 that 7-year-old Edward and his 6-year-old brother were established with their own independent household at Ludlow castle in the care of a governor.[7] Here, they were taught to read and write, and their tutors impressed upon them the need 'to increase and grow to virtue, and to speed the better in all matters and things that we shall use, occupy and exercise', as they wrote to their father in 1454. Duke Richard himself also took an interest in his sons' education. Later that summer Edward and Edmund wrote to their father:

> you command us by your said letters to attend especially to our learning in our young age, that should cause us to grow to honour and worship in our old age, please it your Highness to wit that we have attended our learning since we came here, and shall hereafter; by the which we trust to God your gracious lordship and good fatherhood shall be pleased.[8]

Of course, they were no ordinary schoolboys. Their father's position meant that they had to be groomed for the affairs of state from an early age. Duke Richard's envoys kept them informed of his 'matters and business, and of [his] gracious prevail against the intent and malice of [his] evil willers'. Other aspects of the boys' life were more whimsical. At Easter 1454 the boys told their father:

> we thank your noblesse and good fatherhood for our green gowns, now late sent unto us, to our great comfort, beseeching your good lordship to remember our porteux [breviaries], and that we might have some fine bonnets sent to us by the next sure messenger, for necessity so requires. Over this, right noble lord and father, please it your highness to wit that we have charged your servant William Smyth, bearer of this, to declare unto your nobility certain things on our behalf, namely concerning and touching the odious rule and demeaning of Richard Croft and of his brother. Wherefore we beseech your gracious lordship and full noble fatherhood to hear him in exposition of the same, and to give full faith and credence to his relation.[9]

Here, Edward showed early signs of the concern for his appearance that would characterise him in later life. At the same time, the boys' complaint about the Crofts (boys from the local gentry being brought up alongside them in the Duke of York's household) demonstrates that even if the two young princes were being prepared for a future as great magnates, they were essentially boys in their early teens, and their concerns those of their age.

Few details of Edward's early education can be established for certain, but it may be assumed that it did not differ too sharply from that of any other young nobleman. The provisions Edward himself later made for his own son and heir, as well as for the young aristocrats who were brought up in the royal household, may provide some clues. In the upbringing of these boys, heavy emphasis was placed not only on the physical skills they would need – the lessons in riding, jousting and armoured fighting – but also on finer things. They needed to learn courtly manners, with particular emphasis on their conduct at table, and the rules of the other formalities of the royal court and household. During meals they might hear stories read that were illustrative of 'virtue, honour, cunning, wisdom, and deeds of worship', and those entrusted with their care were instructed to restrict their conversation to similar themes and to avoid inappropriate talk. There was also room for more formal training in variety of subjects, including languages, music and dancing, and perhaps also the practicalities of estate management and a rudimentary understanding of the law. Emphasis was placed on regular attendance at the principal divine offices of the day, and provision was made for deeper theological instruction by sermons preached on important feast days, as well as formal teaching of 'all spiritual cunning'.[10]

A number of books were provided for Edward, possibly at an early date: the volumes he owned before he became king included a composite volume containing medical treatises, a glossed version of the pseudo-Aristotelian *Secreta Secretorum*, and a more practical formulary, a collection of templates for legal documents.[11] Even in 1463 he attributed sufficient importance to this collection to place the works in the care of a dedicated household official, some years before his experience of the ducal and aristocratic libraries of Burgundy is thought to have sparked a taste for the collecting of illuminated manuscripts of the highest quality. By the end of his life, Edward's royal library was substantial: no fewer than 45 volumes surviving today can be attributed to him with some degree of certainty, including historical works like the chronicles of John Hardyng, Jean de Froissart and Jean de Wavrin, French versions of classical authors such as Josephus's *Jewish Wars* and the works of Julius

Caesar, and didactic works, both religious and chivalric, like St
Augustine's *City of God* and Alain Chartier's *Breviary of Noblemen*.

More problematic is the question of which, if any, of these texts
Edward ever read: books were presented and dedicated to kings, expand-
ing their collections beyond the range of their personal interests.
Nevertheless, it is now generally accepted that, far from being ignorant
or poorly educated, many members of the later medieval aristocracy
possessed extensive book-learning, and it has been suggested that
Edward developed a particular interest in alchemy that was reflected in
the books he owned: in the dedication to Edward of his *Ordinal of
Alchemy*, the alchemist Thomas Norton maintained that the king had
specifically asked for the text.[12] Edward learnt to read Latin (unlike his
mother, who was said to have 'little intellect' in that language)[13] and
French, and evidently acquired a degree of proficiency in both: not for
him the 'French of Stratford le Bow' for which Chaucer derided his
prioress. At Picquigny in 1475 Edward was able to answer Louis XI of
France 'in good enough French', as the otherwise critical Philippe de
Commynes recorded, and spent a long time in private conference
with the French king,[14] while in September 1481 he attended a public
disputation in the university of Oxford, and responded 'fluently and
inventively' to a formal address (presumably delivered in Latin).[15]

Formal instruction aside, it was inevitable that the young Edward
should learn something of his family's history and traditions from the
castles and manors in which he grew up, the chapels and churches
where he worshipped, and the armorial bearings, funeral monuments
and achievements and other imagery that filled them. The political
classes of late medieval England were deeply conscious of their history
and heritage, and by them defined much of their private and public
personae. In Duke Richard, and consequently also in Edward, were
united a number of noble and royal bloodlines: in the direct male line,
Richard of York was the grandson of King Edward III's fourth son,
Edmund, Duke of York. His mother, Anne, Countess of Cambridge,
was the daughter of Roger Mortimer, Earl of March, so Duke Richard
was also the lineal descendant and male heir of Edward III's second
son, Lionel, Duke of Clarence. Harking back to the more distant past,
the Mortimer line also united the blood of the de Clare Earls of
Gloucester and the de Burgh Earls of Ulster with that of the Welsh
Princes of Gwynedd.[16]

Not all these family traditions were auspicious in equal measure. While Duke Richard's paternal uncle, Edward, Duke of York, had died on the battlefield of Agincourt, he had previously been accused of disloyalty to Richard II, as well as being subsequently implicated in a conspiracy against Henry IV. Worse still, Richard of York's father, Richard, Earl of Cambridge, had been executed as a traitor in August 1415, after seeking to orchestrate a rebellion against Henry V in favour of his brother-in-law, Edmund Mortimer, Earl of March. Indeed, the name of Mortimer itself had become a symbol of rebellion in Lancastrian England. Although by the time of Richard II's deposition the family's reputation had recovered from the blemish of Roger Mortimer's involvement in the deposition of Edward II – so much so that Earls Roger (*d*.1398) and Edmund (*d*.1425) Mortimer could realistically be regarded as King Richard's heirs – their very position in the line of succession made them likely, if not always willing, focal points for opposition to the Lancastrian kings. Time and time again the standard of rebellion had been raised in the name of Mortimer, junior cadets of the family often colluding in the conspiracies, and even in 1450, a quarter of a century after the death of the last Mortimer Earl of March, the family name was still sufficiently evocative to be apparently adopted by the leader of the Kentish rebels.[17]

If considerations of this lineage shaped Richard of York's, and subsequently Edward's, perception of their position in the English polity, as well as other men's expectations of them, at the time of Edward's birth the Duke of York was first of all, and undeniably, the greatest English magnate of his day. As such, he could be expected to play a prominent political role, and it was inevitable that his father's position in the English polity would also leave its mark on the early life of his son and heir. By September 1445, when Edward was just over three years old, he and his brother Edmund were formally recognised as Earls of March and Rutland respectively.[18] Seven years later, Edward at least nominally made his first appearance on the political stage. After his abortive challenge to the Duke of Somerset's power at Dartford in 1452, York had been placed under arrest, but was soon released, as popular rumour in London would have it, because the ten-year-old Edward was said to be marching on the city at the head of 10,000 armed men. There was nothing inherently incredible in this suggestion. The sons of the late medieval aristocracy were expected to grow up early. King Henry VI, who had succeeded to the throne in infancy, had been declared an adult at the age of 15, Edward III had replaced his father on the throne aged just 14, and Richard II, who at the age of 10 had been meant to lead a retinue to fight in France, was also just 14 when he faced the revolting peasants at Blackheath.[19] Certainly, the young Edward was at his father's side when he rode into London at the head of his household troops in January 1454 to open parliament on behalf of the incapacitated Henry VI.[20] For the time being, however, Edward and Edmund returned to Ludlow and their studies, and little is heard of them until the autumn of 1459, when Edward was 17 years old.

EXILE AND RECOVERY

In the intervening years, the rivalries of the leading English nobles, which Henry VI's ineffective leadership and successive bouts of illness, combined with the queen's meddling, had done little to contain, had found an outlet in open fighting in the north, the southwest, and a street battle at St Albans that claimed the lives of the Duke of Somerset, the Earl of Northumberland and Lord Clifford. The uneasy truce which prevailed after York's second protectorate of 1455–6 was meant to be given permanence by a ceremonial reconciliation in 1458, but a year later the rival lords were once again rallying their armed retainers. Matters came to a head in October 1459. York and his principal supporters, the Neville Earls of Salisbury and Warwick, respectively the brother and nephew of Edward's mother, had assembled their forces at York's castle at Ludlow. Here, the entire ducal family was also assembled. Already, on 23 September, Salisbury had been confronted by a royalist army under Lord Audley at Blore Heath, and Henry VI's main force, under the king's personal command, was not far behind. At Ludford Bridge, just outside Ludlow, the two armies faced each other.

It was clear that a renewed armed confrontation was imminent. During the night of 12 October alarming news arrived. Probably reluctant to fight the king himself, part of the Yorkist forces, drawn from the ranks of the Calais garrison and led by one Andrew Trollope, had defected to the royal army. It was clear that the Yorkist lords could not hope to overcome the superior force facing them. Rapid action was necessary. It was agreed that York himself, accompanied by his second son, Edmund

Earl of Rutland, would ride into Wales and seek to take ship to Ireland. York's heir, Edward, Earl of March, would have to separate from his father and brother, so that – should either be captured – the court party would be unable to decapitate the Yorkist cause at a single stroke. Edward thus went with his uncle Salisbury and cousin Warwick to seek shelter at Calais, where the latter was still captain of the garrison, and which – despite the defection of Trollope and his men – could be expected to remain loyal. The three earls headed for southern Wales, took ship, and landed in northern Devon. From here, a local esquire, John Dynham, took them safely across the county to Nutwell on the Exe estuary, where his widowed mother procured a ship to take them across the Channel to safety. After a brief stop in Guernsey, where Warwick's retainer John Nanfan held the governorship, the fugitives made for the more easily defensible fortress of Calais, where they arrived on 2 November.[21]

Richard of York's fortunes had reached their lowest point yet. Although on discovering their leaders' flight the Yorkist troops surrendered, and with few exceptions received a pardon, the town of Ludlow and the duke's neighbouring estates were given up to pillage by the king's soldiers. The Duchess of York and her three younger children were taken and placed in the protective custody of the duchess's sister, the Duchess of Buckingham. On 20 November a hastily summoned parliament met at Coventry, and completed the rout of the Yorkist party by attainting the leaders, including Edward and his brother Edmund, of treason and declaring their estates forfeit to the king. With the Duke of York sidelined in Ireland, it was the energetic Earl of Warwick who now seized the initiative, and set about restoring the fortunes of the Yorkist party. By age and experience, the Earl of Salisbury was the natural leader of the refugees in Calais, but the prime responsibility for the defence fell to Warwick as captain of Calais, the last English foothold on the European mainland. For half a year, Edward found himself much under his older cousin's tutelage.

At the age of 31, Richard Neville had already gathered extensive military experience, first on the battlefields of France and latterly as commander of the Calais garrison. This experience was soon required, for while they were at large the Yorkist lords represented a threat to Henry VI's government, even when under attainder and deprived of their lands in England. As Henry IV had demonstrated in 1399, the island kingdom was not immune to invasion by a man who might command any form of residual loyalties within the realm. In the immediate term, the Duke of York in Ireland represented less of a threat than the lords in Calais, who were not only poised for an attack across the straits, but in the interim could seriously disrupt commerce by raids on shipping in the Channel. It was imperative that they should be dislodged.

Even before Ludford Bridge Warwick had been formally stripped of the captaincy of Calais, which was instead granted to the Duke of Somerset. Yet Warwick had entrusted the custody of the town in his absence to his uncle, William Neville, Lord Fauconberg, who ignored the government's instructions to deny entry to his nephew. Thus, when Somerset approached Calais to take up his post, his flotilla was driven back by the guns of the town and of the tower of Rysbank at the entrance to the harbour. The duke was reduced to landing at the far western end of the English enclave, and eventually managed to gain entrance to the lesser fortress of Guisnes, but with little hope of assaulting Calais itself, not least because a storm and the collusion of some of the captains and sailors of the vessels carrying his men and supplies put them into Warwick's hands.

Somerset nevertheless sought to take Calais by storm, but saw his attacks beaten back time and time again. Nor did attempts to send reinforcements to Guisnes meet with more success. In the early hours of 15 January 1460 John Dynham led a raid from Calais to Sandwich, where Richard Wydeville, Lord Rivers, was preparing a naval force to sail to Somerset's aid. Dynham not only carried off Rivers' entire fleet, ships, men, supplies and all, he even succeeded in seizing Rivers, his wife, the Dowager Duchess of Bedford, and their son, Sir Anthony Wydeville, in their beds.[22] Rivers and his son were taken to Calais and brought before Salisbury, Warwick and Edward that same night. In the course of a stormy interview all three took it in turns to harangue the captives. The scene captured the popular imagination in London, from where one correspondent described how

> my Lord of Salisbury berated [Rivers], calling him a knave's son, that he should
> be so rude as to call him and these other lords traitors, for they should be
> found the king's true liegemen, when he should be found a traitor etc. And my
> Lord of Warwick berated him and said that his father was only an esquire, and
> brought up with King Henry V, and since then he himself had been made by

marriage, and also made a lord, and that it was not his place to have such language of lords of the king's blood. And my lord of March berated him in like wise. And Sir Anthony was berated for his language by all three lords in like wise.[23]

Bad luck continued to dog the English government. In March Lord Audley and the Somerset esquire Humphrey Stafford were dispatched to reinforce Somerset at Guisnes, but were forced by a storm to take shelter in the harbour of Calais, where they were promptly arrested and imprisoned.[24] By now, the lords at Calais felt sufficiently secure for Warwick to sail for Ireland to take counsel with the Duke of York. In his absence, Somerset attempted a fresh attack on Calais, but was roundly defeated at Newnham bridge on 23 April, incurring heavy losses in the process. In June Lord Fauconberg, John Dynham and Sir John Wenlock led a second raid on Sandwich, where fresh reinforcements for the Duke of Somerset under Osbert Mountfort, an experienced veteran of the French wars, were being mustered. Mountfort's men were killed or dispersed, and Mountfort himself carried off to Calais and executed, while Fauconberg took control of the port of Sandwich as a bridgehead for an imminent invasion.[25] On 26 June Salisbury, Warwick and March landed at Sandwich, and were met by a welcoming committee of the Kentish gentry, who addressed themselves to the young Earl of March as York's son and heir. Edward, who had as yet little experience of dealing with such formal public speeches, turned to Warwick for advice how to respond, and it was his older cousin who answered on behalf of the invaders.[26] The earls then proceeded towards Canterbury, meeting no resistance along the way. Rather, old and new supporters began to flock to their banners. Already their cause was the subject of popular ballads, and Edward's fame was being proclaimed alongside that of his father, uncle and cousin. Shortly before the arrival of the Calais lords at Canterbury a ballad posted on the city gates celebrated:

> Edward, Earl of March, whose fame the earth shall spread,
> Richard, Earl of Salisbury, named prudence,
> With that noble knight and flower of manhood
> Richard, Earl of Warwick, shield of our defence,
> Also little Fauconberg, a knight of great reverence;

> Jesu restore them to their honour that they had before,
> And ever we shall sing to thy High Excellence,
> *Gloria, laus et honor Tibi sit Rex Christe Redemptor!*[27]

Before long, Edward was separated out from his kinsmen and endowed with some of the virtues previously ascribed to them:

> E for Edward, whose fame the earth shall spread,
> Because of his wisdom named prudence,
> Shall save all England by his manliness,
> Wherefore we owe to do him reverence.

> M for March, true in every trial,
> Drawn by discretion that is worthy and wise,
> Conceived in wedlock, and coming of royal blood,
> Joined unto virtue, excluding all vices.[28]

Much strengthened in numbers the invaders continued towards London. Although some of the citizens attempted to persuade their fellows that guns should be placed at the bridge to deny the earls access, it was eventually agreed to admit them to the city. On 2 July Edward, Warwick and Salisbury rode into London accompanied by, among others, the papal legate, Francesco Coppini. The convocation of the clergy of the province of Canterbury was then in session at St Paul's, and this gathering was first to hear the earls' justification from Warwick's mouth.

There was, however, not now time to concentrate on winning hearts and minds. Henry VI's council had been meeting at Coventry when news of the invasion arrived. The king and his councillors moved to Northampton, while messengers were hurriedly sent out to gather armed men, promising those who would respond unlimited plunder in the south-eastern counties which openly favoured the Yorkist lords. These promises bore fruit and by 7 July a substantial force, mainly recruited by the Earl of Northumberland and Lords Clifford, Neville, Roos, Egremont and Dacre in the north, had assembled outside Northampton.[29] Meanwhile, Thomas, Lord Scales (Edward's own godfather who remained loyal to Henry VI), and Robert, Lord Hungerford, had withdrawn into the heavily garrisoned Tower of London, and raised the drawbridge. From the fortress, they began to pound the city with cannon fire, causing considerable damage and the death of a number of Londoners.

For the moment, however, it was the threat posed by the royal army at Northampton that was more pressing. The Earl of Salisbury was thus entrusted with the keeping of London and the siege of the Tower, in which the Londoners readily joined, while Warwick and March, joined by an array of lords and bishops, made their way towards Northampton. The Yorkist force probably outnumbered their opponents, but their leaders nevertheless made a last-ditch attempt to parley with the king rather than openly fighting him. For some time, heralds and bishops went to and fro, but in the event the attempt at mediation failed, probably not least because there were some in either camp who wanted to see the matter settled once and for all.

On Thursday, 10 July, the two armies were drawn up in battle order just outside Northampton. The Yorkist forces were organised into three divisions, commanded respectively by Warwick, his uncle William Neville, Lord Fauconberg, and Edward – his first independent command. In a first display of what for some years was to become Edward's regular convention, the Yorkist lords issued orders that the king and the common soldiers should be spared, and only lords, knights and esquires killed. The engagement lasted for barely half an hour before it was decided in the Yorkists' favour by the defection of Edmund, Lord Grey of Ruthin, who had commanded the royalist vanguard. The king's army broke up in confusion, as many of the remaining soldiers took to flight. The royalist leaders sought safety about the king's person, but to no avail: the Duke of Buckingham, the Earl of Shrewsbury, Viscount Beaumont and Lord Egremont were killed near the royal tent.[30] Their leading enemies dead, Edward and Warwick presented themselves before King Henry and, pledging their loyalty, led him a prisoner in all but name into Northampton, before returning to London with him on 16 July. Three days later, the garrison of the Tower also surrendered.

YORKIST ASCENDANCY

In a remarkable reversal of their fortunes, the Yorkist lords now controlled both the capital and the king, and could exercise the government of the realm in Henry VI's name. A wholesale replacement of the personnel of the royal household and the great officers of state followed. Salisbury became the king's chamberlain; his younger son, the Bishop of Exeter, was made chancellor; and the Duke of York's brother-in-law, Viscount Bourgchier, became treasurer; while Warwick himself received a series of more junior offices.[31] Nevertheless, within days of the battle of Northampton, rumours were circulating that the victorious lords would seek to make the Duke of York's son king, passing over the Lancastrian Prince Edward, whose paternity was now openly being called into question.[32]

But Edward of York's day had not yet come. Although in fifteenth-century England young nobles were expected to grow up early, at 18 he was still young and inexperienced. As at the landing at Sandwich, it was in the first instance his older cousin Warwick to whom he looked for guidance. Following the surrender of the Tower, Warwick had returned to Calais until parliament should meet,[33] leaving Edward at least temporarily to play an enhanced role in the king's council.

In early September the Duke of York landed near Chester, accompanied by Edmund of Rutland and John, Lord Clinton, but otherwise bringing only a small retinue of men wearing the blue and white livery of the duchy of York. In the first instance he rode south, passing through Ludlow, from where he had so ignominiously fled a year earlier, before being eventually reunited with Duchess Cecily at Hereford. For several more weeks York meandered through the marches, ostensibly executing the king's special commission to pacify the region, and in the process gathering retainers to his banner.

Eventually he set out for London, and his true intentions soon became clear. When he reached Abingdon he exchanged the arms and banner of the Duke of York for those of the King of England, and with his sword borne upright before him (a privilege of the reigning monarch) approached London. When York reached the city, a parliament summoned in Henry VI's name, but heavily dominated by York's supporters, had already been in session for three days. Scarcely pausing to receive the formal welcome of the citizens of London, York rode straight to Westminster and strode into the parliament chamber where the lords were assembled, marched up to the throne and laid his hand upon it, as if to claim possession. If he had hoped for immediate acclamation, he had miscalculated. The lords, even those who had supported him and gone into exile for him, stood in shocked silence. This was eventually broken by Archbishop Bourgchier of Canterbury, who welcomed him, asking whether he wished to see the king.

York's conduct up to this point had been unambiguous: his progress towards London could hardly be understood as anything but an open bid for the throne. Englishmen had become accustomed to the idea that a king might be deposed for misgovernance, and the word in the streets of London was that Henry VI's deposition was imminent and that York himself – rather than one of his sons, as had been mooted previously – would be king. York did not now intend to give any indication that he still regarded Henry VI as the rightful king. Giving a haughty, if evasive reply, he stalked out of the parliament chamber, and proceeded to take possession of the royal apartments for himself. Finding the doors of the king's chamber barred, he broke them open by force. Henry VI, already alarmed by the commotion, withdrew into the rooms previously assigned to his queen.

There still remained the problem of the lords' reluctance to meet York's claim with the required enthusiasm. More subtle means were evidently needed to soothe their consciences, but Duke Richard was not a man of subtle means. He had convinced himself that the throne was his by right, and if England could not see that this was so, it must be made to see it. For several days parliament was kept busy overturning the acts of the Coventry parliament of the previous year, before York – his attainder now reversed – addressed the lords once more. This time, he went so far as to sit on the royal throne itself, before declaring to the assembled magnates that the crown was his by right of inheritance. Once more, his declaration was met with silence. Once again, York had to withdraw.

Reluctant to be publicly humiliated a third time, on 16 October the duke submitted a written exposition of his title to the lords, requesting a speedy reply. The lords equivocated. Several peers had caught wind of what was to be asked of them and had wisely absented themselves from the house on that day, and those who remained decided that the matter fell beyond their competence. It was thus decided to consult King Henry, who at last moved to defend his crown and ordered the lords to seek out objections to York's claim. The lords now turned to the king's justices and other senior lawyers, all of whom declared the business to be beyond their competence. Having failed to pass the buck to either the king or the professional lawyers, the lords themselves drew up a list of objections to York's claim. York responded, reiterating his claim. After more than a week, a compromise was finally agreed. Henry VI would retain the throne for his life, thus overcoming the scruples of the lords who had sworn allegiance to him as recently as the previous year. The Duke of York would be declared his heir, setting aside the rights of Henry's son, and the lords would swear to uphold York's succession. On All Saints' Day (1 November) a solemn ceremony was staged at St Paul's cathedral. Henry VI wore his crown, York walked in procession, Warwick bore the sword before the king, while Edward of March carried the monarch's train.[34]

To York, the arrangement held out slim hope that he himself would ever wear the crown, for he was 10 years older than Henry, and could not expect to outlive him with any degree of certainty. The arrangement instead favoured the 18-year-old Edward, 20 years Henry's junior, who was likely to live to succeed him on the throne. What York had to console himself with were the reality and trappings of power, if not of kingship. Henry VI was removed from the royal palace at Westminster to the lesser quarters of the Bishop of London's palace, while York took full possession of the royal apartments.

In all of this, Edward had been very much a junior partner, the lead being taken by his older and more experienced cousin Warwick, and the latter's father, Salisbury, until York himself had returned from Ireland. He had taken his seat on the king's council, but as a young newcomer among many older and more experienced men.[35] One account nevertheless suggests that he, who throughout his life displayed a clear sense of how to win hearts and minds, attempted, albeit in vain, to dissuade his more impetuous father from the usurpation on which the latter had clearly set his heart.[36] All the same, the late summer and autumn of 1460 were happy days for Edward. While his father and their Neville and Bourgchier kinsmen were engaged about the rule of the kingdom, Edward rode daily across London bridge to Southwark to visit his younger siblings, 14-year-old Margaret, 12-year-old George and 8-year-old Richard, who were staying in Sir John Fastolf's former house there.[37] This family idyll was not to last.

Henry VI might have accepted the compromise of October 1460, but Queen Margaret was not inclined to see her son disinherited without a fight. When informed of the agreement that her husband had endorsed by a messenger of the papal legate Coppini, the queen replied with a letter, which Coppini later described as displaying 'too great passion'.[38] Margaret began a series of diplomatic manoeuvres designed to elicit military support from the Kings of France and Scotland, but ultimately to no avail.

Yet there were also English lords who could not accept the October settlement or the Duke of York's supremacy. Chief among these was Henry Beaufort, Duke of Somerset, for whom control of the government by the very lords who had been responsible for his father's death in 1455 was clearly unacceptable. Others could not accept the ascendancy of long-standing local rivals in the wake of York's triumph. Thomas Courtenay, Earl of Devon (the son of York's ally of 1452), linked to the queen's household by marriage, was threatened by the presence of his father's enemy, Lord Bonville, in the Yorkist camp, while Henry Percy, Earl of Northumberland, faced the prospect of seeing his family's long-standing rivalry with the Nevilles in the north settled once and for all to his detriment. By early December Somerset and Devon had gathered their tenants in the south-west and marched to an appointed rendezvous at Hull, where they were to join forces with Northumberland, the Duke of Exeter, and Lords Clifford, Dacre, Roos, Neville, Greystoke and Latimer.[39]

It was evident that the parliamentary settlement could not be enforced by peaceful means. On 9 December York set out for the north to meet the queen's challenge head on, accompanied by his second son, Edmund of Rutland, and his brother-in-law, the Earl of Salisbury. Edward of March was despatched to the west to raise armed men on his family's estates in Wales and the marches, while Warwick and the Duke of Norfolk remained in the south-east to protect London and the seat of government at Westminster. Edward spent Christmas at Shrewsbury.[40] The festivities had not ended, when devastating news arrived. On 30 December at Wakefield the Duke of York had engaged a Lancastrian army led by the Duke of Somerset, the Earl of Northumberland, and John, Lord Clifford. York had been defeated, and he and Rutland had been killed in the fighting. Edward's uncle, the Earl of Salisbury, had been taken prisoner and beheaded after the battle, and his head had been placed alongside those of York and his son over the gates of the city of York.

HEIR TO THE THRONE

However shocked Edward might have been by the news of his father's and brother's deaths, he had little time to mourn his loss. He was now the Duke of York, and more than that, he now represented York's claim to the crown. The fate of his relatives at Wakefield left little doubt that

Queen Margaret would not rest until she had removed all claimants who stood between her son and the throne. Immediately after Wakefield, her army had begun the march south towards London. Edward immediately made preparations to intercept her with the troops that he had gathered from his marcher lordships, when he received news of a further army under Henry VI's half-brother, Jasper Tudor, Earl of Pembroke, and James Butler, Earl of Wiltshire, advancing from the north.

On 2 or 3 February[41] the two forces met at Mortimer's Cross, not far from Edward's castle at Wigmore. On the day before the battle a meteorological phenomenon (known as parhelia) caused three suns to be seen in the skies. Many of Edward's followers were distraught at this portent, but Edward proceeded to deliver to them the first of many eve of battle speeches he would make over the coming years. We have no reliable account of what he said, and his actual words were probably not altogether too different from Henry V's rousing battle cry at Agincourt ('Felas, lets go!'),[42] but one near-contemporary chronicler recorded the following, more elegant, version:

> Be of good comfort, and fear not. This is a good sign, for these three suns stand in token of the Father, the Son and the Holy Ghost, and therefore let us have a good heart, and in the name of Almighty God go against our enemies![43]

On the following day, the Lancastrians were routed, and Pembroke and Wiltshire fled from the battlefield. A number of the principal captured leaders were summarily executed in the market place at Hereford. Edward adopted the 'sun in splendour', the portent of his first independent military success, as one of his devices, but even while he celebrated his victory, events elsewhere were rather less favourable. Faced with news of the queen's advance from York, the Earl of Warwick, now the principal Yorkist magnate left in London, had had parliament dissolved, and had hastily gathered what support he could muster in the city. On 17 February, his forces suffered a bloody defeat in the streets of St Albans. Warwick himself escaped, but several other leaders, including Edward's kinsman, John Bourgchier, Lord Berners, and Warwick's brother, John Neville, were taken prisoner.

When Edward received news of his cousin's defeat, he turned his force east and made for London. At Chipping Norton he met Warwick,[44] who provided him with news of the king and queen's movements, and perhaps also with further details of the disaster at Wakefield that had deprived them both of their fathers. If Edward had not already made up his mind as to what was to be done next, Warwick did much to help him do so: Henry VI, now back under his wife's control, needed to be deposed, and Edward would be king in his place. If the thought of wearing the crown provided him with some comfort, other worries came to the fore. Edward 'was sorry that he was so poor, for he had no money, but the substance of his supporters [*mayny*] came at their own expense'.[45] Yet, when Edward and Warwick entered London on 27 February 1461,[46] the reception they received was more than encouraging. Public opinion in the south had for some time been favourable to the Yorkist lords, but the ravages of Queen Margaret's army and the incautious licence to plunder granted to the northerners had entered the public imagination, and turned the people further against the Lancastrian party. On 23 January the Norfolk gentleman Clement Paston wrote to his brother John:

> In this country every man is well willing to go with my lords here, and I hope God shall help them, for the people in the north rob and steal and are planning to pillage all this country, and give away men's goods and livelihoods in all the south country, and that will ask for mischief. My lords that are here have as much as they may do to keep down all this country, more than four or five shires, for they would be up on the men [in the] north, for it is for the well of all the south.[47]

And about the same time the papal legate Coppini summed up the atmosphere in London:

> we have seen and know full well that all the people are incensed and in the worst possible humour against those who do not desire peace. There are two reasons for this: firstly, the countless acts of cruelty related of [the Lancastrian party], whereas [the Yorkist lords] were not cruel, but received into favour those who wished to come; secondly because they recognise and know that his Majesty and the [Yorkist] lords with him and ourself with them are really disposed to an honest and honourable peace, salutary for both parties. Therefore if your influence with [Queen Margaret's supporters] does not suffice, their cause will be in the worst possible case, because the feelings of the people are incredibly incensed against them, and they will see more than two

hundred thousand desperate men rise against them, who are constantly assembling, offering to devote their goods and their persons in such an honest and just cause.[48]

Popular ballads further stirred up emotion, and painted Edward, the 'Rose of Rouen', as the hope of salvation from the imminent danger:

The northern men made their boast, when they had done that deed,
'We will dwell in the south country, and take all that we need.
These wives and their daughters, our purpose they shall serve' –
Then said the Rose of Rouen, 'no, that work shall I forbid.'
Blessed be the time, that ever God spread that flower.[49]

By virtue of the parliamentary settlement of the previous year, Edward was already heir to the throne in succession to his father. Had the Lords and Commons still been in session, a further act of parliament might have been sought. But parliament had disbanded in confusion some days earlier, in the wake of Queen Margaret's approaching army. There was no time to summon a parliament in which to stake Edward's claim to the crown; if anything, York's experience in the previous year made such a course of action seem unadvisable. Better far to present the Lords and Commons with a *fait accompli* at a later date. Another way of securing popular acclamation had to be found.

On Sunday 1 March the chancellor, Edward's cousin George Neville, Bishop of Exeter, addressed an undoubtedly carefully orchestrated assembly of soldiers and London citizens in St John's Field. He expounded Edward's title to the throne, and read a list of articles to show the ways in which Henry VI had broken the agreement of October 1460 and otherwise shown himself incapable of ruling. He then asked his audience whether they believed that Henry was worthy to continue to rule as king. When the predictable answer in the negative came, the able demagogue demanded to know whether the crowd would accept Duke Edward as king in Henry's stead, and duly received the assembly's enthusiastic acclamation.

Edward himself had carefully remained out of sight at Baynard's castle; he had no wish for an open repetition of his father's humiliation in the previous year. He was, however, soon put out of his misery, when messengers from the assembly in St John's Field arrived to inform him of the people's decision. Edward received them with the courtesy which was to become a mark of his rule, and 'thanked God and them'.[50]

Over the next two days plans for the formal kingmaking were hastily finalised. On Tuesday 3 March proclamations were made in London, summoning the people to assemble at St Paul's on the following morning. At the set time, Edward arrived in solemn procession accompanied by the Yorkist lords. At the cross, Bishop Neville once more asked the assembled people whether they would have Edward as their king, and received the same enthusiastic answer as three days earlier. Having received the people's acclamation, Edward made his way into the cathedral to hear a *Te Deum*, before riding to the Palace of Westminster. In Westminster Hall he took the king's seat in the marble chair of the King's Bench, clad in royal robes, wearing a cap of estate and holding the sceptre in his hand. Always something of a barrack-room lawyer, he personally expounded his title to the throne, and was rewarded for a third time with the enthusiastic acclamation of those assembled, which had eluded his father in the previous autumn. Edward of York was now King Edward IV.

3

THE ESTABLISHMENT OF EDWARD'S RULE, 1461–5

CRUSHING THE LANCASTRIAN RESISTANCE

Edward had been formally recognised and acclaimed as king, and sitting in the marble chair of the King's Bench with sceptre and cap of estate had publicly donned some of the trappings of royal power. To be the king was one thing, however; to be accepted as the king quite another. Henry VI had reigned – infant, boy and man – for more than 38 years, and two generations of Englishmen had never known any other king. To many, arguments over the legitimacy or otherwise of Lancastrian rule were merely academic. Henry VI and his predecessors had been accepted as lawful kings, and the allegiance that had been sworn to them was not easily abandoned. As Richard of York had discovered in the summer of 1460, few men were prepared to set their anointed king aside lightly.

Yet Henry VI's rule had also become synonymous with the military misfortune in France and domestic disorder over which he had presided, whether incapacitated or not. There was a degree of pragmatism about, and if Henry was personally popular, many of the leading lords of his council were not. It seemed to many that the grass might be greener elsewhere, and that this happier prospect was personified by the young Edward. Unquestionably, he looked every inch a king: the handsome and vigorous 19-year-old hardly needed the trappings of royalty to draw a crowd. Contemporaries were greatly struck by his splendid physique (he was over six foot three inches tall and broad shouldered) and good looks, both attributes inherited from his Plantagenet ancestors, which were only marred slightly in his later years by an overindulgence in food and drink.[1] In the days before his accession the word in London was: 'Let us walk in a new vineyard, and let us make us a gay garden in the month of March with this fair white rose and herb, the Earl of March.'[2] In April 1461 an Italian merchant in London wrote to an acquaintance in Bruges:

> I am unable to declare how well the commons love and adore him, as if he were their God. The entire kingdom keeps holiday for the event, which seems a boon from above. Thus far he appears to be a just prince, and to mean to amend and organise matters otherwise than has been done hitherto; so all comfort themselves with hopes of future well-being.[3]

Yet the adoration described by the Italian was not universal. Many thought like the London notary John Clerk who, when urged by his neighbours to come and see Edward's coronation procession to Westminster, had crudely replied: 'Twat and turd for him: I would as readily see the hunting of a duck, as him!'[4] Men like Clerk could be left to the local courts to deal with. Far more dangerous was the challenge to Edward's title presented by Henry VI, now once more at liberty and in his wife's control. If Edward's throne was to be secure, they needed to be crushed, and quickly at that.

In the week after his proclamation, Edward hurriedly set about borrowing money from the Londoners and others who would help, and on 11 March he sent an army under Lord Fauconberg north in pursuit of the Lancastrians. Two days later, he himself followed, raising forces as he went. On 28 March, the two armies met at Towton in Yorkshire. Initial skirmishes proved indecisive, and at sunrise on Palm Sunday, 29 March 1461, the two forces clashed in freezing weather and driving snow. The battle was to be one of the bloodiest of the Wars of the Roses. It lasted until 10 o'clock at night, but by the end of the fighting Edward had emerged victorious.

The battle represented a considerable personal triumph for the young king, who alongside the Duke of Norfolk, the Earl of Warwick and Lord Fauconberg had been in the thick of the battle, 'first fighting like common soldiers, then commanding, encouraging and rallying their squadrons like the greatest captains', as the chancellor, Bishop Neville of Exeter, reported to Bishop Coppini in Flanders. The Lancastrian Earl of Northumberland and Lords Dacre and Welles were killed in the fighting, and the Earls of Devon and Wiltshire were taken and beheaded after the battle. Unlike King Edward, Henry VI, Queen Margaret and their son, Prince Edward, took no part in the battle, and awaited the outcome at York. When the news of the defeat came, they hurriedly slipped away into Scotland.[5] The following morning Edward and his army entered York in triumph. They were met by Warwick's brother, Lord Montagu, Lord Berners, one of Edward's Bourgchier kinsmen, and an old servant of his father's, Sir Thomas Charlton, who had been taken prisoner at St Albans and dragged off to York by the queen's army. Now, Montagu and Berners asked pardon for the citizens of York, which Edward gracefully granted. With the defeated Lancastrian leaders still on the loose in the north, Bishop Neville believed that the victorious lords would remain in York for some time 'to reorganise matters in those parts', and indeed himself set out to join the king there.[6]

As the harsh weather of the battlefield of Towton gradually gave way to spring and early summer, Edward set out on a progress north to Durham and Newcastle, and then through Lancashire, Cheshire and the north midlands, which had displayed strong Lancastrian loyalties. Eventually the victors turned towards London, where Edward's coronation was scheduled for the end of June. The march south was a boisterous one, somewhat to the detriment of those, wealthy or poor, whose lands and possessions lay along the way. Edward was surrounded by a number of friends of his own age, such as Humphrey Stafford, and political concerns such as the impact of a marauding army on the sympathies of the peasantry along the way could for the time be set aside.[7]

Back in London, it was time for further celebration. On Friday 26 June Edward entered his capital in state, and was conducted to the Tower by the mayor and aldermen in their scarlet robes, as well as some 400 citizens robed in green. That evening and the following morning, Edward knighted his two young brothers, 12-year old George and 9-year-old Richard, along with 30 others, including young nobles such as John Mowbray, the Duke of Norfolk's 17-year-old heir, and John Stafford, a younger son of the dead Duke of Buckingham, along with more seasoned servants such as Walter Blount and the two newly appointed chief justices, John Markham and Robert Danby.[8] Later on Saturday, George was elevated to the dukedom of Clarence, as befitted the brother and heir presumptive of a king. After a feast in the Bishop of London's palace, Edward rode in procession to Westminster, preceded by the 32 new knights in blue gowns with white hoods, and tokens of white silk lace on the left shoulder,[9] and on the Sunday at Westminster the Archbishops of Canterbury and York placed St Edward's crown on his head.

Yet, while the victory at Towton had removed the immediate threat of Queen Margaret's army, it had not eliminated the problem of residual Lancastrian resistance in the further-flung parts of Edward's dominions. A number of lords and strongholds still maintained their allegiance to Henry VI and were prepared to fight for it. In the Calais marches, a garrison of Somerset's soldiers under Thomas Hussey continued to hold out at Guisnes until 24 October 1461, when it surrendered in return for a full royal pardon.[10] More dangerously, in spite of Edward's personal sojourn in and progress through the north and the north-western midlands, the north and the west continued to be in upheaval. Scotland, under the regency of the Dowager Queen Mary of Guelders during the minority of King James III, had provided a refuge for the defeated Henry VI and his queen, and had offered them military assistance in return for the cession of the pivotal border fortress of Berwick-upon-Tweed. A number of northern and Welsh strongholds held out in King Henry's name. In Northumberland, the deaths of two successive Percy earls in the Lancastrian cause at St Albans and Towton and the imprisonment of their heir in the Tower had done little to inspire Yorkist loyalties.

In June 1461 a Scottish-Lancastrian raid on Carlisle was successfully repelled, and at the end of the same month Henry VI himself, accompanied by Lords Dacre, Roos and Richemont-Grey, had to be dislodged from Brancepeth Castle. Alnwick and Dunstanborough Castles surrendered in the autumn of 1461, but within months the Lincolnshire rebel Sir William Tailboys recaptured Alnwick for Henry VI, while Humphrey, Lord Dacre of Gilsland, holed himself up in his family's castle at Naworth. In Wales, the Lancastrian resistance was led by Henry VI's half-brother, Jasper Tudor, Earl of Pembroke. Here also a number of strongholds, including the castles of Harlech, Carreg Cennen, Denbigh and Pembroke, continued to hold out in the Lancastrian cause. On 30 September 1461 Pembroke castle surrendered, and two weeks later a royal army defeated the main Lancastrian force in Wales under Pembroke and the Duke of Exeter at Twt Hill near Caernarvon. Denbigh Castle had surrendered by January 1462, but Carreg Cennen Castle held out until May of that year, and Harlech Castle remained unsubdued even longer, until 1468.

In both theatres of war Edward entrusted the suppression of the Lancastrian opposition to loyal lieutenants. In the north, command fell to the Earl of Warwick and his able younger brother, John Neville, Lord Montagu, while in Wales William, Lord Herbert, and Walter Devereux, Lord Ferrers, were put in charge. Edward himself was already displaying a reluctance to come to the further corners of his dominions which would characterise his approach throughout his reign. There were sound reasons for this: the Lancastrian garrisons in the northern and western castles presented a real threat, but they were by no means the only challenge to his rule. In the south-west, where nearly all regional magnates had strong Lancastrian leanings, there was unrest stirred by the nobles and gentry who had escaped from Towton, and in East Anglia the de Vere Earl of Oxford was hatching a plot which was uncovered in the early days of 1462.[11] Edward's journey back to Westminster after Towton thus took in Lancashire, Cheshire and the northern midlands, while the aftermath of the coronation saw him progress through Kent and then westward through Sussex and Wiltshire to Bristol, where he presided over the trial and execution of the Devon rebel Sir Baldwin Fulford. From Bristol he rode northwards into the Welsh Marches, but far from taking any personal part in the campaign against the rebel strongholds in the principality he made his way to his childhood home at Ludlow, and remained there until early October, when it was time to return to Westminster for the opening of parliament.[12]

Fulford's execution was a rare example of the king's personal exaction of the supreme penalty for treason. Not only was Edward keenly aware of the need to reconcile former Lancastrian loyalists to give his rule as broad a base as possible, he was also personally predisposed toward such an approach. Clearly, an example needed to be made of some of the leaders of the resistance, and prior to that of Fulford Edward had personally presided over the execution of his father's old enemy James Butler, Earl of Wiltshire, at Newcastle on 1 May 1461. On most other occasions, however, he was ready to receive even former enemies who had been at the heart of the Lancastrian regime into his allegiance. Thus, Bishop

Lawrence Booth of Durham, who had been Queen Margaret's chancellor and had been dismissed as keeper of Henry VI's privy seal after the Yorkist victory at Northampton in July 1460, was appointed the new king's confessor in April 1461. The Lancastrian constable of Dunstanborough, Sir Ralph Percy, a younger brother of the Earl of Northumberland killed at Towton, who had held his castle for Henry VI into September 1461, was allowed to retain his post. Henry Beaufort, Duke of Somerset, who had consistently opposed the Yorkist cause since his father's death at St Albans in 1455, was not only accepted into Edward's allegiance after his surrender in December 1462 but was almost instantly placed in a position of command alongside the Earl of Warwick at the siege of Alnwick Castle, held by his own recent friends under Robert, Lord Hungerford.[13]

This readiness on Edward's part not only to pardon, but indeed to place trust in, men with an unambiguous track-record of opposition to his rule has been regarded as one of the young king's principal political mistakes in the early years of his reign. But far from arising from Edward's youthful inexperience, let alone – as one recent commentator has tried to suggest – from a homoerotic infatuation with the Duke of Somerset,[14] there were sound political reasons for seeking to reconcile former enemies to the new regime. Edward, as Michael Hicks has pointed out, still badly needed to broaden the base of his support among the nobility and gentry. Moreover, the pardoning of men like Somerset was not a poorly considered isolated decision by the king, nor was their defection inevitable. Rather, Somerset was pardoned in gradual stages: he had initially to prove his new loyalties at the siege of Alnwick, and only then was the reversal of his attainder sanctioned by the Lords and Commons in the parliament of 1463. Moreover it was Somerset himself who – having judged the Lancastrian defeat in the north inevitable – had made the initial overtures to come to terms with the king in the winter of 1462.[15]

With the benefit of hindsight, Edward's policy of reconciliation with Somerset and his northern allies proved a failure and disastrously prolonged the fighting in the north. Although the departure of Queen Margaret from Scotland in April to seek assistance at the French court allowed Edward to negotiate a truce with the Scottish regent and thus to cut off support for the Lancastrian defenders of Naworth and Alnwick, who surrendered in July, the gains made during the summer of 1462 were soon lost again. On 25 October Margaret of Anjou landed near Bamborough and, although she had only a small following rather than the French army she had hoped for, in subsequent days the Northumbrian castles one by one opened their gates to her. Edward, who during the summer's campaign had progressed no further north than Lincoln, deemed the situation sufficiently serious to set out for the borders himself at some speed. On 19 November he reached York and pressed on to Durham, only to be struck down by measles. While the disease was not life threatening, it confined the king to his chamber for some weeks. He was unable either to return south or to play any further part in that winter's campaign, command of which thus once again fell to the Earl of Warwick.[16] One by one the earl methodically and successfully starved the rebel garrisons into submission. News of a relief force of Scots and Frenchmen failed to reach the defenders of Dunstanborough and Bamborough, who agreed to a conditional surrender on Christmas Eve. Alnwick continued to hold out until early January, when the Franco-Scottish relief army appeared in the vicinity; the Earl of Warwick, his men demoralised by the cold and damp of the Northumbrian winter, did nothing to prevent the defenders marching out of the castle and withdrawing into Scotland.

By the end of 1462 Edward's victory seemed all but complete, and the king (now recovered from his illness) and his Neville allies headed south to oversee obits and obsequies for their kinsmen killed at Wakefield two years earlier. It was from this position of strength that the king clearly thought he could afford to be generous to his defeated enemies. Thus, the Duke of Somerset and the constable of Dunstanborough and Bamborough, Sir Ralph Percy, both of whom had been taken when the two castles surrendered at Christmas, were received into the Yorkist king's allegiance; before long Percy was restored to his command, while Somerset and his men were added to Warwick's siege army at Alnwick.

Within months this proved to be a miscalculation, and the situation in the north was soon more precarious than it had been even a year earlier. In March Sir Ralph Percy allowed a force of French and Scottish mercenaries to take back Bamborough and Dunstanborough for Henry VI, and in May Sir Ralph Grey allowed the Lancastrian Lord Hungerford to re-occupy Alnwick. An attempted assault on Newcastle was beaten back by the citizens, but the Scots were now ready once more to support the Lancastrian cause, and before the end of June an army personally led by the 11-year-old King James III and the regent, Mary of Guelders, and accompanied by Henry VI and Queen Margaret crossed the border and laid siege to Norham Castle.[17]

Edward now asked both parliament and the convocation of the clergy of the province of Canterbury for substantial grants of money to fund a major expedition against the Scots, which – it was widely believed – might go so far as to end Scotland's existence as an independent kingdom. In mid-July Edward himself set out northward, but he only got as far as Northampton before news arrived that the Earl of Warwick, Lord Montagu and the Archbishop of York had relieved Norham and had pursued the invaders across the border. Margaret of Anjou and her son escaped to Berwick and at the end of July sailed for Sluys, leaving Henry VI behind in Scotland. It is not clear at what point Edward abandoned his plans for an attack on the Scots (if, indeed, he had ever harboured such a plan). As late as mid-August he issued letters summoning urban levies to assemble at Newcastle on 13 September, and provision for the supply of a royal fleet to be sent against the Scots continued at least until the end of August. The king himself briefly returned to the south to issue instructions to the ambassadors who were about to cross the Channel for negotiations with the French and Burgundians, but he was back in Yorkshire by the end of September, and remained there until early in the new year.

In the meantime, it had evidently become apparent that in spite of parliament's grant of £37,000 a full-scale campaign against the Scots could quite simply not be afforded. For much of the first two and a half years of the reign Edward's finances had been shored up by loans amounting to over £35,000 from the Londoners, the Calais staplers, the clergy and others, and there were urgent financial obligations to be met, among them the payment of the wages of the Calais garrison. It was to this end that much of the money granted by parliament (of which about half had been collected in early August) was diverted, in direct contravention of the conditions attached by the Commons to their grant. This flagrant misuse of the funds caused widespread popular discontent which found one outlet in parliament. The Commons reassembled in November and successfully pressed for the reduction of their grant by £6,0000, as well as the delay of the payment of the second half of this sum until March 1464.[18]

Simultaneously, however, popular disgruntlement with Edward's government resulted in open disorder in a number of regions during the winter of 1463–4, unrest deemed sufficiently serious to demand the king's personal progress through both the east and west of his realm. The local restlessness was rapidly seized upon by the remaining Lancastrian loyalists for their own ends. In December 1463 the Duke of Somerset left northern Wales and rejoined his former associates at Bamborough. Within a few months, Edward's opponents had reasserted their position in the north and had retaken Norham castle in Henry VI's name. Once again, Edward proved reluctant to come north in person, concentrating his energies instead on the quashing of unrest further south, and placing his faith in the military prowess of Lord Montagu and his own diplomacy. It was imperative that negotiations with the Scots should succeed in depriving Henry VI's adherents of support from across the border. In mid-April Lord Montagu was despatched to the Scottish frontier to ensure that King James's ambassadors should safely reach a planned meeting at York on 20 April. On the way, they were twice way-laid. Although Montagu successfully evaded a first ambush near Newcastle, on about 25 April he encountered a rebel army led by the Duke of Somerset, Lords Roos and Hungerford, and Sir Ralph Percy at Hedgeley Moor. Forced to offer battle, Montagu succeeded in routing the rebels and killing Percy, although the other rebel leaders fled to fight another day. That day came sooner than expected.

It is not clear when or where the news of Montagu's triumph at Hedgeley Moor reached Edward. He evidently had not been informed even two days after the battle, when he finally set out for the north in person. He reached St Albans on 28 April and, as we will see, on May Day he was briefly delayed by some personal business at Stony Stratford in Northamptonshire, but on 5 May he reached Leicester, where his army had been ordered to assemble. On 14 May he moved on to Nottingham, and it was there that fresh messengers from Lord Montagu reached him. While at Newcastle, Montagu had been informed that the Northumbrian rebels had made a sortie from Alnwick and had pitched their camp two miles from Hexham. Montagu and his lieutenants, Lords Greystoke and Willoughby, had immediately marched to meet them with all the forces at their disposal, and on 15 May had succeeded in routing the insurgents completely. Most of the rebel leaders, including the Duke of Somerset, Lords Hungerford and Roos, and a number of other prominent Lancastrians, were taken during the battle or rounded up in subsequent days, and summarily executed.[19]

These executions literally decapitated the Lancastrian cause in England, and by the end of June 1464 all the Northumbrian castles were in Edward's hands. In Wales, Harlech Castle alone held out for another four years until August 1468. In England, Henry VI remained at liberty, but while he could be used as a figurehead, he lacked the energy to assume personal leadership of the dwindling numbers still loyal to him. For some months he continued to find shelter with supporters in northern England, but on 13 July 1465 he was captured near Bungerly Hippingstones in Lancashire and taken to the Tower.[20] With the rival monarch in his custody, Edward's rule of England should have been secure.

THE RE-ESTABLISHMENT OF ROYAL AUTHORITY

For almost 40 years since the accession of the infant Henry VI, English government had lacked the leadership of a competent adult king. Now government had to be reinvented, centring on the person of a competent and vigorous, if also inexperienced and in some respects self-indulgent, monarch. The king's youth – he was still only just 19 years old – and inexperience were not lost on external observers, who concluded that others must rule the king, and by implication England, and who saw themselves vindicated by the sway that Warwick and his kinsmen unquestionably held in many areas of government. In April 1461 an Italian commentator in Flanders was prepared to give the benefit of the doubt to the 'just prince' who meant 'to amend and organise matters otherwise than has been done hitherto', but others were more critical. Nicholas O'Flanagan, the Dominican Bishop of Elphin, wrote to the papal legate Coppini in April 1461 that the king's mother held him 'at her pleasure',[21] while in March 1464 the French king's governor of Abbéville in Picardy reported sarcastically to his master, Louis XI, that England had 'but two rulers – M. de Warwick and another, whose name I have forgotten'.[22]

Yet, as Charles Ross and others have rightly argued, those who wrote Edward off as a mere puppet in Warwick's hands were mistaken about the true balance of power. If Edward chose to give his cousin a free hand on the periphery of his realm, he nevertheless retained the freedom to end this arrangement at his pleasure. Edward, in Ross's words, 'was very much king in fact as well as in name'.[23] Fifteenth-century government was very much personal to the monarch. Kings were expected to, and did, rule in person. Historians have rightly pointed to Henry VI's personal responsibility for his downfall, whether – as some would have it – because of the wilful and inconsistent nature of his intervention in the government, or – as others have suggested – because of his inability to exercise the personal rule required of him for the smooth functioning of the administrative machinery. Edward IV exercised his authority with vigour from the outset. The sheer number of government documents, warrants, orders and letters signed by the king's own hand bear witness to the amount of administrative business he faced and addressed from the first days of his reign. If under Henry VI the royal sign manual had been an occasional form of authorisation, and the king's personal authority had been conferred chiefly by the royal signet, which could – if necessary – be wielded by the secretary in response to some sign of acquiescence on the part of the dysfunctional monarch, Edward's initial frequently appeared on warrants, orders and bills, regardless of whether or not they were later also authorised by the signet or another royal seal.

In other areas of governance Edward also fulfilled the functions expected of him. He presided over the council and the opening of parliament, and he displayed a strong personal commitment to the restoration of law and order. The breakdown of the law in the provinces and Henry VI's inability to re-enforce it had been a particular cause of criticism of the deposed king's government; in 1455 Edward's father, the Duke of York, had been appointed protector for a second time explicitly to deal with the disorder that was sweeping the south-west. Edward was deeply conscious of the importance of restoring the law throughout the realm as a measure of his kingship, and of the part that he as king had to play in doing so.[24] Time and time again, Edward's commitment to the administration of justice was the theme of show-piece political statements made by the king or on his behalf. In October 1461 the Norfolk gentleman Clement Paston reported to his brother John how Edward had exclaimed that day:

> We have sent two privy seals to Paston by two yeomen of our chamber, and he disobeys them; but we will send him another tomorrow, and by God's mercy, if he does not come then he shall die for it. We will make all other men beware by him how they shall disobey our writing. A servant of ours has made a complaint of him. I cannot think that he has informed us all truthfully, yet

that notwithstanding we will not suffer him to disobey our writing; but since he disobeys our writing, we may believe the better that his conduct is as we have been informed.[25]

In December, Edward's personal address to a delegation of the parliamentary Commons was followed by a statement by Chancellor Neville announcing a series of measures ordained by the king to re-establish law and order, and sworn to by the lords. These measures were to be published throughout the realm, and the king himself would go on a progress through the kingdom, and would hear the grievances of all who wished to complain of breaches of the law. In March 1462, the royal judge William Yelverton, presiding over the sessions of the peace at Norwich, was at pains to describe to the assembled parties how the king had taken him by the hand and personally thanked him for his diligence in encouraging the community of Cambridgeshire to complain of corrupt officials, and had asked him to do likewise in Norfolk.[26] In April 1463, the widely reported sermon preached in the presence of king, lords and commons by Bishop Neville at the opening of parliament took as its theme the text 'Let those who judge the land prize justice' from the Book of Wisdom. The following February a royal messenger, wearing a collar of the king's livery, stood next to the presiding judge at the shire house at Norwich while a royal letter was read, promising that the king himself would come around Easter to punish the principal disturbers of the peace and to pardon lesser offenders.[27] In May 1468 the second session of the parliament elected in the previous year was opened by the new chancellor, Bishop Stillington of Bath and Wells, with a philosophical speech about the nature of justice, emphasising how much Edward had done to restore peace. A year later Edward, entreated to intervene in the Paston family's quarrel with the Duke of Norfolk, was reported to have replied that he would 'neither treat nor speak for [the Pastons], but let the law proceed'.[28]

Nor did Edward intend these to remain empty words. By the time his first parliament assembled, the king had already undertaken a judicial progress into the south-west and the marches, and further progresses followed in January 1462 into Kent, and in March through Cambridgeshire and Huntingdonshire into Lincolnshire. In order that he might be seen to be dispensing justice at the heart of his realm as well as in its provinces, in October 1462, in a gesture much commented upon, Edward even sat in person as judge in the marble seat of King's Bench – trying cases of rape.[29]

Yet even the most vigorous and active of kings could not be everywhere at once, and could not execute every detail of the government of his realm in person. It was a characteristic of Edward's rule that he showed considerable reluctance to progress to the further-flung corners of his dominions except in times of extreme need. Even then, he was often reluctant to go the whole way. It is notable that although Edward personally set out to campaign against his Scottish and Lancastrian opponents on no fewer than four separate occasions between 1461 and 1464, he turned back and failed to arrive on the scene every time.

Contemporary commentators interpreted this failure to fulfil the role of the soldier-king as a personal shortcoming in the young monarch, arising from his laziness and love of leisure. Modern scholarship by contrast has read it, probably accurately, as part of a deliberate policy, which saw the king focus his attention in the heart of his realm and, in particular, personally spend much time on the details of government at the administrative centre, while leaving the rule of the regions to trusted lieutenants. There was nothing inherently new in this approach. The Lancastrian court's movements had for much of the time been restricted to meanderings around the Thames valley, while attempts were made, especially in the 1440s, to use existing administrative structures, such as the duchy of Lancaster, headed by trusted officers to rule the regions where possible. Where Henry VI's government had failed conspicuously was at the centre, where the king and his council had shown themselves unable to provide strong and coherent leadership that the king's lieutenants in the provinces might look to. This specifically was a mistake that Edward was aware of and that he was determined not to repeat.

Genuine the young king's intentions might be, but his efforts were hampered by his shaky hold on the throne. While large parts of the realm did not yet acknowledge the king's authority, he could not afford to antagonise any of his leading magnates. Thus, as the East Anglian Paston family discovered, Edward was not prepared, or at least not able, to uphold their rights against the Dukes of Norfolk and Suffolk even in the face of the most flagrant breaches of the law on the part of these magnates.

EDWARD'S GOVERNMENT AND ITS PERSONNEL

It was the young king's very focus on ruling from the heart of his kingdom that misled foreign observers watching from the periphery into
believing him to be under the control of his greatest subject, the Earl of
Warwick, or indeed of his mother, for it was on the periphery that he
was content to rely on lieutenants, chief among them Warwick, rather
than intervening in person. Of course, contemporary commentators were
correct in their assessment of Edward's youth and inexperience. What
little practical knowledge he possessed even of the administration of a
noble estate, he had gathered from a distance by observing the activities
of his father's officials during his time at Ludlow. But it soon became
evident that Edward intended to be his own man. To this end, he could
not afford to be seen to be ruled by a narrow group of his nobles, least of
all by a man as openly ambitious as the Earl of Warwick. He thus needed
to counterbalance the power of the earl and of his Neville kinsmen by
other great men loyal to him, and to bolster their ranks by the elevation
of new men who owed wealth, status and influence to him alone.

The early months of the reign saw a number of the Duke of York's
old supporters as well as more recent converts to Edward's cause
rewarded with grants of lands, and in a number of instances elevation
to or within the peerage. Eight new barons were created (lords
Cromwell, Hastings, Herbert, Lumley, Montagu, Ogle, Stafford of
Southwick and Wenlock), while three barons (lords Ferrers of Chartley,
Morley and Scales) were recognised in their wives' right. Edward's
kinsmen William Neville, Lord Fauconberg, and Henry, Viscount
Bourgchier, were elevated respectively to the earldoms of Kent and
Essex, while the king's younger brothers were created dukes of Clarence
and Gloucester on the eve of the coronation. Other creations followed.
In June 1464 Edward's trusted lieutenant in the north, John, Lord
Montagu, was rewarded with the earldom of Northumberland, and
over the following five years, a further five barons (Dunster, Dynham,
Maltravers, Mountjoy, Welles) were added to the lowest rung of the
peerage, while lords Grey of Ruthin, Rivers, Herbert and Stafford, as
well as the Duke of Suffolk's heir, were raised to the earldoms of Kent,
Rivers, Pembroke, Devon and Lincoln.

The creation of a new Yorkist peerage aside it was also imperative not
to penalise men simply on account of their past allegiance to Henry VI,

who had after all been accepted as the rightful and anointed king of England for no less than 38 years. The new king not only needed the support of the magnates in the regions; crucially, he also needed the experience of seasoned royal servants to assist him in the governance of the kingdom he had so suddenly acquired.

At his accession, Edward IV was a young man, and it was thus natural that he should surround himself with young nobles. Several of his new creations at the start of the reign, like Humphrey, Lord Stafford of Southwick, Walter Devereux, Lord Ferrers of Chartley, and Humphrey Bourgchier, Lord Cromwell, were in their twenties; others, including men who would become central to his rule, like the chamberlain, Lord Hastings, John Neville, Lord Montagu, and the Earl of Warwick himself, were in their early thirties. The younger of these men were congenial companions for Edward, but they had scarcely more experience of matters of state, or even of the management of a great estate, than the king himself. There was little in this youthful and testosterone-driven circle that promised the return to stable government that the kingdom so badly needed. A number of more experienced men thus took a central part in government. The treasurership remained in the hands of Henry Bourgchier, now Earl of Essex, a man in his mid-fifties, who had previously held the office during the Duke of York's second protectorate in 1455-6. The chancellor, Bishop George Neville of Exeter, was still a young man, but at least had the benefit of a clerical education and five years at the helm of his bishopric. Neville – like the keeper of the privy seal, Robert Stillington, archdeacon of Wells, and the king's secretary, James Goldwell, archdeacon of Essex – had first taken office in the aftermath of the battle of Northampton, and like them thus had at least cut his teeth in office during the months of Yorkist rule in Henry VI's name in the second half of 1460.

The chief justices of two of the principal royal law courts at Westminster were replaced in the early months of the reign: the chief justice of King's Bench, Sir John Fortescue, had gone into exile with Henry VI and Queen Margaret, while the chief justice of common pleas, John Prysot, had died in May 1461. Their replacements (John Markham and Robert Danby) were experienced men of law, who had each served as puisne judges in their respective courts for a number of years. By contrast, the replacement of the chief baron of the Exchequer, Peter Ardern, in September 1462 had rather clearer political overtones. His successor,

Richard Illingworth, had not previously held judicial office, but had done private service as a member of the Earl of Warwick's council. No changes were made to the lower ranks of the judiciary, other than to replace the two newly promoted chief justices.

As might be expected, sweeping changes were made to the king's household. Even the senior officers who had been put in place in Henry VI's household by the Yorkist regime of the late summer of 1460, such as the steward, John, Lord Beauchamp, the treasurer, Sir Walter Skull, and the controller, Sir Thomas Charlton, were replaced at Edward IV's accession. That the carvers, knights and esquires of the body, whose duties required daily attendance upon and close personal contact with the monarch, should also be replaced was only natural.

There was more continuity in the lower echelons of the royal household. Many of Henry VI's serjeants and grooms of the *domus providencie*, the departments responsible for the day-to-day provisioning of the king and his entourage, made a smooth transition into Edward's service. Similarly, there was little change in the middling and lower ranks of the Westminster bureaucracy, among the clerks, prothonotaries, filacers and secondaries. It is hard to overemphasise the importance of continuity in the clerical ranks of the Chancery and Exchequer for the smooth running of an inexperienced king's government, and such continuity prevailed. For the most part, the clerks and other officers who had taken up their posts under Henry VI remained in office, some of them for the entire duration of Edward's reign, and even beyond. When they were replaced, their replacements were normally career civil servants who had risen through the ranks of the lesser clerical hierarchy, rather than overtly political appointments.

Some of the great offices of state had, of course, to be granted to Edward's principal supporters as rewards. Thus, Edward's uncle William Neville, the new Earl of Kent, became steward of the household, the newly ennobled Lord Wenlock became chief butler of England, and Warwick himself acquired or retained a whole host of offices, including those of Great Chamberlain and Admiral of England, the captaincy of Calais, the wardenships of the Cinque Ports, and the East and West Marches towards Scotland, and the chief stewardship of the Duchy of Lancaster. Taken together, this bundle of offices made Warwick the supreme military commander both within England and around its shores.[30]

THE SETTLEMENT IN THE REGIONS

If Edward was to rule from the centre, important decisions needed to be taken to ensure that his authority could percolate down into the regions, still in turmoil from the civil war that had gone before. The aftermath of Towton saw many of the traditional leaders of local society executed, disgraced or in flight, and new arrangements were needed. In the north of England, the final years of Henry VI had seen a breakdown of the precarious balance of power between the Percy earls of Northumberland and the Neville earls of Salisbury and Westmoreland and their respective cadets. The traditional rivalry of the two families had been allowed to break out into open violence in the early and mid-1450s. This had led the feuding dynasties into rival camps during the open civil war at the end of the decade, and had seen the Nevilles, who had sided with the Duke of York against the court, emerge victorious. Henry Percy, third Earl of Northumberland, had died at Towton and posthumously been attainted by parliament. His estates were confiscated, and many of them were assigned to Warwick and his brother John, Lord Montagu, who three years later was also granted the comital title. Between Warwick's earldom of Salisbury and his brother's earldom of Northumberland the Nevilles had full control of the north, contested only by the remaining Lancastrian rebels in the Northumbrian castles.

Equally problematic was the position in the south-west of England, a traditionally unruly region which had been troubled for much of Henry VI's majority. The executions of William, Lord Bonville, after the second battle of St Albans, and of the Earls of Devon and Wiltshire after Towton, had removed three of the principal magnates in the region from the scene, and the continued Lancastrian loyalties of lords Hungerford and Moleyns and the dukes of Somerset and Exeter ruled them out as viable leaders of a Yorkist settlement. The solution adopted in the first place apparently sought to avoid the creation of any pre-eminent magnate in the region, perhaps with a view to an eventual restoration of the heirs of some of the executed peers to their ancestral titles, in line with Edward's policy of reconciling former Lancastrians wherever possible. To this end, the heirs of Courtenay and Hungerford were allowed to recover a share of their families' forfeited lands and for much of the 1460s seem to have lived quietly enough.

In the first instance, Edward looked to a collegiate solution. The redistribution of the lands at the king's disposal in 1461 took account of the leading place of the Nevilles in his circle. The importance of the bishopric of Exeter – held by Warwick's brother George Neville – was considerable, when so many of the secular magnates in the region had been removed from the equation. Bishop Neville, however, was serving as Edward's chancellor, and was unlikely to spend much time in his diocese. Neville influence in the region was thus buttressed by a grant of 50 of the forfeited manors of the executed Earls of Devon and Wiltshire to his uncle, William Neville, Lord Fauconberg and now Earl of Kent. Also increased was the influence of Edward's youthful friend Humphrey Stafford, who was created Lord Stafford of Southwick and endowed with a further substantial share of the forfeited Courtenay estates. It was he who emerged pre-eminent in the region when the deaths, in quick succession in 1462 and 1463 of Kent and another south-western peer, the ageing William, Lord Botreaux, without male heirs, necessitated a reorganisation of the power balance in the region.

Further Courtenay lands were now given to Stafford, much to the chagrin of another of Edward's early supporters, John Dynham of Nutwell, who in 1459 had helped to spirit the young Earl of March away from the disaster of Ludford, but who had not received the rewards some others, including Stafford, had been able to claim. Only in 1464 were some of the Hungerford lands settled on Dynham, who was eventually elevated to a peerage in 1467, but did not emerge as a serious political force in his native south-west until the 1470s. In 1465, the translation of George Neville to the archbishopric of York and his replacement by John Booth, a half-brother of the Bishop of Durham, removed the remaining Neville influence from Devon and Cornwall. In 1469 the execution for treason of the Courtenay and Hungerford heirs paved the way for the grant of the comital title to Humphrey Stafford, who had by now emerged as the king's unquestionable and trusted lieutenant in the region.

In the midlands Warwick's long-standing rivalry with Humphrey Stafford, Duke of Buckingham, was decided in Richard Neville's favour by Buckingham's death in the battle of Northampton in 1460. In the eastern midlands Edward created a new power base by granting a range of duchy of Lancaster offices and some of the forfeited estates of the Earl of Wiltshire, Viscount Beaumont and Lord Roos to his confidant William, Lord Hastings, the chamberlain of the royal household.[31]

In the east of England Edward's brother-in-law, the Duke of Suffolk, his uncle, Henry Bourgchier, Earl of Essex, and the Mowbray dukes of Norfolk, a family with long-established ties to the house of York, held sway. The region should thus have presented few problems. Yet East Anglia in particular had long been an unsettled part of the realm, and it continued to present problems to the new king. The parliamentary elections of 1461 in Norfolk witnessed disturbances. In 1462 John de Vere, Earl of Oxford, who had ostensibly acquiesced in Edward's accession, was found guilty of treason and executed, together with his son and heir. Even the Duke of Norfolk, one of the mainstays of Edward's rule in the area, was not above resorting to open violence to get his own way, as when he laid siege to and forcibly took possession of the Paston castle at Caister, thus demonstrating the limits of royal authority in the face of the king's reliance on the power of local magnates.

In Wales and the Marches, where Edward's own earldom of March gave the crown considerable sway, the Yorkist victory had removed as an active political force the Talbot Earl of Shrewsbury (who had been killed at Northampton fighting for King Henry, leaving his heir a minor of 12), while Henry VI's half-brother, the Tudor Earl of Pembroke, continued to stir up unrest for much of the 1460s, but was eventually also forced into French exile. The new king's principal lieutenants were Sir Walter Devereux, recognised in his wife's right as Lord Ferrers of Chartley, and above all William, Lord Herbert, who was granted many of the lands of the Tudor earldom of Pembroke and in 1468 received the comital title itself.

Although this rearrangement of regional power was highly favourable to Warwick and his Neville relatives, in many respects it also represented an assertion of Edward's own will. Thus the settlement in Wales ran contrary to Warwick's ambition of consolidating his holdings in Glamorgan by the acquisition of the Duke of Buckingham's neighbouring lordships in south Wales, since these lands were placed under the control of Lord Herbert. In the midlands, similarly, the influence of Warwick's great fiefdom was counterbalanced by the estates granted to William, Lord Hastings, whose hand was further strengthened by his appointment to the stewardship of the Duchy of Lancaster honour of Leicester, of which Warwick was stripped in his favour.[32]

ECONOMIC POLICY

Along with the restoration of law and order in the regions, an area of government in desperate need of monarchical attention was commercial policy. Like the administration of justice, this was an area of policy in which Edward took a strong personal interest. The loss of Lancastrian France had left much of the English trade with the continent in ruins, and from the point of view of the English merchant community it was imperative that measures should be taken to protect its interests. Edward was very willing to lend an open ear to the grievances of the English traders. He was under no illusion about the importance of commercial finance to the stability of his rule – from the outset of his reign loans and gifts from the citizens of London and from the merchants of the Calais staple had been central to financing his quest for the crown. Nor, indeed, was Edward above filling his coffers by engaging in trade himself. Throughout his reign, factors buying and selling cloth, wool and tin on his behalf did much to help make the regime solvent. In his later years, the king was actively encouraging English merchant adventurers to seek new markets on the Barbary and Guinea coasts of Africa, and there has even been a suggestion that a licence granted in 1480 to a group of Bristol merchants may have resulted in the discovery of America in the following year.[33]

In setting commercial policy, the chief problem faced by any medieval English monarch was the diversity of interests of the various groups and associations within the merchant community, and, indeed, the ways in which the requirements of those groups diverged from the needs of the crown. Thus the merchants of the staple[34] as far as possible sought to have all cloth exports from England channelled through Calais, whereas the more loosely organised merchant adventurers' companies that had formed in several English towns sought to protect their unrestricted trade with foreign markets. In competition with both, and consequently deeply resented, were communities of alien merchants, above all Italians and the merchants of the Teutonic Hanse.[35] From the crown's point of view, the trade of the staplers needed to be protected, as their revenues financed the strategically vital garrison of Calais, but Edward, like his predecessors, also relied upon the Italians for loans of money, while the Hansards had a monopoly on the trade in goods from the

Baltic, such as tar and ashes which were crucial to the English cloth manufacturing industry.

The preoccupation of the reign's first parliament with the necessary constitutional settlement precluded any broad discussion of commercial issues and the king reserved to himself judgement on the one matter that did arise – the confirmation of the privileges traditionally enjoyed by the merchants of the Hanse. By contrast, in Edward's second parliament of 1463–5 mercantile policy loomed large. Among the measures passed during the course of this assembly were acts concerning the size of broadcloths, the wool trade, the import of grain and the trade with Burgundy, as well as measures protecting the privileges of various crafts and London livery companies. The 11 statutes of 1463–5 were followed in 1467 by an act of parliament protecting the interests of English cloth-iers by placing a ban on the export of woollen yarn and unfinished cloth. Yet if Edward readily acquiesced in the protectionist legislation demanded by the parliamentary Commons, he was politically astute enough to circumvent the restrictions placed on his Italian friends and creditors by the grant of special licences, and at no point subjected his foreign policy to the demands of the native merchant community.

Characteristically, what was perhaps the most drastic commercial measure of Edward's first reign was not enacted in full parliament, but was instead agreed upon by an unelected great council of lords and other hand-picked representatives held at Reading in the autumn of 1464. This was a full re-coinage of the currency of the realm, ostensibly on the pretext of the severe shortage of bullion in England. The measure amounted to nothing less than the most drastic devaluation of the English coinage in more than a century, as the face value of the currency was increased by a quarter. A pound of silver now produced 450, rather than 360 pennies, and the gold noble was reckoned at 8s 4d rather than 6s 8d. Popular discontent was immediate, not merely on account of the debasement of the coinage, but also for the quite practical reason that people who were accustomed to the duodecimal base of the currency 'could not reckon that gold ... so quickly as they did the old gold'.[36] This latter grievance was one that Edward and his advisers were pre-pared to redress, so in April 1465 a new and attractively designed gold coinage was introduced, consisting of a gold noble (or royal) worth 10s, a half-noble and a quarter-noble, as well as two new coins, the angel and the angelet, respectively valued at 6s 8d and 3s 4d.[37] From the king's point of view, the recoinage was a success. Not only did it add more than £17,000 in minting charges to his private coffers, it also put into circulation even in the furthest-flung parts of the realm new coins intimately associated with the new king's image. The reform did little to alleviate the shortage of circulating coins, but it played an important part in stimulating the export trade, since the devaluation of the currency meant that English goods were now 25 per cent cheaper.

There was, however, one aspect of economic policy with which Edward signally failed to come to grips. This was the management of his own finances. It was a staple of medieval English political discourse that the king should live of his own: that is, that the revenues of the crown estates and the fee farms of the shires and boroughs of England should pay for the maintenance of his household. Only in exceptional circumstances, such as war, could the community of the realm be asked for extra funds by way of taxation. As, however, the king was also expected to show his grace to his subjects by grants of the lands and offices at his disposal, the real income he could expect to draw was much diminished, and successive kings were reduced to diverting taxation granted for war to other uses, regularly reaping displays of popular discontent in return. The Lancastrian kings in particular had found themselves in almost permanent financial crisis, not least because of the heavy financial demands of the sustained fighting in France throughout most of the first half of the fifteenth century.

At Edward's accession, a very different picture presented itself. On learning of his father's death, Edward had complained to Warwick about his poverty; within a few months, however, his position had changed dramatically. Not since the days of the Norman kings had an English monarch united such vast estates in his hands as were now at Edward's disposal. Richard of York had been the greatest landowner of his day, and had left his son not only the extensive estates of the duchy of York, but also those of the Mortimer earldom of March. With Edward's accession to the throne, he acquired also the royal duchies of Cornwall and Lancaster (the latter held by Henry VI as his patrimony, but now incorporated and settled on Edward and his successors as kings), and the earldom of Chester. An act of attainder passed by parliament in November 1461 condemned the new king's opponents to forfeiture of their lands: Edward thus gained control of the lands of the dukedoms of Somerset, Buckingham and Exeter, the earldoms of Devon, Wiltshire,

Northumberland and Pembroke, the viscountcy of Beaumont and the baronies of Hungerford, Roos, Clifford, Richemont-Grey, Welles, Neville and Dacre, as well as the possessions of a range of lesser men. Naturally, the king was not at liberty to keep all of these lands himself. Apanages needed to be provided for Edward's mother, the Dowager Duchess of York, and his surviving brothers, the newly created Dukes of Clarence and Gloucester. The supporters who had won Edward the throne needed to be rewarded with generous grants of land, and from time to time old adversaries needed to be won over by restoration to their inheritances.

As a result, by 1463 Edward had granted away most of what he had acquired and was unable to meet pressing commitments such as the payment of the Calais garrison. The seemingly secure footing on which the crown's finances had been placed in 1461 had been lost once more. The goodwill that the king's efforts to restore good governance had generated allowed him to approach Parliament for a subsidy in support of an invasion of Scotland, which was granted. When, however, the lack of ready money in his coffers forced Edward to divert the taxation to pay the wages of the Calais soldiers, the commons' goodwill, and with it the king's popularity, rapidly evaporated. Moreover, much of Edward's patronage had been focused on a narrow group of associates. The Nevilles had been more than generously rewarded for their support, and generous grants of forfeited lands had built up the power of Edward's chosen regional lieutenants, Lords Herbert and Stafford.[38] Any future restorations of reconciled former opponents or substantial grants to relatives and supporters (such as, for instance, Edward's as yet only 11-year-old and poorly endowed younger brother Richard, Duke of Gloucester) would require either a reorganisation of royal patronage or the alienation of further crown lands. This, like the disgruntlement of the commons at the misuse of taxation, threatened future destabilisation of Edward's rule.

THE BALANCE OF ACHIEVEMENT

In the early years of his reign Edward had done much to restore the authority of the English crown, while at the same time securing his dynasty's grip on it. Much of this was his personal achievement. While he was happy to leave trusted lieutenants like Warwick, Montagu and Herbert to fight residual insurgency in the outlying corners of his dominions, the king himself concentrated on the monarch's duties at the centre. He took a personal interest in the problems of the English merchant class, and ostentatiously made the restoration of the law one of his personal priorities. He was generous in rewarding his and his father's supporters with grants of lands and titles, but wherever possible sought to reconcile the adherents of the defeated Lancastrian dynasty to his rule. If contemporaries were struck by Edward's considerable, and to some minds even excessive, generosity in dealing with his opponents, they could not deny that it was underpinned by sound political considerations.

However, Edward's efforts to reconcile former enemies were not uniformly successful. Some old Lancastrians proved irreconcilable. Equally, in his management of the crown's finances and the vast estates that came into his hands at his accession, Edward was guilty of some serious mistakes in the early stages of his rule. The redistribution of lands and offices was focused on a narrow circle of men, and arguably, too much was handed out too rapidly. To some extent, Edward was the victim of circumstance. Beyond question, he needed to create a new aristocracy beholden to him alone; equally, he needed to reward his supporters, who had put their lives and fortunes on the line in supporting his father and him in their quest for the crown; certainly, he needed to reconcile former Lancastrians and restore them to their patrimonies in order to give his rule a broad base and remove opposition to it.

All this required grants of lands and offices. As a result, by 1464 Edward had little left for himself: the problem of finance that had dogged his Lancastrian predecessors now returned to haunt him. The crown's financial mismanagement had long concerned the people of England, who had been asked repeatedly to make up for their rulers' administrative deficiencies through taxation; any semblance of a return to the bad old ways was likely to cause popular discontent. By 1464, consequently, the measures which Edward had taken, in many respects successfully, to secure his rule, were threatening to undermine that very rule in the future.

4

FOREIGN POLICY, THE KING'S MARRIAGE AND THE BREAK WITH WARWICK, 1461–8

However pressing Edward's domestic concerns in the early years of the reign were, the young king could not afford to ignore their wider dimension beyond the boundaries of his realm. The Lancastrian resistance could hardly have proved as resilient or continued for as long as it did without the support of foreign rulers, and it was clear that Edward urgently needed to come to grips with the intricacies of diplomacy and develop his foreign policy. To a late medieval monarch, the conduct of foreign relations was a personal preserve, concerned above all with relationships among the crowned heads of Europe. Yet fifteenth-century foreign policy was no straightforward affair. The frequent changes of dynasty in England aside, throughout the century the political and dynastic map of Europe was also in flux elsewhere.

At the centre of the continent, the Emperor Frederick III had reigned in succession to his father Albrecht II since 1440 and would become the longest-ruling occupant of the imperial throne in its 1,000-year history, but the Roman crown continued to be elective, and there was no guarantee that the electors would in time be bribed into accepting Frederick's son and heir, the Archduke Maximilian, as his successor. Italy, nominally part of the empire, was fragmented into numerous largely autonomous states and principalities. The aristocratic republics of Genoa and Venice aside, the ruling families of many of the smaller territories looked to the papacy to lend legitimacy to their often precarious succession. The last Angevin king of Naples, Réné, father to the former English Queen Margaret, had been replaced by King Alfonso V (*d*.1458) of Aragon in 1443, but Alfonso had been without legitimate issue and had been succeeded on the Neapolitan throne by his bastard son Ferdinand I (*d*.1494), who in his turn was followed successively by his three sons, two of whom were deposed or forced to abdicate. In Urbino the Montefeltro dukes had to rely on the authority of the pope to legitimate the succession of Federico III (*d*.1482), bastard brother of Duke Oddantonio (*d*.1444), and both men owed their ducal titles to successive pontiffs. In Milan the first Sforza duke, Francesco I (*d*.1466), could legitimate his succession in 1450 after the brief interlude of the short-lived Ambrosian republic by his marriage to the daughter of the last Visconti duke, but one of Francesco's three sons and two of his grandsons, all of whom in turn succeeded to the dukedom, suffered the ignominy of deposition. In Savoy, Duke Amadeus VIII had abdicated in 1440 to become antipope to Eugenius V, but had been succeeded without problems by his son Louis. Isolated examples of stability and unchallenged and legitimate successions were provided by the Este dukes of Ferrara, Gonzaga marquesses of Mantua, and – from their respective seizures of power in the 1430s and 1450s until the 1490s – the Medici rulers of Florence and Sforza dukes of Milan.

Elsewhere in Europe, the French crown continued to be disputed between the house of Valois and the kings of England, while in Scandinavia the succession in both Denmark and Sweden was contested throughout the fifteenth century. In 1439 King Erik IX of Denmark, Sweden and Norway had been deposed and replaced by his nephew, Christopher III, who in turn was followed on the Danish throne in 1448 by Christian I, a distant relative, on whose death in 1481 the country experienced a two-year interregnum. The troubles of successive Swedish monarchs made England seem peaceful, as native pretenders and the kings of Denmark contested the throne for much of the second half of the fifteenth century and beyond. A rare example of increasing dynastic stability was provided in the Iberian peninsula where the marriage of Ferdinand, the heir of Aragon, to Isabella, sister and heiress of the last Trastamara King of Castile and Léon, Henry IV (*d*.1474) the Impotent, in 1479 created a Spanish kingdom unified except for the small Pyrenean kingdom of Navarre.

This dynastic uncertainty throughout the western world threatened to undermine the traditional means of princely diplomacy, the marriage alliance between ruling houses. Much could be lost by family ties with a ruler who could not retain his throne. Nevertheless, princes and princesses continued to be used as bargaining chips and guarantors of truces and treaties, and during the 1460s Edward did not hesitate to use his brothers George and Richard and his sister Margaret in this way, while in the second decade of the reign he had at his disposal a growing brood of his own children that might be employed in this manner.

The King of England did, however, have another useful diplomatic tool at his disposal. The language and imagery used by the courts and aristocracy of Christian Europe continued to be that of chivalry, and the fourteenth and fifteenth centuries had seen the emergence of a number of monarchical orders of chivalry, knightly fraternities whose members bound themselves more or less tightly to the service of a particular prince. The most prestigious of these orders was the Order of the Garter, founded by Edward III in 1348 and presided over by his successors on the English throne. Admission to the Garter with its strictly limited membership of 24 knights had become a chivalric accolade coveted across political boundaries. This was in keeping with the intentions of Edward III: three of the 'founder' knights of 1348 had technically been foreigners, and in subsequent decades subjects of foreign princes were regularly admitted to the order.[1]

Yet, since the order's statutes imposed upon the membership a requirement of loyalty to the king of England as sovereign, the admission of foreign rulers themselves was eschewed. This changed under Henry IV, when the Garter was bestowed upon a succession of Portuguese kings and princes, who, by virtue of the marriage of Henry's sister to King João I (d.1433) of Portugal, could be regarded as part of the extended English royal family. The same was true of Henry III (d.1406) of Castile, another of Henry IV's brothers-in-law, and King Erik IX (dep. 1439, d.1459) of Denmark, Henry's son-in-law. Only under Henry V was an independent foreign ruler, the Emperor Sigismund (d.1437), admitted, and in subsequent decades Sigismund's successors, as well as other continental princes not directly connected with the house of Plantagenet, were added to the order.[2] Nevertheless, the requirement of loyalty to the English king continued to be of concern to intended recipients, and a number of foreign princes offered the Garter declined to accept, most notably Philip the Good of Burgundy.

The depletion of the ranks of the order during the civil war gave Edward scope to make extensive use of the Garter in his foreign diplomacy. The election to the order in 1463 of Francesco Sforza, Duke of Milan, and Ferdinand I, king of Naples, and four years later of Ferdinand's chamberlain, the count of Monte d'Orizo, forged important alliances in the Italian peninsula directed at an eventual encirclement of France. Similarly, following his marriage to Edward's sister in 1468, Charles the Bold of Burgundy was persuaded to accept the order which his father had declined. Ostentatious display of the English king's munificence and magnificence was an integral part of the diplomatic impact of the award of the order to an individual. While the sovereign made annual gifts of robes for the feast of St George to all the knights companion of the Garter, foreign companions had to be provided with the other insignia of the order, the mantle, the collar and the garter itself, all of which had to be of exquisite quality to do the sovereign credit.

FOREIGN POLICY 1461-5

While Edward was still struggling to secure his grip on the English crown, foreign policy of necessity had to be subordinated to more pressing domestic concerns. Indeed, during the first years of the reign, international relations were tightly bound up with the defence of the throne against the Lancastrians, as England's traditional enemies, France and Scotland, sought to take advantage of the factional strife that rocked their neighbour by offering support to the tottering Lancastrian dynasty. Throughout the fifteenth century, England's close entanglement with her old enemies, France and Scotland, and with the French crown's great feudatories, the dukes of Burgundy and Brittany, provided the key to her foreign policy.

The weakening of the kings of France by the Hundred Years' War against the English had given the two dukes a degree of political autonomy, which they sought to preserve in the face of the revitalised French monarchy's endeavours to reintegrate them fully into the French state. By a series of judicious marriages, the dukes of Burgundy had acquired a host of territories outside the confines of the French king's suzerainty, and the conglomerate of territories and lordships thus assembled by the mid-fifteenth century did much to enhance their political independence from the French crown.

From an English point of view, matters were complicated by commercial considerations. To England's cloth merchants, the markets of Flanders were vital, and if they were to be protected, good relations with Burgundy were imperative. Arguably, there were other potential markets for English cloth. In October 1464 the trade with Flanders was dealt a blow when Duke Philip of Burgundy embargoed the import of English cloth into his dominions. One obvious solution seemed to be to find new trading partners in the French king's realm, but an underlying, deep-running, popular antagonism against France inclined mercantile opinion in England to seek a diplomatic solution which would restore the cloth trade to Flanders, and this was eventually found.[3]

To the advantage of England and her young monarch, Scotland was itself torn by faction, while the accession in July 1461 of the wily Louis XI of France, whose father Charles VII had shown favour to his Lancastrian kinsmen, appeared to herald a new era of improved Franco-Yorkist relations. From the outset, Edward sought to exploit the disaffection of several leading Scottish nobles with the government of Scotland, conducted by the dowager queen, Mary of Guelders, in the name of the young James III, to force the Scottish crown to abandon its support for Henry VI and Queen Margaret. Queen Mary showed herself open to an agreement, but Edward's efforts were repeatedly frustrated by the opposition of the able Bishop of St Andrews, James Kennedy, who himself took charge of the young James III after Mary's death. Similarly, however, Louis XI soon proved himself a master at playing off the rival factions in England against each other, offering limited military support to Margaret of Anjou, while at the same time stringing along the Duke of Burgundy, who sought to bring about an understanding between Louis and Edward.

It was only in early 1463, when the French king had evidently decided that the Lancastrian cause was lost, that he lent an open ear to Philip of Burgundy's efforts. The result was a treaty signed at Hesdin in October 1463, by which Louis agreed to cease any further assistance to the Lancastrians. Privately, he went even further, assuring the English envoys that not only would he countenance an English attack on Scotland without offering France's traditional ally any assistance, but in the event of a proper agreement between him and Edward IV, he might even be prepared to assist in the conquest of the northern kingdom.[4] Abandoned by Scotland's principal ally, Bishop Kennedy had no option but to open negotiations with the English. In December a truce was signed and more formal discussions were begun, in return for which Scotland agreed to cease its support of the Lancastrians.

In the diplomacy of these early years, a bargaining chip that had been placed on the table time and time again was the hand in marriage of England's handsome young monarch. There was nothing unusual in this. With the exceptions of John and Henry IV, who had married before there was much likelihood that they would ascend the throne, and of the Black Prince, who – had he lived to inherit the crown – would in Joan of Kent have brought an Englishwoman to the throne as his consort, every English king since the Norman conquest had found his wife abroad, and there was every reason to suppose that Edward, too, would seek a foreign alliance for his dynasty. Even in 1445, when there had as yet been little expectation that the then 3-year-old would succeed to anything more than his father's admittedly vast dukedom, there had been a proposal for a marriage to Madeleine or Joan, the infant daughters of Charles VII of France, an initiative intended to strengthen the ties between the ruling houses of England and France.[5] In 1458, probably as part of Henry VI's last-ditch efforts to make peace between his feuding lords, a triple marriage alliance between the young Prince of Wales, a son of the Duke of York and the Duke of Somerset and three continental brides was proposed, but successive approaches to the Duke of Burgundy and the King of France met with no response.[6]

Once Edward was on the throne, the search for a suitable bride began in earnest. In October 1461 English ambassadors made overtures to the Burgundians, proposing a match between the young king and one of the unmarried sisters of the Duke of Bourbon. These were nieces of Duke Philip of Burgundy's and sisters-in-law to his heir, Charles, Count of Charolais, the future Duke Charles the Bold. The Burgundians showed no interest, and a year later, in 1462, Warwick, who had taken it upon himself to seek out a bride for his royal cousin, put forward the unappealing suggestion that Edward might marry the regent of Scotland, the middle-aged Dowager Queen Mary of Guelders, in a renewed triple alliance, which would see his sister married to King James III of Scotland, Mary's son, and one of James's sisters to one of his two younger brothers. Happily for Edward, the Scots (other than Mary herself) proved no more enthusiastic than the Burgundians had been, and spared him from a union that offered little hope of an heir.[7]

In the interim, Louis XI of France had realised the threat that an Anglo-Burgundian marriage alliance, should it ever come about, posed to his realm's security, and sought instead to negotiate a marriage that would renew the ties between England and France severed by the deposition of Margaret of Anjou's husband. During the tripartite negotiations between England, France and Burgundy in September 1463, Edward's ambassadors themselves suggested that Louis XI might like to marry his daughter to their king. The French king declined this offer, pointing out – not without justification – that at little more than 3 years of age the Princess Anne was too young for such a union. He proposed instead one of the sisters of the French queen, a daughter of the Duke of Savoy, as a suitable bride.[8] Before long the Burgundians, to whom an Anglo-French marriage was as unpalatable as an Anglo-Burgundian one was to Louis XI, attempted to re-open negotiations over the Bourbon marriage they had previously turned down. A further possibility that was mooted about this time, but which ultimately came to nothing, was a proposal that Edward might marry a daughter of the Count of Foix.[9] In the spring of 1464 Warwick was pursuing yet another scheme, a proposal for Edward's marriage to Isabella, half-sister of King Henry IV of Castile,[10] but it was the alliance with a sister of the French queen that seemed to hold increasing promise. In July Louis XI of France paraded his queen's sisters before Edward's ambassadors, Lord Wenlock and Richard Whetehill, expressing the earnest hope that the young king might choose one of them as his bride.[11]

THE KING'S MARRIAGE

The diplomatic dimension aside, with Lancastrian resistance in the north crushed and Henry VI safely locked in the Tower, the question of Edward's marriage now also acquired domestic importance. Although the king had two young brothers who could have succeeded him in the event of his sudden death, and although within living memory Henry V and Henry VI had been unmarried and childless for much of their reigns, it was nevertheless imperative that the young Yorkist monarch should marry and secure his dynasty's hold on the crown by producing an heir. Few had forgotten the part that the lack of an undisputed adult male heir had played in the troubles of Henry VI's final decade, and it was clear that Edward's –

and thus the house of York's – grip on the crown needed to be strengthened sooner rather than later by a flock of royal children.

Nor was Edward naturally predisposed against marriage. The young king shared none of his predecessor's purported reservations about women – far from it, he sought and courted them. It was an open secret that the king was 'a man who would readily cast an eye upon young ladies and love them inordinately',[12] 'given to bodily lust, whereunto he was inclined by his own disposition'.[13] Indeed, the Italian observer Dominic Mancini was told not long after Edward's death:

> He was licentious in the extreme: moreover it was said that he had been most insolent to numerous women after he had seduced them, for, as soon as he grew weary of dalliance, he gave up the ladies much against their will to the other courtiers. He pursued with no discrimination the married and unmarried the noble and lowly: however he took none by force. He overcame all by money and promises, and having conquered them, he dismissed them.[14]

According to Thomas More, Edward himself had boasted that he had three mistresses, 'one the merriest, another the wiliest, the third the holiest harlot in his realm'.[15] Perhaps the best known of these was Elizabeth Shore (who has entered the popular imagination courtesy of the sixteenth-century dramatist Thomas Heywood as Jane Shore), the wife of a London merchant, who survived into More's day.[16] Another was Eleanor Butler, daughter of John Talbot, Earl of Shrewsbury, and widow of Thomas Butler, son of Ralph Butler, Lord Sudeley; to this woman, so it was later claimed, Edward had actually been betrothed.[17] A third was Elizabeth Lucy, an otherwise obscure lady thought to have been the daughter of the Hampshire gentleman Thomas Waite.[18] These well-known dalliances aside, there were others. The early seventeenth-century antiquary Sir George Buck ascribed to Edward a liaison with an otherwise obscure Katharine de Clarendon.[19] Periodically, the diet accounts of the royal household name the householder with whom the king stayed when travelling around his realm. On occasion, these were women, probably widows. Thus, on 24 February 1464 Edward stayed at the house of Alice Farwell at Ware, on 3 December 1465 he was with Elizabeth Thrower at Hertford, while on 4 May 1466 his hostess was Agnes Baldwyn at Leyton. On that occasion, it may be significant that the queen, who not long before had been travelling with Edward, had then apparently parted from his company.[20] In his amorous exploits, the king was assisted not only by his close friend Lord Hastings, who as chamberlain was instrumental in controlling access to the monarch's person, but later also by his stepsons, and his queen's brother, Sir Edward Wydeville. These congenial companions not only encouraged Edward's sexual adventures, but – along with other courtiers – reaped their rewards when the king passed on to them the mistresses of whom he had grown tired.[21]

It was, of course, not uncommon for members of the late medieval European nobility, whether married or unmarried, to engage in sexual relationships outside the marital bed and to father children out of wedlock. Such aristocratic bastards were often openly acknowledged, and might receive settlements of land or be married to heiresses. Edward himself fathered at least three such children: generally accepted is the identity of Arthur, Edward's son by Elizabeth Lucy, née Waite, who seems to have been brought up in the king's household in the 1470s, when clothing was provided for him at the king's expense alongside his half-brother, the young Prince of Wales.[22] (After 1485, Arthur was taken into the household of his half-sister Elizabeth, then Henry VII's queen, and in 1523 he was created Viscount Lisle after marrying the heiress of the Lisle family.) A bastard daughter, Grace, was taken into the household of Edward's queen, while another, Elizabeth, married Thomas, the son of George, Lord Lumley.[23] Yet, if illicit liaisons out of wedlock were widely accepted as the norm, Edward apparently went a step further: he was prepared to use an offer of marriage as a means of securing the favours he sought. This, it was later claimed, had been the case with Eleanor Butler, and may also have applied in the case of Edward's eventual queen, Elizabeth Wydeville, who had resisted Edward until their marriage had been solemnised. This solemnisation had taken place clandestinely, and in the presence of only the bride's mother as a witness, and it is a matter of some debate whether the young king had entertained hopes of denying the match later.

If this was so, Edward's hopes were soon dashed. Negotiations for a French or Castilian match were ongoing when in September 1464 rumours began to circulate that the king had already married in secret and had taken an Englishwoman to wife. On 14 September Edward arrived at Reading abbey, where a great council was to meet. In subsequent days the shocked assembly was presented with the truth. Six months earlier, the king had indeed married, and had taken one of his own subjects to wife. The lady in question was no mere commoner: she was the daughter of Jacquetta of Luxemburg, Dowager Duchess of Bedford, by her second husband, Richard Wydeville, Lord Rivers. Nevertheless, Edward had unquestionably married far beneath him. The Wydevilles were relative newcomers to the peerage, and what was more Elizabeth Wydeville was no virgin: she was the widow of Sir John Grey, by whom she had two sons. Just four years earlier, Edward himself had berated the captive Rivers for his presumption in accusing lords of the king's blood of treason, when he himself was the son of a mere esquire, made good by marriage. All this he had now evidently set aside.

Edward had kept St George's day (23 April) at the Tower of London, but four days later had ridden north into Hertfordshire. He had spent two days at St Albans, before on 30 April continuing to Stony Stratford, where he lodged at the house of one John Hekelyng. Probably from there, he made his way to Lord Rivers' residence at Grafton Regis, where early on May day the marriage took place privately, witnessed only by the bride's mother and a few selected attendants.

Although Edward could hardly have anticipated it on that spring morning, his marriage was to become one of the defining factors of his reign. Squandered diplomatic potential aside, from the outset it placed severe strain on the king's relations with his subjects, not least because it called the king's judgement into question. Throughout England, and western Christendom the news of the king's marriage was greeted by howls of outrage. According to Polydore Vergil

> all men incontinent wondered, that the nobility truly chafed, and cast out open speeches that the king had not done according to his dignity; they found much fault with him in that marriage, and imputed the same to his dishonour, as a thing to which he had been led by blind affection, and not by rule of reason.[24]

On 3 October Lord Wenlock wrote to the Franco-Burgundian agent Jean de Lannoy that Edward had taken a wife

> at his pleasure, without the knowledge of those who should have been called for council; for that reason it is to the great displeasure of several great lords, and also of the greater part of his council.[25]

In the same month some Venetian merchants arriving in Bruges from London reported that

> [t]he greater part of the lords and the people in general seem very much dissatisfied at this, and for the sake of finding means to annul it, all the peers are holding great consultations in the town of Reading, where the king is.[26]

And even in distant Danzig on the Baltic Sea, the otherwise pragmatic merchant chronicler Caspar Weinreich recorded that

> this winter King Edward in England took to queen a nobleman's wife, and she was also crowned against the will of all the lords. Some people said her husband had been killed in battle; some said he had been pushed off the bridge at Rochester; some also said that he had been beheaded during the previous Parliament. He was a mere knight; and the king fell in love with the woman when he dined with her frequently. And although royal custom in England demands that the king should take in marriage a virgin, whosoever she might be, but of legitimate birth, and no widow; yet the king took this one against the will of all his lords.[27]

Nor did the splendour in which Elizabeth Wydeville sat in Edward's court let men and women, great or insignificant, forget her background. In the months after Edward's death, Dominic Mancini heard that Edward had married 'a lady of humble origin, named Elizabeth, despite the antagonism of the magnates of the kingdom, who disdained to show royal honours towards an undistinguished woman promoted to such exalted rank',[28] and about the same time, some 20 years after the marriage, Queen Isabella of Castile, spurned by Edward in Elizabeth Wydeville's favour, commented acidly on the 'mere widow' whom he had chosen.[29]

Nobody complained louder than the king's mother. Cecily Neville, who four years earlier had stood to become queen, who proudly styled herself 'the right high and right excellent Princess, the king's mother and late wife to Richard, rightful King of England and of France and Lord of Ireland',[30] and who just three years earlier had had the young king 'at her pleasure',[31] now faced the prospect of being displaced as the first lady in the kingdom by a woman whom she, with some justification, regarded as unsuitable. This prospect was unbearable, and to some extent affected her judgement. In 1483 the Italian visitor

Dominic Mancini heard that on learning of her son's marriage Cecily

> fell into such a frenzy, that she offered to submit to a public inquiry, and asserted that Edward was not the offspring of her husband the Duke of York, but was conceived in adultery, and therefore in no wise worthy of the honour of kingship.[32]

Yet the volume of the initial complaints about Edward's unsuitable bride should not obscure the highly pragmatic attitude of much of the nobility to the *fait accompli* of the king's marriage. Like Lord Wenlock, most peers rapidly concluded that 'since the matter has proceeded before anything could be done about it, one must tolerate it, in spite of ourselves'.[33] It has been suggested that the sole exception to this pragmatic consensus was the Earl of Warwick, but, as Michael Hicks has demonstrated, he too accepted his cousin's marriage as fact without hesitation. Thus it was Warwick himself who conducted the queen at her first public outing in Reading Abbey on Michaelmas day (29 September) 1464; he went on to serve as godfather to the king's eldest daughter, and to preside over the queen's subsequent churching; and his absence from her coronation was an unavoidable result of his diplomatic activity on the continent.[34]

EDWARD AND THE WYDEVILLES

From the point of view of England's landowning classes, one of the principal advantages of a foreign-born queen was that little consideration needed to be given to her relatives, beyond the diplomatic implications of the alliance with a foreign dynasty. An English queen, by contrast, might come with a whole host of kinsfolk, all of whom could lay claim to royal patronage and precedence in accordance with their kinswoman's new status. Elizabeth Wydeville certainly came with such a clan. She had no fewer than 12 surviving siblings, as well as two sons, Thomas and Richard, by her first marriage to Sir John Grey. The extent to which Edward extended his patronage to his wife's relatives to the detriment of others has exercised some debate. An older tradition which tended to emphasise the disproportionate acquisitions of the 'grasping' Wydevilles in the wake of the king's marriage was roundly challenged by J.R.

Lander and Charles Ross in the mid-1970s, but more recent assessment has gone some way to return qualified emphasis to the disproportionate access to royal patronage available to the Wydevilles.

Unquestionably, precedent suggested that the king's newly acquired relatives should be provided for. Queen Elizabeth's sons by her first marriage would one day be half-brothers to a king or queen, and as such could be expected to play an important role in their sibling's court. Although explicitly excluded from the succession, Henry IV's Beaufort half-brothers had been recognised as the monarch's kin, and as recently as 1453 the dynastic importance to the then still childless Henry VI of his half-brothers Edmund and Jasper Tudor, the sons of Queen Katharine of Valois by the obscure Welsh esquire Owen Tudor, had been recognised by their elevation to the earldoms of Richmond and Pembroke and their endowment with the requisite income. Elizabeth Wydeville's sons, Thomas and Richard Grey, at least could thus expect some recognition of their kinship to the royal house, and (although precedent here was more shaky) so could her parents and siblings.

Yet Edward faced a problem. By the time his marriage became public, he had granted away most of the lands that had come into his hands by the forfeitures of 1461 and 1463, as well as much of the royal duchies of Lancaster and Cornwall. If the king wished to extend to the Wydevilles patronage on a lavish scale, he had either to recover lands by compensating the previous grantees financially, or to risk alienating them by depriving them of their grants by force. Neither option was appealing; neither was politically prudent; quite possibly neither was politically viable. Some compromises had to be made. The queen was endowed with estates appropriate to her rank, but had to be content with rather less than her predecessor. Her father, Lord Rivers, was raised to the dignity of an earl and was granted the offices of Treasurer and Constable of England, but did not receive a landed endowment commensurate with his new dignity. It was commonly accepted that the income requisite to support comital rank was 1,000 marks per annum, and Rivers' annuities and the other fees attached to his offices did ensure that he could annually draw far more than that sum. Crucially, however, this was an income personal to the earl and there was no guarantee that it would descend to his son and heir. This heir, Queen Elizabeth's oldest brother Anthony, had some years earlier been recognised as Lord Scales in the right of his wife, a dignity which her inheritance allowed him to support, but prior to his succession to the earldom after his father's execution in 1469 he received only a few minor grants.

If the queen's family was not to be provided for by direct grants of land, there were nevertheless other ways in which the king could, and did, show them favour. Principal among these was the crown's control over the marriages of the heirs and widows of its tenants-in-chief. In the two years between October 1464 and October 1466 the queen's sisters Margaret, Katharine, Anne, Eleanor and Mary respectively married the heirs to the earldoms of Arundel, Essex, Kent and Pembroke and the dukedom of Buckingham. Two other marriages, arranged for two of the younger male Wydevilles, were more openly frowned upon by contemporaries. The queen's younger brother, 20-year-old John Wydeville, was in January 1465 betrothed to the Earl of Warwick's rich and elderly aunt, Katharine Neville, Dowager Duchess of Norfolk, then (as one annalist commented sardonically) a mere 'slip of a girl' of about 65.[35] For her eldest son by her first marriage, Thomas Grey, the queen procured the hand of Anne Holland, daughter of Edward's sister, and heiress to the lands of the dukes of Exeter, even though the girl was already betrothed to the Earl of Northumberland's son, George Neville.[36] In all of this, Edward's personal intervention was crucial: time and time again he used his prerogative to bring about a marriage, augmented marriage portions and brought about property transactions as inducements for the families to whom he wished to link his wife's relatives.[37]

What of the queen herself? As Tony Pollard has recently demonstrated, her character has come down to us painted first, by her near-contemporaries, and in the light of her son's deposition and disappearance in 1483, as that of the *mater dolorosa*, the benevolent queen and helpless mother. Later, under the influence of the propaganda spread first by Warwick in 1471 and again by Richard of Gloucester in 1483, she was depicted as a *femme fatale*, the grasping and scheming head of the rapacious Wydeville clan, who completely controlled her husband.[38] The truth, as Pollard has argued, probably lies somewhere in between. There can be little question that Elizabeth exercised considerable influence over Edward: it is unlikely that he would have consented to their clandestine marriage had he not desired her beyond all *raison d'état*. Various observers spoke of Elizabeth's rather cold beauty and haughty demeanour. Here, it is the eye-witness account of the entourage of the Bohemian nobleman Leo von Rozmital that is the principal source. Rozmital came to England in early 1466 and witnessed the ceremonies for the queen's churching after the birth of Princess Elizabeth. He was particularly struck by the way in which the queen was set apart from the other members of the court, and how even her mother and the king's sister were made to kneel before her. Yet it is not hard to see how Elizabeth's strict adherence to ceremonial, perhaps born out of insecurity and the knowledge of her lack of acceptance by much of the established nobility, might contrast unfavourably with Edward's easy-going affability and light-hearted disregard for form.

EDWARD AND THE NEVILLES

Unquestionably, Edward's need to provide for his new wife's impecunious family had implications for others who might fail to receive grants they could otherwise reasonably have counted on, and one family for whom the king's marriage doubtless had implications were the Nevilles. Ever since the Earls of Salisbury and Warwick had first allied themselves with the Duke of York's cause in the 1450s, their family had taken pride of place among the supporters and councillors of the Yorkist royal line. After Edward's accession, Warwick had become his unchallenged and unchallengeable principal adviser and lieutenant, and while other individuals, such as Stafford, Herbert and Hastings, had also benefited considerably from Edward's munificence, none of them headed a family network that could match that of the fecund Nevilles. Not even the Bourgchier Earl of Essex and his kin, who were in any case part of Warwick's wider family, could compare in influence and royal favour with the earl's immediate relatives. Between them, Warwick and his family controlled the principal offices of state, dominated the defence of the realm against both internal and external enemies, and took a principal role in foreign policy. The king's marriage did not see Warwick's abrupt exclusion from the governance of the realm, far from it. If anything, it merely redressed the political balance which had in the first years of the reign seen the earl become the most over-mighty of over-mighty subjects of the fifteenth century. Warwick continued to be pre-eminent and his brothers continued to enjoy the king's favour, but this favour now had to be shared with others, or more specifically, with the queen's Wydeville relatives.

Plate 1 Anonymous engraving of Edward IV, c. 1470–1. Bayerische
Staatsbibliothek München/2 L.impr.m.c.n.mss. 39, f. IV

Plate 2 An image of Edward IV sitting in judgment; illuminated capital on the opening membrane of Court of Common Pleas plea roll for Michaelmas term 1462. The National Archives, ref. CP40/806 rot.1.

Plate 3 Queen Elizabeth Wydeville, c. 1471–80. Oil on panel 37.6 x 27 cm, British School, 15th century. The Royal Collection © 2007, Her Majesty Queen Elizabeth II.

Plate 4 Edward IV and his family, as depicted in the Royal Window of Canterbury Cathedral. Photographer: Mrs. M. Tucker © Dean and Chapter, Canterbury. With kind permission of the Dean and Chapter, Canterbury.

Plate 5 The misericord from the sovereign's stall in the choir of St. George's Chapel, Windsor, showing Edward IV's meeting with Louis XI of France on the bridge at Picquigny. St George's Chapel Archives & Chapter Library.
© The Dean and Canons of Windsor.

Plate 6 St George's Chapel. Reproduced with kind permission from St George's Chapel Archives & Chapter Library. © The Dean and Canons of Windsor.

Plate 7 Edward IV's tomb in St. George's Chapel. St George's Chapel Archives & Chapter Library © The Dean and Canons of Windsor.

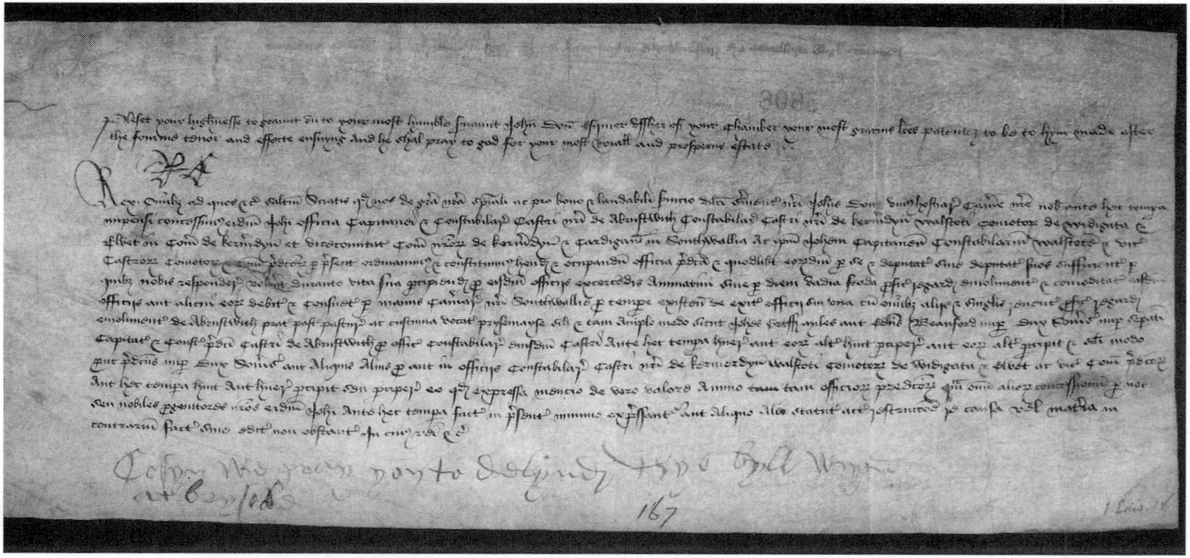

Plate 8 Privy seal letter with Edward IV's autograph. The National Archives, ref. C 81/1487/31.

There is no suggestion that following his marriage Edward consciously turned against the Nevilles as a group, nor, as Michael Hicks has pointed out, that his patronage of his wife's family represented a deliberate policy of providing a political counterbalance to them.[39] The marriage of the Holland heiress to the queen's son in spite of her prior betrothal to the Earl of Northumberland's son might be regarded as a personal slight to the Nevilles, but there is no suggestion that Edward intended deliberate offence to John Neville, or that the latter was more than temporarily put out by it.

There may have been one exception. If by nature Edward was easygoing and keen to avoid conflict, he could occasionally take a dislike to a man, and when he did so, act with considerable ruthlessness. One man to whom he appears to have taken a dislike at an early stage was his ambitious chancellor and cousin, George Neville. Although Neville, still aged only 33, was elevated to the archbishopric of York in 1465, the king and queen did not attend his elaborate installation celebrations that September. On 8 June 1467 Edward himself, accompanied by his brother Clarence and a number of other lords, rode to the archbishop's inn at Charing Cross to demand the surrender of the Great Seal, and thus dismiss the archbishop from the chancellorship. To add insult to injury, the king poured scorn on Neville's ambition for a cardinal's hat by sending him the papal letter announcing the creation of Archbishop Bourgchier as Cardinal of England that same month.[40]

By contrast with Edward's apparent dislike of George Neville, there is little to suggest that he harboured similar feelings towards the Earl of Warwick, who continued to play a prominent role in the government of the realm. Nor, as suggested above, did Warwick take anything less than a pragmatic approach to the *fait accompli* of the king's marriage. Indeed, in marked contrast to the view of near-contemporaries and many modern historians alike, Michael Hicks has of late convincingly argued that Warwick's disenchantment with his cousin's policies (which will form the subject of the next chapter) did not date from the immediate aftermath of his marriage, or even from Edward's – arguably limited – provision for his wife's kin. Still, the removal of Archbishop Neville from the chancellorship undeniably represented a challenge to the primacy in Edward's administration that the king's maternal relatives had enjoyed since 1461. Warwick was too shrewd a man not to realise that his brother's dismissal from office might foreshadow further erosion of Neville influence as time went by.

Indeed, even before George Neville's dismissal, Warwick's pre-eminence in his cousin's council was waning in one important area of policy, that of foreign diplomacy. The removal by the mid-1460s of the Lancastrian threat in the north gave Edward a freer hand to conduct foreign policy than he had hitherto enjoyed, and the king's increased personal attention to diplomatic affairs encroached on the freedom which he had previously accorded to Warwick in the pursuit of his interests. While England had been preoccupied with its internal divisions, in France Louis XI had vigorously pursued his policy of centralisation at the expense of his semi-independent greater subjects, above all the Dukes of Burgundy and Brittany. In 1465 the tension between the French crown and its feudal subjects led to open civil war, which was, however, rapidly quelled by the astute king, albeit at the cost of some concessions. Nevertheless, relations between the French king and his internal opponents remained strained, and each party sought to draw England into the conflict on its side.

It was this choice of continental alliance over which Edward and his cousin Warwick disagreed most fundamentally. From the very outset of Edward's reign, Louis XI had invested heavily in the Earl of Warwick, systematically lavishing flattery and other courtesies upon him, until Warwick came to think himself the 'arbiter of English policy' as which he was being treated by the French king. At least in part as a result of these blandishments, Warwick came to strongly advocate an alliance with Louis XI, and in the autumn of 1465 even went so far as to promise English neutrality, should the king of France chose to deal with his domestic opponents by military means.[41]

Edward, by contrast, showed himself more circumspect. Although occasionally out of touch, he was generally a good judge of public opinion, and public opinion was predominantly opposed to an alliance with France. Over a century of intermittent warfare had generated in England deep-seated popular resentment of the French, and even in the 1460s the trauma of the defeats of a decade earlier was still palpable. Moreover, there were the needs of England's merchants to be considered. To the cloth merchants of the Calais staple and of the City of London, whose loans of ready money continued to be crucial to Edward's solvency, the markets of Burgundy were of the first importance, and they were reluctant to jeopardise well-established mercantile connexions in favour of the as yet untested opportunities that the markets of the French king's realm might offer.

In the first instance, Edward remained aloof from the warring factions across the Channel. In May 1465 he dispatched an embassy headed by Warwick, but also including lords Hastings and Wenlock, to the continent to sound out France, Brittany and Burgundy one by one, to see which would make the most advantageous offer for an English alliance. Otherwise, however, he kept his distance from the civil war in France, and for the time being chose not to commit himself to any form of continental treaty. That August, however, the death of Isabella of Bourbon, second wife of the Duke of Burgundy's heir, Charles Count of Charolais, once more set the wheels of diplomacy in motion. Although – by contrast with his father, Duke Philip – Charles had previously shown himself sympathetic to the Lancastrian cause, he was prepared to consider an alliance with a Yorkist King of England, and in early 1466 he sent messengers to England to open negotiations over a possible marriage to Edward's sister, Margaret. Edward responded by dispatching a fresh embassy under Warwick's leadership to both France and Burgundy. This proved a judicious step, for while no immediate agreement was reached with either, French and Burgundians alike were sufficiently worried by the prospect that Edward might conclude an alliance with the other to improve their own offers sharply and to step up the vigour of their own diplomatic activity.

These activities continued into 1467, and saw Louis XI offer ever more wide-ranging bribes, concessions and inducements to the English, including extensive trading privileges for English merchants in France, a personal pension for Edward IV and a partition of the lands of the duchy of Burgundy. Privately, however, it seems that the French king realised that the tide was turning against him, for he now explored an alternative scheme of bringing about a restoration of Henry VI by using his influence over Warwick to affect a reconciliation between the earl and Queen Margaret. King Louis had not been blind to the marked contrast between the way in which Edward refused to meet his ambassadors, instead leaving contacts with the French to Warwick, and the open arms and public spectacle with which successive Burgundian missions were received (culminating in a celebrated tournament between Duke Philip of Burgundy's illegitimate son Antoine, known as the Bastard of Burgundy, and the king's brother-in-law, Anthony, Lord Scales).

Although Duke Philip's death on 15 June 1467 placed negotiations with Burgundy on a new footing, as his successor drove a rather harder bargain than his father, Edward pressed ahead with his plans for the encirclement of France. A week before Duke Philip's death he had concluded an alliance with Duke Francis of Brittany, and a month later he ratified a similar treaty with King Henry of Castile. About the same time, King Ferdinand of Naples agreed a treaty of friendship.[42] During the autumn of 1467 parliamentary prohibitions of imports of goods from Burgundy were annulled and a commercial treaty concluded, and in February 1468 the terms of the marriage between Duke Charles and Margaret of York (which took place later that summer) were finally settled. Edward had asserted his own foreign policy, and in May 1468 was able to report to Parliament through the mouth of his new chancellor, Bishop Stillington, that he had concluded, or was about to conclude, treaties with Burgundy, Brittany, Aragon, Castile, Naples, Scotland, Denmark and the Empire, and was ready to invade France and restate his ancestors' claim to its crown. His reward was a substantial grant of taxation for the proposed expedition across the Channel.

In return, however, he had made considerable concessions: he had risked unpopularity among the English merchants by abandoning protectionist statutes, and had to borrow widely to find the 200,000 crowns (£41,666 13s 4d) of his sister's dowry. Moreover, Edward's diplomatic successes had come at the cost of alienating the Earl of Warwick. It had not been lost on Richard Neville that he was being sidelined from Edward's diplomacy by being placed in charge of stringing along negotiations for a French alliance, which the king had already decided to abandon, and consequently had been made to look foolish in the eyes of the French king. At the same time others, principally Edward's new noble friends, such as Lords Herbert, Stafford and Mountjoy, and the queen's kin, Earl Rivers and his son, had taken pride of place in the ceremonial that surrounded the negotiations with the Burgundians. If the removal from office of Warwick's brother, who seems to have acted as his spokesman at court while he himself was abroad, was seen against this backdrop, Richard Neville could reasonably conclude that the political influence that he coveted above all, and indeed had long regarded as his birthright as one of the 'lords of the king's blood', had diminished, was diminishing, and ought to be increased.

It is uncertain whether, as the Burgundian chronicler Jean de Wavrin suggested, Warwick was even at this date floating the possibility of replacing Edward on the throne by his brother Clarence, but it seems unlikely. The earl was too shrewd a politician not to realise the constitutional difficulties that such an arrangement would present. What is rather more evident, though, is that he saw in his young cousin Clarence the means of shoring up his own position. Not long after Edward's accession Clarence had been placed under the earl's tutelage (in which he would later also be joined by his younger brother, Richard of Gloucester) and had taken up residence in the Warwick household. It was undoubtedly here that the seeds were sown of the enmity for his brother's queen and her family that he was to conceive. An attractive, intelligent and charming youth, during the 1460s Clarence clearly developed an exaggerated view of his own importance. Although Edward provided him with estates worthy of the king's eldest brother (and, until the birth of Princess Elizabeth, heir-presumptive), Clarence nevertheless displayed jealousy of the rather more limited provision made for his younger brother, Richard of Gloucester, and in 1462, still aged only 14, apparently persuaded his brother to transfer to him the valuable Honour of Richmond, which had originally been settled on Prince Richard.

Edward's marriage and the birth of his first two daughters, Elizabeth and Mary, in 1466 and 1467 affected Clarence's position in more ways than one. On the one hand, he was no longer heir presumptive to the English crown (although in an age of high infant mortality the lives of two young girls represented no great distance from the throne). On the other hand, however, the king's injudicious squandering of his own capital in the dynastic marriage market of Europe gave his eldest brother a new importance as the most eligible bachelor in England. This was something that Warwick, then much preoccupied not only by international marriage diplomacy but also by the need to find suitable husbands for his own two daughters, cannot have failed to impress on his young cousin. Indeed, if – as the Italian Dominic Mancini heard in 1483 – the then 15-year old Clarence had been 'sorely displeased' at his brother's marriage, and had 'vented his wrath ... conspicuously, by his bitter and public denunciation of Elizabeth's obscure family; and by proclaiming that the king, who ought to have married a virgin wife, had married a widow in violation of established custom',[43] it is hard not to suspect that he was giving voice to what he had heard in Warwick's household.

The diplomatic negotiations of the mid-1460s saw a series of glittering prizes dangled before the young duke in the form of a string of proposals for a foreign marriage. Among these one stood out: betrothal to Charles of Burgundy's only daughter and heiress by his first wife, which could eventually have seen George rule as Duke of Burgundy in her right. In the event, however, all these proposals were abandoned. Were Clarence to marry a member of the English nobility, the obvious candidate was the elder of Warwick's two daughters, Isabel. If, as seemed possible, the earl failed to produce a son, the vast estates of the earldoms of Warwick and Salisbury would ultimately be shared between his two daughters, and would have combined with Clarence's already extensive lands to make him rich beyond imagination.

Warwick also had good reason to seek to marry his daughters to the king's brothers. His family's standing and wealth, and the likelihood that much of the latter would descend to his daughters, meant that only a bridegroom of ducal or at least comital rank would do. However, the marriages arranged for Queen Elizabeth's kin between 1464 and 1466 had so greatly depleted the English marriage market that the two royal Dukes of Clarence and Gloucester remained the only viable candidates for the hands of the two Neville heiresses. Furthermore, from Warwick's point of view, the prospect of becoming father-in-law to the king's brother offered a chance of strengthening the ties of kinship between his family and the crown that had been weakened by Edward's injudicious marriage, and recovering some of the political ground that he had lost.[44] Yet, whether motivated by diplomatic considerations or by other, obscure, personal reasons, Edward refused to consent to a marriage between George of Clarence and Isabel Neville. Whether Clarence had conceived a fondness for the girl during his time in the Warwick household, or whether Earl Richard had successfully persuaded him of the benefits of the marriage and the girl's likely prospects, the young duke resented his brother's refusal to countenance the union, and came to share Warwick's dislike of the queen's family and the king's friends. Before long, the resultant alliance of the impetuous, if charismatic, young prince and the seasoned and determined warrior and politician proved an explosive one and threatened Edward's rule itself.

5

CRISIS, EXILE AND RETURN, 1468–71

RENEWED TROUBLES, 1468–9

The year 1468 brought Edward a number of successes, both domestically and in foreign policy, that might have cemented his rule for good. In March the Burgundian alliance was affirmed by a treaty agreeing the marriage of the king's sister Margaret to Charles the Bold, and in the early summer parliament agreed a grant of taxation in support of an invasion of France. In August the last Lancastrian stronghold, the Welsh castle of Harlech, surrendered to William Herbert, newly created Earl of Pembroke, following an ambitious but ultimately ill-fated invasion by Jasper Tudor, the former Lancastrian earl.

Yet increasingly there were dissonances. Various parts of England were growing restless once more and rumours of treason and conspiracies were rife. In January 1468 a mob attacked and ransacked one of Earl Rivers' estates in Kent. About the same time there were tales of rebels gathering in Yorkshire around a leader calling himself Robin, in reference to the popular people's hero. Even more menacingly, as the year progressed a number of plots, real or imagined, thought to be intended to bring about a restoration of the Lancastrian dynasty, were uncovered. Men of importance were said to be secretly making contact with the exiled Queen Margaret and her circle in France.

Henry VI was securely locked in the Tower, but his son, Prince Edward, was still in his mother's custody, and at the age of 15 began to represent a credible focus for a potential restoration of the house of Lancaster. Increasingly, Lancastrian agents appeared to be roaming England. Even within weeks of Henry VI's capture in 1465, a man as prominent as the former chief justice and political theorist John Fortescue had secretly crossed the Channel on Queen Margaret's instructions; in 1466 rebels were arrested in the isle of Wight; and in June 1468 a certain Cornelius, a servant of Prince Edward's former receiver general, Sir Robert Whittingham, was apprehended. Under torture Cornelius implicated one of Lord Wenlock's servants, John Hawkins, who in his turn incriminated a number of leading Londoners as well as a former treasurer of Calais, Sir Gervase Clifton, and even his master, Wenlock himself. Among those arrested as a direct result of Hawkins' confession was the alderman of London's Broad Street ward, the former mayor Sir Thomas Cook, who eventually was acquitted of all charges except for misprision of treason, but not before his estates and goods had been plundered by the king's officials and the queen's relatives.[1]

The atmosphere of suspicion and mistrust that prevailed throughout the land was captured by the prior of Crowland Abbey:

> [A]t this period, many nobles and great men of the kingdom, as well as very many bishops and abbots, were accused before the king of treason; the ground being that they had secretly solicited Margaret, the late queen, who was now living in parts beyond the sea, both by letters and with money, to return to the kingdom with a strong force and had made her promises of their advice and assistance.[2]

More specifically, in December 1468 one Godfrey Greene reported from London to his uncle, the Yorkshire knight Sir William Plumpton:

> My Lord [the Earl] of Oxford is committed to the Tower, and, it is said, kept in irons, and that he has confessed many things; and on Monday before St Andrew's Day one Alford and one Poiner, gentlemen to my [lord] of Norfolk, and one Sir Piers Skinner of London were beheaded, and on the morning after Sir Thomas Tresham was arrested and is committed to the Tower, and it is said he was arrested upon the confession of my lord of Oxford; and they say his livelihood, and Sir John Marney's livelihood and various other livelihoods

are given away by the king. Also arrested is Master Hungerford, the heir of the Lord Hungerford, and one Courtenay, heir of the earl of Devon, and many others whose names I do not know, and it is said that Sir Edmund Hungerford is sent for, and also the yeomen of the Crown have ridden into various regions to arrest men that are impeached.[3]

In January 1469 Thomas Hungerford and Henry Courtenay were executed at Salisbury in Edward's presence. Whatever the truth of their treasonable activities, already there was at least one strand of public opinion that blamed the ambitions of the grasping men about the king: 'men', the chronicler John Warkworth recorded, 'said the Lord Stafford of Southwick was cause of the said Henry Courtenay's death, for he wanted to be the earl of Devonshire, and this the king made him afterwards.'[4] Nor did the executions of January 1469 put an end to the unrest.

The chronology of the widespread disorder that swept the north of England in the course of the subsequent year and a half is hard to disentangle, but events appear to have been roughly as follows. In April a large body of insurgents gathered in Yorkshire around a captain known as Robin of Redesdale or Robin Mend-All. They were dispersed by John Neville, Earl of Northumberland, but rapidly regrouped outside his reach in Lancashire, while the earl was detained in the East Riding, where another army of malcontents assembled under a captain called Robin of Holderness. This latter rising was effectively crushed by Neville, and it leader captured and beheaded. The same was not, however, true of Robin of Redesdale, who towards the end of June began to move southwards and to attract substantial numbers of recruits to his cause. But what was this cause?

According to the most closely contemporary source, Robin of Holderness's men had been Percy supporters who sought the restoration of a member of that family to the earldom of Northumberland. Robin of Redesdale's rising, by contrast, had broader overtones. Although the rebels had strong Neville connexions and Robin himself has been identified with Sir John Conyers of Hornby, the Earl of Warwick's cousin by marriage, many of the rebels harboured grievances that were more powerful in drawing them to rebellion than even the call of the popular Earl of Warwick could have been.[5]

Edward IV had failed to meet the high hopes which had accompanied his accession. In spite of grand gestures such as his personal assumption of the judgement seat of the King's Bench, he had failed fully to establish law and order in the provinces. In spite of his promise to live of his own, reiterated in parliament only in the previous year, he had raised taxes, and moreover had spent on routine costs the money granted by the community of the realm for an invasion of France, while the promised expedition across the Channel had failed to materialise. The fault for all this, according to the conventions of late medieval political discourse, did not directly lie with the king but with the rapacious advisers with whom he had surrounded himself, denying his natural councillors, the 'lords of the king's blood', their rightful place on his council. Unquestionably, the lords who had been displaced from their places by the king's side were thought to be the Nevilles, and their usurpers were named as the queen's Wydeville kin and the king's friends Humphrey, Lord Stafford, and William Herbert, Earl of Pembroke. The questions of the squandered taxes and continuing lawlessness, however, ran deep in the popular psyche and did severe damage to Edward's standing among his people.[6]

The seriousness of the situation in the north, and his personal unpopularity in the region at its root, seem to have escaped Edward in the first instance. As yet, he saw no reason to intervene in person, relying instead on John Neville to bring the rebels under control as he had done in the previous year. In May the king was at Windsor for the feast of the order of the Garter which saw the formal installation (albeit by proxy) of the Duke of Burgundy, and in early June he set out on a pilgrimage to Bury St Edmunds and Walsingham.

While he was still on this progress through East Anglia, the reports from the north grew increasingly urgent. By 18 June Edward had decided that he might have to counter the rebels himself. Having ordered the wardrobe to send equipment and liveries for his army, he slowly proceeded north, summoning armed contingents from his tenants-in-chief and the cities and towns of the realm along the way. On 30 June he reached Fotheringhay Castle, and in the first week of July proceeded via Stamford to Nottingham. Here, at last, he seems to have begun to appreciate the full extent of the rebellion that faced him, as well as the likelihood that his own brother, Clarence, and his cousin Warwick were complicit in it. Nevertheless, he doggedly refused to believe in his kinsmen's guilt. On 9 July he dispatched two of his household men, Sir Thomas Montgomery and Maurice Berkeley of Beverstone, with letters to Clarence, Warwick and the Archbishop of York, summoning them to come into his presence, and assuring Warwick of his confidence that 'you should not be of any such disposition towards us, as the rumour runs here, considering the trust and affection we bear towards you.'[7]

While Edward awaited the arrival of Warwick and Clarence, he also gathered an army to crush the unrest. Two of the very 'new men' vilified by the rebels, William Herbert, Earl of Pembroke, and Humphrey Stafford, the new Earl of Devon, were ordered to deal with Robin of Redesdale. Edward himself remained inactive at Nottingham, either still refusing to believe in Warwick's and Clarence's guilt, or quite simply unaware of what was happening in the south.

At the time of Edward's summons, Warwick and Clarence had already crossed the Channel to Calais, where on 11 July Archbishop Neville married the duke to Warwick's elder daughter, Isabel. On the following day, they issued a manifesto in the form of a letter attached to the northern rebels' petition, taking it upon themselves to promote the northerners' grievances before the king.[8] Finally, they openly summoned all their supporters to join them at Canterbury on 16 July. From Canterbury, Warwick's army rapidly advanced by way of London towards Coventry.

Still, Edward remained immobile. In the interim, the Earls of Devon and Pembroke had lost no time in raising men to counter the threat from the north, and had joined forces near Banbury in Oxfordshire. Yet the character of the men Edward had elevated now became the source of their downfall, and by implication, that of their king. The two earls quarrelled, and while the story that their disagreement arose over a lodging where there was 'a certain damsel' may be apocryphal, it is certainly not out of keeping with what we know of the two men's disposition at other times. It may even reflect a certain lasciviousness among the young men of Edward's court that was far removed from the ideal courtly love of chivalric romance, and tolerated, if not actively encouraged by the bon-vivant young king. In any case, the result of the two earls' quarrel was that Stafford withdrew his contingent by some distance. On 25 July at Edgcote Herbert's levies were routed by the rebels, and he and his brother, Sir Richard Herbert, taken and executed at Northampton the following day. It is not clear what part, if any, Stafford's south-westerners played in the battle, but in its aftermath the new Earl of Devon rapidly took to his heels and made for his West-country estates.

The news of the disaster at Edgcote found Edward, who had finally set out to join Devon and Pembroke, at Olney in Buckinghamshire, and whatever its effect on the king himself, it caused many of his men to desert him. Moreover, there now arrived an armed contingent led by Archbishop George Neville himself, who had not forgotten the slights of two years earlier and relished the opportunity of exacting his revenge by conducting the king first to Coventry and a few days later to Warwick Castle a prisoner.[9] Edward now found himself in a predicament similar to that in which he had seen Henry VI ten years earlier, when he and Warwick had conducted the king from the battlefield of Northampton back to London, with all outward signs of the respect owed to the reigning monarch, but in effect holding him prisoner. Edward cannot have failed to ponder the fate of his hapless predecessor, who was still held in the Tower in much reduced circumstances: 'not worshipfully arrayed as a prince and not so cleanly kept as should seem such a prince', as was found a year later.[10]

In the first place, however, and probably to the considerable chagrin of his ally, the ambitious Clarence, Warwick showed no sign of wishing to deprive Edward of his throne. Instead, he set about completing the destruction of his rivals about the king. On 12 August Earl Rivers and Sir John Wydeville were executed at Coventry, five days later the Earl of Devon was apprehended and beheaded at Bridgwater in Somerset, and around the same time Sir Thomas Herbert, the Earl of Pembroke's brother, was executed at Bristol. While Queen Elizabeth and her children remained unmolested in London, her mother, the Dowager Duchess of Bedford (and now also Dowager Countess Rivers), was arrested and charged with witchcraft.[11]

Having decimated the king's new men and the queen's relatives, Warwick was once more his cousin's principal adviser. But he was no more than that. With the exception of those removed (most notably the executed Earl Rivers, who was replaced as treasurer by Sir John Langstrother, Prior of St John in England), the king's council remained largely the same as it had been before the dramatic summer of 1469. Robert Stillington remained chancellor, and Thomas Rotherham kept the privy seal. Edwardian loyalists like Lords Dynham, Mountjoy, Dacre and Ferrers and Sir John Howard remained on the council. Yet they remained in London, separated from the king at Warwick, from where he was moved to Middleham Castle in mid-August.

For the time being, Warwick was able to rule in Edward's name, issuing orders to the council in London from the north. Before long, however, he had to realise that there were limits to what could be done through a captive king. It is not certain how far the earl was prepared to go. Already the precedents of the depositions of Edward II, Richard II and Henry VI had made a menacing appearance in the manifesto he had issued from Calais.[12] During the summer of 1469, rumours (probably actively spread by Warwick) of Edward's supposedly illegitimate birth began to circulate, and by early September the Milanese ambassador to the French court believed that Warwick had decided to deprive his cousin of the crown, probably in favour of his own son-in-law, the Duke of Clarence.

Certainly, Warwick intended to follow the precedent of 1460 in so far as to place the measures he took on a secure footing, and in the face of opposition from some who thought this step imprudent he summoned a parliament to meet at York on 22 September.[13] This assembly never met, for before long Warwick discovered what sleeping dogs he had inadvertently awoken. The long-standing Lancastrian loyalist Humphrey Neville of Brancepeth took the opportunity of the general turmoil in the north to raise a fresh rebellion in the cause of Henry VI. Elsewhere men sought to abuse the captive king's impotence by settling their own affairs in the same way as they had done under Henry VI. In traditionally unruly East Anglia, the impetuous young Duke of Norfolk laid siege to the Paston family's castle at Caister in Norfolk, and curtly informed the Duke of Clarence, who had written to him on behalf of the royal council offering arbitration, that he would give up his quest for the forcible acquisition of Caister 'for no duke in England'.[14]

Whether in control of the king or not, Warwick and his allies could not command the respect and authority that was accorded to an active monarch. Although the council eventually succeeded in brokering an agreement over Caister that at least prevented further bloodshed, Warwick had to concede his inability to crush Humphrey Neville's rebellion without the king's active involvement.

In these circumstances there was little that the earl could do but acquiesce in Edward's liberation in the first days of September. It is unclear exactly how the king regained his freedom, and how active a part he played in doing so. At the French court it was believed that his captivity had been an easy one, and that he had simply made use of one of the hunting trips which he was allowed to undertake to evade his captors. The usually well-informed Crowland continuator, however, maintained that he had no so much escaped as found himself released with Warwick's express consent.[15] Whatever the truth of the matter, by the middle of September Edward was his own master once more, and rapidly succeeded in raising a force to crush Sir Humphrey Neville's rebels. On 29 September, Sir Humphrey and his brother Charles were beheaded in the king's presence at York.

Already, it appears, he had sent for his younger brother, the now 17-year-old Duke of Gloucester and his brother-in-law, the Duke of Suffolk, as well as the lords of the council in London. In their company he set out for London, and in the second week of October he entered the capital in state, escorted by an impressive array of lords and no fewer than 1,000 mounted men. Notable by their absence were Warwick and the Duke of Clarence, as well as Archbishop Neville and the Earl of Oxford, who had intended to attend upon the monarch, but had been told that Edward would send for them when they were wanted.[16]

Nevertheless, even now that he was once again in full control of his realm, the king proved strikingly reluctant to curb the power of the Nevilles that could so easily have cost him his throne. The reallocation of the Earl of Pembroke's former offices in southern Wales to Richard of Gloucester, the replacement of John Langstrother as treasurer by the Bishop of Ely, and the omission of Warwick and Clarence from the commissions of array issued at the end of October were, as Charles Ross argued, to be expected,[17] and amounted to little more than measures to restore the status quo. There were no more sweeping redistributions of offices or grants of land, nor were any punitive measures taken against the men who had recently shown themselves disloyal, much to the chagrin of some of the king's servants. 'The king himself has good language of the lords of Clarence, of Warwick and of my lords of York, and of Oxford, saying they are his best friends. But his household men have other language,' John Paston, one of the said household men, wrote to his mother in October 1469.[18] Indeed, Edward made a concerted effort to reconcile Warwick and Clarence to his rule. They were persuaded to attend a great council, which convened in London in November, and intermittently sat until February 1470, and agreed to 'peace and entire oblivion of all grievances upon both sides'.[19]

The reasons for Edward's failure to deal decisively with the threat to his rule posed by the Nevilles, and particularly Warwick, are far from clear.

In the short term, he may have had little alternative. The Nevilles controlled the north and without them it would be difficult, if not impossible, to suppress the Lancastrian rebellion raised by Humphrey Neville. The king's other allies were decimated. Pembroke and Devon were dead, as were several of the queen's Wydeville relatives. If Warwick needed Edward to crush the northern rebels, Edward also needed Warwick and his brother, Northumberland. But what probably also came into play was a fatal flaw in Edward's character: a need to be liked, and a consequent inclination to conciliate, which alone seems to explain his dogged refusal to believe in the treason of those close to him, and his readiness to forgive even the most blatant acts of treachery. It was this total faith in his ability to win over opponents that led to the king's undoing when faced by an able and calculating politician like Warwick.

Edward was, it appears, nevertheless not entirely oblivious to the need to create a counterbalance to Neville power in the north of England. Historically, the rule of the region had been shared between the Neville earls of Westmoreland on the one hand, and the Percy earls of Northumberland on the other. The eclipse of the Percy with the death of Henry, Earl of Northumberland, at the battle of Towton, his subsequent attainder, and the grant of the comital title to Warwick's brother, John Neville, Lord Montagu, had left the Nevilles as undisputed rulers of the north throughout the 1460s. The experience of the summer of 1469 may have persuaded Edward that the earlier balance needed to be restored, and he began to make plans for the rehabilitation of the Percy heir.

Various parts of England were, however, still in turmoil. The Duke of Norfolk's assault on Caister castle was just one of several private feuds that turned to open violence in the course of 1469–70. In Lancashire the Stanleys were squabbling with their old rivals, the Harringtons; in neighbouring Yorkshire they felt emboldened to challenge the king's own brother, the Duke of Gloucester; and in Gloucestershire a long-running dispute between the Berkeleys and the Talbots found its outlet in a pitched battle on Nibley Green on 20 March 1470.[20] In Lincolnshire, a dispute between Edward's master of the horse, Sir Thomas Burgh, and Richard, Lord Welles, broke out into open fighting in the spring of 1470, and it was this private squabble that before long sparked renewed civil war on a national scale. During the winter of 1469–70, Lord Welles, his son Sir Robert Welles, and his brothers-in-law, Sir Thomas Dymmock and Sir Thomas de la Launde, had attacked and destroyed Burgh's manor house at Gainsborough. Perhaps as a result of Burgh's complaints, or perhaps still under the impression of the previous year's unrest in the region, Edward decided to intervene and restore the peace in person. Welles and Dymmock were summoned to London to appear before the council, and the king sent letters to various townships requesting troops to assemble at Grantham on 12 March, where he himself would assume leadership of the army.

REBELLION IN THE NORTH

The news of the king's imminent arrival in the north with an army at his back had an unexpected impact. In both Lincolnshire and neighbouring Yorkshire, from where many of the previous year's rebels had hailed, popular rumours spread like wildfire, suggesting that Edward did not simply intent to put a halt to the feuding of Welles and Burgh, but intended a punitive expedition throughout the region for the past disturbances.[21] There has been some debate whether Warwick and Clarence were from the start responsible for spreading these rumours, and thus fomenting renewed rebellion, as the official account of the risings asserted, or whether they merely took advantage of a popular movement that had developed independently of them.[22] Certainly, some of the men involved in the attack on Gainsborough had connexions with Clarence, while Lord Welles was related to Warwick and had been a carver at the enthronement of Archbishop Neville at York five years earlier.[23]

It was, however, Sir Robert Welles who assumed leadership of the excited populace in the north. Although pardoned for the attack on Gainsborough on 3 March, a day later day Welles issued proclamations throughout Lincolnshire summoning the men of the county to assemble at Ranby Hawe near Lincoln two days later 'to resist the king in coming down into the said shire'.[24] As Edward moved north he received alarming news of the numbers of rebels rallying to Welles' banners, albeit tempered by reassuring letters from the Duke of Clarence, stating that he and Warwick were on their way to join his force. In response, Edward ordered Warwick and Clarence, whose complicity he had still not begun to suspect, to array further armed men in Warwickshire and Worcestershire, before he pressed on to Huntingdon, and eventually Fotheringhay castle, which he reached on 11 March.

In the interim, Edward had summoned Lord Welles and Sir Thomas Dymmock from London, and on the king's instructions Welles had written to his son, ordering him to surrender, or see his father and Dymmock executed. This letter reached Sir Robert on the way to Leicester, where he had hoped to join forces with the contingent that Warwick was bringing up from the west, and it caused him in the first instance to turn back towards Empingham. It was here that the rebel army was encamped in full array when Edward's force arrived in Stamford. The king acted swiftly and energetically. As Sir Robert showed no inclination to surrender, he had Lord Welles and Dymmock summarily beheaded, and then immediately attacked the rebels. The insurgents put up little resistance and by nightfall had been completely routed, discarding items of armour and clothing as they fled.

According to the official version of events subsequently issued, the battle and the debris abandoned in the field, provided Edward with powerful evidence of Warwick's and Clarence's complicity in the rising. Some of the rebels, including the leader, Sir Robert Welles, had openly worn Clarence's livery; the insurgents' battle cry as they advanced had been 'A Clarence! A Clarence! A Warrewike!'; and – most damagingly – treasonable letters from Warwick and Clarence were found in one of the helmets discarded on the battlefield. Still, Edward seems to have hoped for an innocent explanation, or at least a possibility of reconciliation: he ordered the duke and the earl to disband the force they had raised on his orders just days earlier, and to come into his presence with no more than the retinues required by their rank. This Warwick and Clarence nominally agreed to do, but they hardly waited for the king's envoy to depart before hastily galloping off in the opposite direction.

At the same time, armed uprisings broke out in two other parts of the kingdom. In Yorkshire, Sir John Conyers, once more assuming the guise of 'Robin of Redesdale', John, Lord Scrope of Bolton, and other supporters and kinsmen of the Earl of Warwick were rallying both the earl's retainers and unconnected malcontents to their banners, while in Devonshire a number of members of cadet branches of the Courtenay family, retained by Clarence, staged a separate rising. Edward once again instructed the loyal John Neville to deal with the Yorkshire rebels, while Lord Dynham and his brother-in-law Lord Fitzwaryn were dispatched to deal with the Courtenays. Both groups of rebels rapidly dispersed, perhaps under the impression of the collapse of their cause at

Empingham, and lacking direction after the flight of Warwick and Clarence. Their central part in stirring the rebellions was becoming more apparent by the day. Among the rebel leaders who had been rounded up in the aftermath of Lose-cote field (as the engagement became known) was Sir Robert Welles, who was examined by the king himself on 14 March and confessed that the duke and the earl had been 'partners and chief provokers of all their treasons', and that they had intended to depose Edward in favour of his brother Clarence.

Nevertheless, the king continued to rely on diplomacy, even if his tone began to grow sterner. There was a further exchange of letters, in which Edward promised to deal with Clarence 'according to the nighness of our blood and our laws', but threatened dire consequences if he and Warwick did not submit and immediately stop stirring rebellion. Warwick and Clarence for their part responded with a demand for a full pardon, not only for themselves but also for all their supporters. A number of magnate retinues, including those of the Dukes of Norfolk and Suffolk, and various local levies had now joined Edward's army, and he answered his opponents' demands sharply and decisively, ordering immediate and unconditional submission.

On 20 March the king led his army northwards towards York to seek out his opponents. By contrast with the numerous magnates who had rallied to the king, Warwick and Clarence signally failed to attract any support among the nobility. Warwick's brother-in-law, John de Vere, Earl of Oxford, who had come under suspicion in the previous year, fled to France without taking any open part in the rebellion; John Talbot, Earl of Shrewsbury, was suspected of complicity with the duke and the earl, but also lay low; and the Lancashire baron Thomas, Lord Stanley, another of Warwick's brothers-in-law, to whom the fugitives appear to have appealed for support in the immediate aftermath of Lose-cote field, when they turned towards Manchester, also failed to take their part. He was in any case preoccupied by a dispute with the Duke of Gloucester, who was approaching his estates from Wales. Most crucially, Warwick's own brother, John Neville, Earl of Northumberland, also remained loyal to Edward. Yet it was at this point, on Lady Day 1470 (25 March), that Edward took the step which he had been preparing for some months, and restored the Percy heir to his ancestral earldom of Northumberland. Obviously, John Neville, whose loyalty in the face of his own brother's treachery had been notable, needed to be compensated, and he was consequently elevated to the newly created marquessate of Montagu and granted some of the south-western lands of the earldom of Devon that had fallen back into Edward's hands after the execution of Humphrey Stafford in the previous summer. Already, Edward had taken other steps to reward John Neville: on 5 January his son and heir, George Neville, had been created Duke of Bedford and betrothed to the king's eldest daughter. In the event that Edward should fail to produce a son, the crown itself might one day pass to John Neville's line.

The king remained in York for five days until 27 March, before decisively setting out in pursuit of his brother and his cousin. The fugitives for their part were heading south through the Welsh Marches and Somerset, and on 3 April reached Exeter. Here, Edward's lieutenants Dynham and Fitzwaryn, sent to deal with the Courtenay insurgency, had allowed themselves to be trapped by a siege laid by another Courtenay cadet, Sir Hugh of Boconnoc, a character of dubious loyalties. On the rebel lords' arrival, the siege was raised and the two loyal peers surrendered to Warwick, but if the fugitives had hoped for a wider rising of the south-west, they were to be disappointed. On 9 April they took ship in neighbouring Dartmouth and sailed for Calais, where Warwick was at least nominally still in command.

This time Edward did not make the same mistake as in the previous year and sprang into action rapidly. He well remembered Warwick's tactics a decade earlier, and was determined not to be caught out in the same way as Henry VI's regime had been. Coastal defences were prepared, Warwick's ships seized, and the authorities of Southampton and the Cinque Ports instructed to repel any attempted assault by the rebels. Similar orders were also sent to Calais, where Warwick's deputy, John, Lord Wenlock, refused to grant him admission, his resolve stiffened by the marshal of the pale, the Gascon exile Gaillard, Lord Duras. In subsequent months, Edward grew suspicious of Wenlock's loyalties, and first placed him under the supervision of Earl Rivers, and subsequently replaced him in post by the newly ennobled John, Lord Howard.[25] At Southampton, Warwick's councillor Sir Geoffrey Gate attempted to secure the earl's ship *Trinity* for his master, but was intercepted and captured by the new Earl Rivers, who like his royal master had not forgotten the lessons learnt ten years earlier. Gate himself was spared, but his men were tried for treason before John Tiptoft, Earl of Worcester, and condemned to death. Their execution was intended to serve as a warning to others who might consider rebellion, and replaced the usual indignities of a traitor's death by the impalement of their heads on stakes driven in through the buttocks of the dead men's suspended corpses,[26] a measure for which the cultured Earl of Worcester was widely reviled by contemporaries.[27] Edward now seemed to be in complete control of his kingdom once more, and the reversal of fortunes that followed was nothing short of remarkable.

Having been turned away from the safe haven of Calais, Warwick and Clarence sought refuge in France, where King Louis XI could always be relied upon to make mischief for an English king. There Warwick soon overcame the initial setback of the loss of his fleet at Southampton when his bastard cousin Thomas Neville defected to him with a naval squadron that had been part of Edward's royal fleet patrolling the Channel under the command of Lord Howard. With these vessels the energetic earl attacked and seized a large convoy of Burgundian ships on 20 April, and although Lord Howard succeeded in recapturing some of the Flemish vessels in subsequent days, Warwick nevertheless returned to the mouth of the Seine with a naval force to be reckoned with.

Now Louis XI brokered a remarkable agreement. The former Lancastrian queen Margaret of Anjou hated few of the Yorkist lords as much as Warwick, whom she rightly regarded as instrumental in depriving her husband of his throne, but was persuaded to consent to an arrangement by which Henry VI's restoration might be brought about. It was agreed that Warwick and Clarence would invade England and would restore Henry to the throne. King Henry's son, the Lancastrian Prince Edward, would marry Warwick's younger daughter, Anne, and thus become Clarence's brother-in-law. On 22 July[28] Warwick knelt before the queen and humbly asked her forgiveness; three days later Prince Edward was betrothed to Anne Neville in Angers Cathedral, and on 13 September Warwick, accompanied by Clarence, Oxford and the Lancastrian Earl of Pembroke, Jasper Tudor, landed on the Devon coast, and proclaimed the restoration of Henry VI.

News of the landing reached Edward in the north, where he had progressed at the end of July to suppress fresh rebellions in Yorkshire and Cumberland staged by Lord FitzHugh, another of Warwick's brothers-in-law, and a number of Neville retainers of gentry rank. It is uncertain whether these risings were really substantial enough to warrant the king's personal intervention at a time when an invasion from France was threatening, but in the south-east (where news of armed northerners always caused panic) it was said that there were 'many folk up in the north, so that Percy is not able to resist them; and so the king has sent for his feed men to come to him, for he will go to put them down.'

Nevertheless, if Edward had allowed himself to be caught up in this general panic, he cannot have been blind to the other threat he faced either. The king's household knight Sir John Paston wrote to his brother:

> Some say that the king should come again to London and that in haste, and, as it is said, Courtenays have landed in Devonshire and rule there. Item, that the lords Clarence and Warwick will attempt to land in England any day, as folk fear.[29]

Certainly there were sound reasons why the king should have chosen to go north, even in the face of urgent warnings of Warwick's imminent strike, not least from his brother-in-law, the Duke of Burgundy. Above all, the risings in the north were present and real, and Edward intended to deal with them in person, as he had done earlier in the year. Moreover, in the north, where the estates of the Neville earldom of Salisbury were concentrated, there was always a danger of residual sympathies for Warwick that might translate into active support of an invasion. By contrast, Edward had no reason to suppose that elsewhere in England Warwick and Clarence would attract any more support than they had done a few months earlier. This, however, proved one of two major miscalculations which within weeks proved the king's undoing.

In stark contrast to the rebels' inability to attract magnate support a few months earlier, their proclamation summoning all able-bodied men to join their army now not only drew sizeable popular levies, but soon saw their cause joined by lords who had previously shied away from open opposition to Edward IV. Within days the Earl of Shrewsbury and Lord Stanley brought their retinues, and the army that approached Coventry in the final days of September was substantial, estimated by the town's local records to have numbered as many as 30,000 men. Even if this number was exaggerated, it seems that the king was unable to match the forces fielded by his opponents. Although Edward still had with him a number of loyal magnates, including his brother Gloucester, Rivers, Hastings and Say, whose armed followings numbered in their thousands, he was failing to attract popular support and could not hope to defeat the army marching against him in an open battle.

It was now that Edward's second major miscalculation came into play. The restoration of Henry Percy to the earldom of Northumberland in March 1470 had been in keeping with Edward's past policy of seeking to reconcile former Lancastrians to his rule, but he had failed to appreciate fully how much this particular title meant to the family pride of John Neville, the long-standing supporter who had been stripped of it in Percy's favour. Neville was an honourable man, but also a man with a strong sense of history and lineage. Elevation to the earldom of Northumberland had represented nothing short of his family's complete victory over their old Percy rivals. The rule of the north, which had so long been contested between the two families, now belonged to the Nevilles, and this was what mattered to John Neville. The Courtenay estates which he received in recompense for those returned to the Percys were certainly no mere 'magpie's nest', and the marquisate of Montagu guaranteed him and his heirs precedence over the restored Percy earl, but they were estates and a title which lacked any connexion to the region that alone had traditionally mattered to the Nevilles.

Had Montagu shared his brother's zeal for the rule of England, he might have been content, but to all intents and purposes he did not. He was a northern lord, and had fought to gain and defend the north for his king. To be shunted south after all he had done, was an insult. To add further injury, following Warwick's flight Edward had treated his estates as if forfeit by attainder, perhaps pending a future act of parliament to this effect. This called into question the position of Montagu and his son as next heirs to the Neville patrimony, the lands of the earldom of Salisbury, many of which were entailed in the male line of the family.[30] In the light of these dual slights, Montagu took the decisive step of declaring for King Henry in front of his troops, and set out to take Edward prisoner.

Initially, the king refused to believe the news, but when it was confirmed, he rapidly appreciated that his position between the two Neville armies was untenable. With a small retinue he fled in a south-easterly direction. Having succeeded in making the precarious crossing of the Wash, in the course of which some of Edward's companions were drowned and the king himself only narrowly escaped with his life, they reached Bishop's Lynn on the night of Sunday, 30 September. Here the party remained for two days, before setting sail in two Dutch hulks and a small English vessel on 2 October.[31] On 6 October Henry VI was brought out of the Tower and formally restored to the throne. Edward's reign was at an end.

EDWARD IN EXILE

The natural place for Edward to seek refuge was the court of his brother-in-law, Charles of Burgundy, and it was for the coast of Holland that the fugitives sailed.[32] The crossing itself was fraught with danger for, Warwick aside, there were also other enemies to be considered. The towns of the Hanseatic league were at war with the English (see below, p. 136), and Edward's small flotilla was intercepted by a number of their ships which chased it all the way to the Dutch coast. On 3 October 1470 Edward and his companions nevertheless landed on the Dutch island of Texel, where they were met two days later by the treasurer of North Holland, Jan van Assendelft, and conducted south to Alkmaar, where they were more formally greeted by the Duke of Burgundy's governor of Holland, Louis de Bruges, Seigneur de la Gruthuyse.

It was unusual for England's fifteenth-century kings to have more than a modest supply of ready money to hand; even small sums paid to servants and messengers in reward were often borrowed from the monarch's entourage. In 1470 Edward had been forced to flee from his kingdom in such haste that there had been no time even to scrape together more than a few clothes. The fugitive king who set such store by his appearance arrived in Holland penniless, reduced to rewarding the captain of the vessel that had taken him to safety with a furred gown he had managed to salvage. Now, Gruthuyse provided new clothes and an escort to The Hague, which the party reached on 11 October.

Already, on 8 October, messengers had been dispatched to Hesdin to inform Duke Charles of the arrival of his brother-in-law, who for a time had been rumoured dead, and on the 10th Edward himself had written to the duke. Yet, if Edward had expected to be welcomed with open arms by his brother-in-law, he was to be disappointed. As king of England, he had been a useful ally to the duke; as a fugitive, he represented something of a political embarrassment. Indeed, even as Edward's party landed in Holland, the Burgundian court was still providing shelter for the dukes of Exeter and Somerset and other Lancastrian exiles.

However willing the duke might be in principle to support his brother-in-law, the more prosaic demands of foreign policy and statecraft meant that the exiled monarch represented above all a threat to relations with England, now under Warwick's control, a problem rendered all the greater by the understanding between Queen Margaret and Louis XI of France. In view of the changed political realities, Charles the Bold did not hesitate long before sending messengers to Calais to express his pleasure at Henry VI's restoration, while at the same time granting Edward a monthly pension of 500 écus. He did, however, steadfastly refuse to meet his brother-in-law in person, and for the time being the exiles remained at The Hague as the governor's guests.

In mid-December, the news of Louis XI's advancing negotiations with Warwick finally persuaded Charles to grant Edward a hearing. From 2 to 4 January they met at Aire, and again on the 7th at St Pol as guests of Jacques de Luxemburg, a kinsman of Edward's queen. Nevertheless, Charles the Bold was still reluctant to take sides openly. Thus he sent Exeter and Somerset back to England with reassurances of Burgundian friendship towards the house of Lancaster, and publicly ordered that no aid was to be given to Edward. Privately, however, Charles provided his brother-in-law with £20,000, and had three ships fitted out for him at Veere. Moreover, he worked to bring about a reconciliation between Edward and the Hanseatic league, which allowed him to hire a number of vessels to escort the Yorkist exiles to England and – if necessary – to provide them with a means of escape back to Burgundy, should the invasion fail. Edward himself kept himself busy by soliciting support from loyal friends in England and elsewhere, appealing to Duke Francis II of Brittany for assistance, and above all seeking to mollify the Duke of Clarence through the good offices of his mother and sisters. In the meantime, Edward remained a guest at Bruges in the house of Louis de Gruthuyse with its splendid library.[33]

Meanwhile, in England Warwick had set about reorganising the government. Edward's key officers of state were replaced by Warwick's trusted supporters: his brother, George Neville, returned as chancellor, while the privy seal was entrusted to John Hals, Bishop of Coventry and Lichfield. Sir John Langstrother, Prior of St John, was restored to the treasurership which he had held during Warwick's ascendancy in the summer of 1469. Clarence once more received the lieutenancy of Ireland from which he had been dismissed after his flight to France. To himself,

Warwick awarded the offices of Admiral and Great Chamberlain of England, with Sir Richard Tunstall restored to the chamberlainship of King Henry's household, which he had held before the battle of Northampton. The Earl of Oxford became steward of the king's household,[34] while Warwick's Staffordshire retainer John Delves replaced Lord Howard as keeper of the wardrobe and treasurer of the household.

This, however, was largely the limit of what the earl could distribute. If a Lancastrian restoration was to be durable, large parts of the Yorkist peerage needed to be reconciled to the new regime, and could not be expected to disgorge the rewards they had amassed during the previous decade in their entirety. Already a problem loomed in the shape of the Lancastrian peers who had gone into exile with Queen Margaret and would look to be restored to their families' property as a reward for their loyalty. Most precarious of all was the position of the Duke of Clarence. Whatever credence the vain and evidently gullible prince had given to the promises that Warwick had made to him, he was not too stupid or deluded to realise before long that there was scant likelihood that he would enjoy greater prominence at the court of a restored Henry VI than he had at that of his own brother, least of all once Queen Margaret and her son returned from France.

Many of Edward's supporters who had not joined him in exile took sanctuary. The heavily pregnant Queen Elizabeth, her mother, the Duchess of Bedford, and her three young daughters sought shelter in Westminster Abbey; the chancellor, Bishop Stillington, the keeper of the privy seal, Bishop Rotherham, and a number of others went to St Martin le Grand in the City of London, where they were joined after the surrender of the Tower to Warwick's lieutenant, Sir Geoffrey Gate, on 3 October, by members of the garrison. One who failed to save himself was the unpopular treasurer, the Earl of Worcester, who was caught hiding in a tree in a Huntingdonshire forest, tried before the Earl of Oxford, and executed on Tower Hill on 18 October.[35]

EDWARD'S RESTORATION

3 March 1471 marked the formal end of the tenth year of Edward's reign, and it was henceforth to mark also the beginning of the recovery of his realm. He was still some weeks short of his twenty-ninth birthday,

and he was once again displaying the energy and determination that had characterised him in the acquisition of his throne a decade earlier. Ever adept at symbolic acts, on 2 March he boarded his ship, the *Antony* – a vessel owned by Louis de Gruthuyse's father-in-law, Henri de Borselle, Seigneur de Veere, the admiral of Burgundy – at Flushing, and even though unfavourable winds delayed the departure of his flotilla for nine days, he refused to return to shore until he was finally able to set sail for England on March 11.[36]

The crossing went smoothly, and the following day Edward's ships anchored off the Norfolk coast near Cromer. Prudently, the king did not immediately go ashore in person, but instead sent two East Anglian knights, Sir Robert Chamberlain and Sir Gilbert Debenham, and other local men to sound out the loyalties of the population. Although they put on a brave face, the news they brought was dispiriting. Warwick had anticipated Edward's landing. Over the course of the preceding weeks he had rounded up the Dukes of Norfolk and Suffolk, Edward's Bourgchier relatives and any other local men of influence whom he suspected of residual loyalty to Edward, and imprisoned many of them in London. With all potential Yorkist supporters out of the way, the road was clear for John de Vere, Earl of Oxford, who had borne a grudge against Edward ever since the execution of his father and elder brother in 1462, to control East Anglia.

Edward refused to be disheartened, but realised that a landing in Norfolk offered little prospect of success, weighed anchor, and set a course for the north. Within hours, this decision seemed to have been disastrous. A storm arose which continued for two days, and it was a rather bedraggled fleet that was scattered about the mouth of the Humber on 14 March. Edward lost contact with his ships, and was left with no choice but to land with the small, if handpicked, retinue who had sailed with him in his flagship. The spot he chose for his landing, like the date of his departure from Holland, was steeped in symbolism: Ravenspur in Holderness was the very point at which Henry of Derby had landed 72 years earlier to claim the crown as Henry IV.[37]

This was no accident: Edward knew his history. In a further echo of Henry IV, who in 1399 had let it be known that he only came to claim his paternal inheritance, the Duchy of Lancaster, Edward had it put about that he merely came to reclaim the dukedom of York, wore an ostrich feather (the Prince of Wales's badge), and in the face of the watching crowd was heard crying 'A King Henry! A King and Prince Edward!' If this device did not win him supporters, it at least gave him clear passage through a country that was not necessarily favourable to his restoration to the throne, and bought him time in which to rally those still loyal to him.

These, however, were in the first instance few and far between. Edward spent his first night back in England in 'a poor village, two miles from his landing place', surrounded by just the 500 men who had landed with him. On the following morning, they were joined by the 500 men of Richard of Gloucester's and Earl Rivers' retinues, but if the king had hoped that the people of Yorkshire would join his cause, he was disappointed. The county levies had been arrayed on Warwick's orders to prevent the exiles from landing, and the best residual Yorkist loyalties could achieve was to prevent them from openly attacking the invaders. Nevertheless, Edward refused to give up hope that enough armed support to defeat Warwick could eventually be raised, and resolved to march on the city of York. The reaction of his erstwhile subjects along the road was less than encouraging. Both Beverley and Hull refused to open their gates to him, and when his small force reached York on 18 March, the citizens took some persuading before they would allow him entry. Only Edward's charm and repeated assertions that he sought to recover nothing but his father's duchy eventually won them over.

On the following day, the invaders moved south towards Tadcaster, and from there towards Wakefield and Sandal, hereditary possessions of the house of York. This was a daring move, for their road led not far past Pontefract castle, where Warwick's brother, the Marquess of Montagu, was in residence. Now, however, Edward's apparent error of judgement in restoring the Percy Earl of Northumberland paid a handsome dividend, for Montagu was evidently unable to muster a force large enough to challenge the invader in a region where men traditionally followed the lead of a Percy. Northumberland, however, remained inactive, and raised no opposition to Edward's landing.

In the Yorkist heartland around Wakefield, the numbers of Edward's army began to grow, but as yet only slowly. By way of Doncaster Edward marched on to Nottingham. Here, finally, came an indication that the hoped-for supporters might yet materialise when two local knights, Sir William Parr and Sir James Harrington, arrived with a company of some 600 men. At the same time, the invaders' morale received another much-needed boost when it became apparent how easily the resolve even of some of the leading Lancastrian magnates might be shaken. The Duke of Exeter, the Earl of Oxford and Viscount Beaumont had assembled some 4,000 men from East Anglia at Newark, but, mistaking Edward's scouts for the vanguard of his entire army, the leaders abandoned part of their men and fled in the dead of night.

From London, Warwick had observed events in the north with growing concern, and had made for his own midland strongholds in Warwickshire. There he had assembled a substantial force with which to crush Edward once and for all but, all too aware of the brittleness of the alliance of die-hard Lancastrian and former Yorkists over which he presided, as yet refused to give open battle. Instead, he decided to await the arrival of further reinforcements and in the face of the approaching Yorkist army withdrew into the fortified town of Coventry. By contrast with the caution displayed by Warwick, Edward moved with speed and determination. He took his force, such as it was, straight to the walls of Coventry. He was not blind to the divisions among his opponents, and sought to deepen them at every opportunity. Warwick repeatedly refused battle before the gates of Coventry, and even turned down offers of a full pardon, unless Edward agreed to extensive conditions. This Edward was reluctant to do, and his hand was strengthened when he was able to repel an attack by an army under the Duke of Exeter and the Earl of Oxford.

At this point, the Duke of Clarence, who had spent several weeks meandering around the south and southern midlands while deciding how to extract himself from his predicament, made his move. Throughout the period of Edward's exile, there had been feverish efforts, led by the king's mother, Duchess Cecily of York, and his sister, Margaret of Burgundy, to bring about a reconciliation between Clarence and his brother. By the spring of 1471 it had become apparent even to the vain Clarence that he had little to gain from the imminent return of Queen Margaret and Prince Edward of Lancaster, and much to lose. Nevertheless, anxious not to find himself on the losing side, he maintained his support for Warwick's regime, and in the middle of March 1471 began to rally his retainers, ostensibly to help fend off his brother's invasion.[38]

By the end of March Clarence had made up his mind. On 2 April he led his forces from Burford towards Edward's army, then encamped at Warwick. On the following day, the king advanced to meet him. On the Banbury road between Burford and Warwick the brothers drew up their men in battle order, and then each advanced towards the other with a small following, which on Edward's side included Richard of Gloucester, Lord Hastings and Earl Rivers. When the two groups met, Clarence fell to his knees before his brother, who raised him up and kissed him. Greetings were also exchanged between Clarence and Gloucester and the other nobles in their retinues. At this point, a cry of 'Long live King Edward!' went up, trumpets were sounded, and with a cheer the two armies united in the cause of Edward's restoration.[39]

His force strengthened by Clarence's men, Edward was now in a position to march on London. The atmosphere here was one of confusion. Aware of the impending invasion, in the first weeks of 1471 Warwick had placed under arrest all the lords whom he (rightly) suspected of loyalties to Edward. Chief among these were the Dukes of Norfolk and Buckingham, the Earl of Wiltshire, and the king's Bourgchier relatives, the Earl of Essex, the Archbishop of Canterbury and Lord Cromwell, but also William Grey, Bishop of Ely, and Walter Blount, Lord Mountjoy.[40] On Monday in Holy Week Edmund Beaufort, Duke of Somerset, his brother John, Marquess of Dorset, and John Courtenay, Earl of Devon, rode west out of the city to await Queen Margaret's landing in the West Country. With Warwick, Montagu and Beaumont holed up at Coventry, the only Lancastrian leaders left in the city were the ancient Lord Sudeley and a gaggle of prelates, headed by the chancellor, Archbishop Neville. And, of course, there was King Henry VI. On Wednesday Neville and Sudeley made a last desperate attempt to play this sole remaining trump card. They assembled the few men they had at their disposal and staged a formal royal progress around the traditional circuit through the city in a vain effort to persuade the Londoners to rally to their – still personally popular – monarch.

The spectacle failed to produce the desired effect. Whether it was the small number of retainers that accompanied the king or his own appearance – Henry was by this stage so detached from what was happening around him that he had to be led by the hand by the archbishop – the Londoners thought it wise not to commit themselves. News of Edward's approach had already spread through the city. On Palm Sunday John Mowbray, Duke of Norfolk, had taken the opportunity of the high mass to slip away quietly and make his way to his East Anglian estates to rally his tenants and retainers in support of Edward's cause. Two days later, the nobles and gentry whom Warwick had imprisoned in the Tower had overcome their guards at night, and by daybreak on Wednesday the fortress itself was in their hands. In the streets of London, chaos prevailed. Some still openly sported Warwick's ragged staff badge, but others had already wisely cast this off and were openly showing their allegiances.

Around midday on Maundy Thursday, Edward entered his capital. He rode straight to St Paul's to give thanks, before making his way to the neighbouring bishop's palace, where King Henry was lodged. The meeting of the rival monarchs was brief and formal, before Edward ordered that Henry be returned to his cell in the Tower. With King Henry, Edward found his cousin, Archbishop Neville, babbling profuse and semi-coherent excuses. There was no time to listen to the shifty prelate's pleading. Along with John Hals, the keeper of Henry VI's privy seal, Neville was despatched to the Tower. As Edward and his retinue entered London, his chancellor and keeper of the privy seal, Bishops Stillington and Rotherham, the Earl of Essex's son and heir, William, Lord Bourgchier, and other knights and esquires came out of sanctuary, while the nobles and knights who had been interned by Warwick also emerged and joined their king's banner.

Edward spent Good Friday in London, while waiting for further men to rally to his cause. Among those who arrived were Lord Howard and Lord Hastings' brother, Sir Ralph, who had taken sanctuary at Colchester and brought welcome reinforcements, and the two sons of John Bourgchier, Lord Berners, who brought a contingent from Kent. But time was running out. Before midday on Easter Saturday news came that Warwick had at last left Coventry and was heading for London with all possible speed to engage Edward before he could increase his strength much further. The king hastily ordered his forces, said by some to number as many as 20,000 men and by others as few as 7,000, to muster in St John's Field, and about four o'clock set out in the direction of St Albans. About three hours later, Edward's vanguard made contact with Warwick's outriders in the vicinity of Hornsey Park and there was a brief skirmish, but the settling dark prevented a fully fledged battle that night. In the dark, both armies pitched their camps just a short distance apart, each uncertain of the other's exact position. Throughout the night Warwick fired his guns in Edward's approximate direction, but as the king had given orders that no fire should be returned and anything that might give his army's location away avoided, the hostile artillery overshot his camp.

Battle commenced about four o'clock in the morning, when the two armies could make each other out in the first light, with an exchange of fierce artillery and archery fire. Visibility continued to be hampered by a thick fog. Warwick's force outnumbered Edward's, and the severity of the shower of arrows caused a number of the king's men to break away from the rear, yet in the poor conditions few noticed and the main line of the royal army held. Edward's personal leadership played a crucial part in steadying his men's resolve. Fighting 'about the midst of the battle' he 'manly, vigorously, and valiantly assailed them, in the midst and strongest of their battle, where he, with great violence, beat and bore down before him all that stood in his way'.[41]

What eventually decided the engagement in Edward's favour was the mistrust that still persisted between old Lancastrian loyalists and former Yorkists in Warwick's force, which made them susceptible to any suggestion of treachery in their ranks. Crucially, in the thick fog the two armies had not lined up perfectly opposite each other, with Warwick's army overlapping on the western end and Edward's in the east. The resulting superiority of force at either end caused the lines of battle gradually to wheel about. In the early stages of the battle, the Earl of Oxford's division drove back that of William, Lord Hastings, and caused its ranks to break and the men to take to flight. Oxford was unable to prevent his men from pursuing their fleeing opponents, and it took him some time to rally them and return to the main battlefield. Here, Montagu's division had for its part pushed back Edward's centre, with the result that the battle lines stood at an angle to their previous alignment.

The accident of Oxford's return in the morning twilight and fog now combined with existing suspicions to turn the engagement in Edward's favour. Unaware of the shift of the lines of battle since his departure, Oxford came up on the flank of Montagu's division, rather than, as he intended, finding Edward's rear. In the poor light Montagu's men mistook Oxford's device of a star with streams for the Yorkist sun with streams and attacked. When Oxford's men found themselves under attack from the same Neville men who had so recently been staunch adherents of King Edward, they naturally assumed the worst, raised a cry of treason and turned to flight.

The confusion now turned into a rout of Warwick's army, in which Montagu was killed. The Duke of Exeter was seriously wounded and left for dead on the field, but eventually recovered and was imprisoned in the

Tower. Viscount Beaumont, Oxford and two of his brothers fled to Scotland to fight another day. On Edward's side, the principal casualties were Lords Cromwell and Say and the heirs of Lord Berners and Lord Mountjoy, Sir Humphrey Bourgchier and Sir William Blount. Warwick himself fled, but was apprehended and killed by some of Edward's men near Barnet wood, probably against the king's will.[42]

A triumphant Edward returned to London, carrying with him the bodies of Warwick and Montagu, which were put on display in St Paul's cathedral to quash the rumours that the earl had escaped alive which were already circulating. Yet there was little time for celebration. In the west, Devon and Somerset were still at large, and before long news arrived that Queen Margaret had landed at Weymouth, bringing with her the now 17-year-old Prince Edward: an alternative king, should any harm come to Henry VI, and a rallying point for any remaining Lancastrian loyalists. Edward's response was, once again, prompt and vigorous. Commissioners were ordered to raise fresh troops in the shires, and on 24 April Edward himself set out from Windsor, where he had celebrated St George's day, and headed west. The queen's army, consisting principally of south-western Beaufort and Courtenay retainers, was marching north towards the River Severn, intending to cross over into Wales and join up with a force that was being raised there by Jasper Tudor. On Edward's orders, the governor of Gloucester Castle, Sir Richard Beauchamp, denied the queen's men passage through the town to the Severn bridge there, forcing them to continue their march onwards to Tewkesbury. Here Edward caught up with them on the evening of 3 May.

In the early hours of the following morning Edward prepared his army for battle. Richard of Gloucester was placed in charge of the vanguard and William, Lord Hastings, took command of the rearguard, while Edward himself led the main body. A detachment of 200 spearmen was sent to search a wooded hill to the left of the king's army for any concealed Lancastrian forces. Having opened the battle by showering the Lancastrian vanguard under the Duke of Somerset with arrows and artillery fire, Edward was able to crush this contingent, not least by the timely intervention of the 200 spearmen who had found the wood clear of enemies. The two other Lancastrian divisions had up to this point apparently failed to engage in support of Somerset's men, and at least one later chronicler believed that the Lancastrian leaders now began to quarrel among themselves, and that Somerset personally brained

John, Lord Wenlock, one of the commanders of the Lancastrian centre, with his battleaxe.

What is certain is that under the impact of Edward's concerted assault the queen's army disintegrated and turned to flight. Among those killed on the battlefield or in flight were John Courtenay, Earl of Devon, John Beaufort, Marquess of Dorset, and, most devastatingly for the Lancastrian cause, Henry VI's son, the Prince of Wales. Several of the leaders found their way back to the abbey and sought sanctuary in the church. This proved a bad miscalculation, for Tewkesbury Abbey did not possess the franchise of a sanctuary, and in any case the pursuing Yorkists, still flushed with battle and killing, were impossible to stay. Edward himself was evidently less than proud of what followed, for in the official account of the battle circulated on the continent he was at pains to emphasise that he had granted his 'free pardon' to his enemies in the abbey church.[43] The reality, as reflected in the chronicle of Tewkesbury Abbey, was different. Edward's men stormed into the church, brandishing weapons, and killed a number of the fugitives then and there. According to Warkworth's chronicle, the king himself was with them, sword in hand, and had to be stopped in his tracks by a priest bearing the sacrament.

Characteristically, Edward did not take long to regain his composure and to concentrate on what – for the time being – mattered more than revenge. He set about knighting more than 40 of his supporters in reward for their valour on the day, and then returned to the abbey for a mass of thanksgiving. Yet his opponents had not been forgotten, and Edward was intent that the principals would not be given the opportunity to make trouble again. Consequently, two days later Somerset, Sir Hugh Courtenay and Sir John Langstrother were tried before the Dukes of Gloucester and Norfolk as constable and marshal of England. The predictable sentence was death, and they were immediately executed on a scaffold set up in the centre of the town. They were, however, spared the indignities of drawing and quartering, and their bodies were given honourable burial. Several members of the inner Lancastrian circle, including Queen Margaret's chancellor in exile, the former chief justice John Fortescue, were granted their lives and later pardoned.

The Lancastrian cause had now been effectively (as well as literally) decapitated, but Edward's troubles were not yet over, for news now arrived of two separate risings in Kent and in the north. On 7 May, the day after the execution of the Lancastrian leaders, Edward set out for the north. On the following day he reached Worcester, where he received news that Queen Margaret had been found hiding in a 'poor religious place' and had been taken into custody. On 11 May the king arrived in Coventry, where he remained for three days waiting for fresh troops, but was much reassured two days later by the arrival of the Earl of Northumberland, who was able to report that in the absence of Neville leadership and faced with his own opposition, resistance had collapsed. Northumberland had taken the rebel leaders captive, and the north was now quiet.[44]

There was, however, one further pocket of resistance to be dealt with, and this was not only more dangerous than the northern rising had proved to be, it threatened the capital directly. In the early days of 1471 Thomas Neville, an illegitimate son of Warwick's brother, William Neville, Earl of Kent, known after his father's earlier title as the Bastard of Fauconberg, had gone to sea with a flotilla to patrol the Channel against a possible invasion by Edward and his supporters. As this had failed to materialise, he had remained largely inactive while the fate of England was being decided on the fields of Barnet and Tewkesbury.

Rather late in the day, he sprang into action. On about 2 May 1471 he landed in Kent with some 300 men from the Calais garrison loyal to Warwick, and marched inland, rallying support as he went. Above all on account of his renown as a sea captain and commander at Calais, Warwick continued to enjoy a degree of popularity in the notoriously volatile county of Kent and the Cinque Ports, but men also rallied to Fauconberg's standard from further afield, until his army numbered between 2,000 and 3,000 men. By way of Canterbury, this force made for Sittingbourne, from where the Bastard wrote to the London authorities, demanding passage through the city. The Londoners, however, had already received news of the events at Tewkesbury and flatly denied the demand.[45]

It is unlikely that the Bastard was unaware of what had happened, and in the light of his persistence in his assault on London it is possible that his objective was not passage through the city, or even its sacking, but the rescue of Henry VI from the Tower.[46] On 12 May Fauconberg's ships sailed up the Thames, and succeeded in burning some alehouses near St Katharine's, while his main force attacked the Southwark end of London bridge. However, the city was well defended both by the mayor and aldermen and by the constable of the Tower, Lord Dudley, and the rebel attack was beaten back without much difficulty.

The following day, Fauconberg marched west towards Kingston bridge. Here, however, he was met by Earl Rivers with an armed force, and forced to turn back. Even now, Edward and his main army had not yet left Coventry. Only on 14 May did the king send an advance force of 1,500 men to assist the threatened capital, and only on 16 May did he himself set out with the main body of his army. On the same day that the royal vanguard left Coventry, Fauconberg renewed his assault on London. Pounding the city with their artillery, the rebels simultaneously attacked at three points. While one detachment once more assaulted the bridge, two other contingents that had been ferried across the Thames attacked the Aldgate and the Bishopsgate. Although at one point it seemed as though the attackers might prevail, eventually the joint efforts of the citizens and the earls of Essex and Rivers in the city and the Tower succeeded in repulsing them with considerable losses to their numbers. Fauconberg now withdrew his army to Blackheath, but sent his fleet ahead to Sandwich. On 18 May he too rode for the port, accompanied only by the remnants of the professional detachment from the Calais garrison, leaving the rest of his rebels to disperse quietly to their homes. From Sandwich he dispatched his soldiers back to Calais, while he awaited the king's arrival.[47]

On 21 May Edward made a triumphant entry into London at the head of his army. The mayor and leading aldermen were rewarded for their steadfast defence of the capital with knighthoods, and the captive Queen Margaret taken to the Tower. There, Henry VI died that same night, most likely killed on Edward's instructions. Although the official version of events attributed the former monarch's death to 'pure displeasure and melancholy', contemporaries were under no illusion as to what had really happened. 'King Edward has not chosen to have the custody of King Henry any longer,' the Milanese ambassador at the French court wrote to the Duke of Milan on 17 June. 'He has caused King Henry to be secretly assassinated in the Tower, where he was a prisoner. ... He has, in short, chosen to crush the seed.'[48]

This urgent business settled, Edward set out into Kent. On 26 May Richard of Gloucester received the Bastard of Fauconberg's submission at Sandwich, while on the same day Edward himself entered Canterbury in state, accompanied, as on the occasion of his entry into London, by an impressive array of lords. There, the king personally presided over the first trials of some of the Kentish rebels, and stripped the corporations of Canterbury and Sandwich of their liberties and privileges.

Edward was now master of his kingdom once more. With Warwick dead, he was, perhaps for the first time, truly master of his own kingdom. His throne and the future of his house looked more secure than ever. The Lancastrian royal family had been all but exterminated, and the possibility that Henry VI's distant kinsmen, the Tudors, might reassert the line's claim was a remote one. While Edward had been in exile, Queen Elizabeth had given birth to the desired heir, a Yorkist Prince of Wales. On 3 July 1471 peers and prelates assembled in the Parliament Chamber at Westminster to swear their allegiance to the young prince as King Edward's eventual successor. Among them were not only staunch supporters, but also reformed former rebels like Archbishop Neville.[49] Edward had recaptured the initiative. He had recaptured his kingdom, and he recaptured the imagination of his people.

6

RE-ESTABLISHING THE
REGIME, 1471–5

PACIFYING THE REALM, 1471–3

Edward might be king once more, but now the government of the realm needed to be reconstructed. Late medieval royal government was a deeply personal affair, and the interruption of Edward's reign had disrupted the work of the king's law courts and all other government activities that depended for their functioning on the monarch's command. The solution found was characteristically pragmatic: the readeption was treated as a non-event, and Edward's reign was deemed to have been uninterrupted by his absence. The formula adopted suggested that the king had 'for certain necessary and urgent causes and affairs specially moving and concerning us, progressed to the parts beyond the sea out of our realm of England, leaving no lieutenant or keeper of the said kingdom in the same realm'.[1]

At the head of the administration, most of the great officers of state who had been dismissed in October 1470 returned to office. Robert Stillington returned to the chancery, and Thomas Rotherham once more received the privy seal. William Hatcliff resumed his duties as the king's secretary. The loyal and experienced Earl of Essex became treasurer once more, and he continued in office for the remainder of Edward's reign, becoming one of the longest-serving holders of the office in the entire fifteenth century. In marked contrast to ten years earlier, changes were now also made in the lower ranks of the administration. At the exchequer, all four tellers, the key officials handling the day-to-day flow of money were at least temporarily replaced with members of the king's household (Sir John Scott, Thomas Vaughan, Sir John Fogge and Richard Fowler), while Treasurer Bourgchier naturally also put in place his own choice of under-treasurer (Fowler) and clerk of the receipt (Thomas Bulkeley). The Westminster courts saw the dismissal of a number of justices, but apart from the chief justice of common pleas, Robert Danby, who for much of his career had been closely associated with the Nevilles, those leaving office were mostly elderly men who had served on the bench since before 1461.[2]

More important than the line-up at the centre were the changes to the rule of the regions, where the bloodletting among the king's early associates and the eclipse of the Nevilles had left vacancies. In the north, the Earl of Northumberland could be rewarded for his services at the time of Edward's return, but his power was counterbalanced by the grant of extensive estates to the king's younger brother, Richard of Gloucester, who increasingly emerged as the greatest landowner not just in the north, but in all of England. In the troublesome south-west, Edward's more volatile brother Clarence was allowed a degree of pre-eminence, but the day-to-day control of the region fell on to the more reliable shoulders of John, Lord Dynham, his brother-in-law, the young Fulk, Lord Fitzwaryn (both of families long-established in the region), and the king's stepson, Thomas Grey, Marquess of Dorset, who had successively married the two great West-Country heiresses of Henry Holland, Duke of Exeter, and William, Lord Bonville. In Wales and the Marches, where in the 1460s William Herbert, Earl of Pembroke, had held sway as the king's virtual lieutenant, a new arrangement was also required, as in 1471 Herbert's son and heir was barely 16 years old. Although the young earl was initially allowed to succeed to his father's title, the act of resumption of 1473 stripped him of part of the lands he held by royal grant, and in 1479 he was forced to exchange the earldom of Pembroke for that of Huntingdon. His former title was instead conferred on the Prince of Wales, to whom the rule of Wales belonged at least in name. In practice, the prince's authority was exercised by his tutor, the king's brother-in-law Anthony, Earl Rivers.

Yet, if during his first reign Edward had placed his trust in individuals rather than institutions, the second reign saw a change in his attitude, at least as far as the rule of some of the further-flung regions was concerned. From an early date, the young Prince of Wales was set up at Ludlow with an independent household and council, and this council began to exercise a wide-ranging jurisdiction, not only in Wales, but also in the prince's duchy of Cornwall in the south-west of England. The authority of the prince's Welsh and Cornish councils was strengthened by the inclusion of the leading magnates in their respective regions, such as Walter Devereux, Lord Ferrers, and the Duke of Buckingham in Wales, and Lord Dynham in Cornwall.[3] In the north, the judicial activity of the prince's council was mirrored by that of the council of the Duke of Gloucester, which, on account of Duke Richard's exceptional position as the king's effective lieutenant in the region was invested with a quasi-viceregal authority that went beyond that commanded by other magnates' councils, and in some respects prefigured the council in the north given formal shape by Henry VIII in the 1530s. To ensure effective control of those areas where the establishment of such conciliar rule was less practical than in the traditionally volatile north and west, royal castles, manors and other estates throughout England were increasingly placed in the hands of reliable royal servants, who if necessary could be trusted to report any seditious rumblings and would allow any renewed rebellion to be crushed immediately.[4]

CONTINUED LANCASTRIAN PLOTTING

The deaths of Henry VI and his son, Prince Edward, in May 1471 should once and for all have removed the Lancastrian threat to Edward's throne. The remaining claimants' titles were at best tenuous, and arguably far weaker than Edward's own. Henry IV's descendants in the male line had become extinct with Henry VI's death, and even of John of Gaunt's blood only female lines remained. Two of these lines were represented by distant foreign princes, who showed little interest in becoming involved in the dynastic struggle for the crown of England: John of Gaunt's daughters Philippa and Katharine had respectively been queens to King João I of Portugal and Henry III of Castile, and their descendants (Alfonso V of Portugal and Henry IV of Castile) now ruled their respective kingdoms. Henry IV's younger sister Elizabeth had married John Holland, Earl of Huntingdon, and her claim to the Lancastrian inheritance was now represented by Henry Holland, Duke of Exeter, a prisoner in the Tower since his removal from sanctuary in London in the aftermath of the battle of Barnet.

John of Gaunt's children by Katharine Swynford had been formally excluded from the succession, and after the execution of Edmund Beaufort, Duke of Somerset, were represented by the descendants of John of Gaunt's daughter Joan, the wife of Ralph Neville, Earl of Westmoreland (Edward himself was descended from Joan through his mother) on the one hand, and by Margaret Beaufort, daughter of John Beaufort, Duke of Somerset (*d.* 1444), and her only son on the other. It was on this son, Henry Tudor, Earl of Richmond – on his father's side Henry VI's nephew of the half blood – that any hope of a Lancastrian challenge now became focused. Inexperienced and without tangible resources, Henry possessed one important asset in his resourceful uncle Jasper Tudor, Earl of Pembroke. Pembroke had failed to join forces with Queen Margaret at the time of the battle of Tewkesbury, but had kept control of a number of Welsh castles, from where, with the aid of Louis XI of France, he could continue to make mischief.[5]

Also still at large was John de Vere, Earl of Oxford, whose livery badge had cost the Lancastrians the battle of Barnet. He had fled into Scotland after the disaster, and from there made his way to the French court. With French support, Oxford was raiding the marches of Calais by the spring of 1472, and was evidently in communication with some prominent well-wishers in England. Among these was an old associate, the earl's brother-in-law, George Neville, Archbishop of York. Edward had long disliked his shifty cousin, and although he had been prepared to pardon the archbishop for his part in the events of 1469–71, the rumours of renewed disloyalty gave the king the excuse he needed to deal with Neville once and for all. On the night of 25 April 1472 the archbishop was expecting the king's arrival at his manor of the Moor in Hertfordshire on the following day for a hunting party, but instead was summoned to attend upon the king at Windsor. There he was charged with treason, placed under arrest, sent to the Tower, and forthwith dispatched across the channel for imprisonment in the castle of Hammes in the Calais marches. The considerable treasure that Neville had amassed (said to amount to over £20,000) was seized, and the archbishop's richly jewelled mitre was broken up and converted into a new crown for the king.[6] The news of the archbishop's sudden downfall caused some popular consternation. On 30 April 1472 Sir John Paston wrote to his younger brother that

> my lord Archbishop was brought to the Tower on Saturday at night, and on Monday at midnight he was conveyed to a ship, and so into the sea, and as yet I cannot understand whither he is sent, nor what has befallen him. Men say that he has offended; but as John Foster says, some men say nay. But all his men are dispersed, every man his way, and some that are great clerks and famous doctors of his go now again to Cambridge to school.[7]

Although thus deprived of his principal contact in England, Oxford continued to plot in France. With the support of Louis XI and the Hanseatic league he succeeded in equipping a fleet, and on 28 May 1473 attempted a landing at St Osyth in Essex, the region of his family's traditional power. Repelled by the Earl of Essex and Lords Dynham and Duras, he spent some months harassing shipping in the Channel before descending on the Cornish coast and seizing the island fortress of St Michael's Mount in September 1473. The choice of landing place was no accident. The Mount's strategic value aside, the south-west had tradition-ally harboured Lancastrian sympathies; many Cornishmen, including the greatest landowner in the county, Sir John Arundell of Lanherne, had fought for Henry VI in 1471. Yet it was Arundell (who had been par-doned by Edward on payment of a substantial fine) who was hurriedly instructed to dislodge Oxford, acting alongside Sir Henry Bodrugan, a wealthy Cornish knight of more reliable Yorkist sympathies.

Worryingly for the king and council, however, it was not Arundell who hampered their efforts by showing himself sympathetic to Oxford's cause, but Bodrugan, who was left in sole charge of the siege after Arundell's sudden death in late 1473. Rather than starving Oxford's men into submission, Bodrugan allowed the garrison to be supplied with enough provisions (so it was discovered) to allow the fortress to hold out for more than six months. In December Bodrugan was replaced by the sheriff of Cornwall, John Fortescue, a nephew of Henry VI's former chief justice. Fortescue conducted the siege with more vigour than Bodrugan had done, but shrewdly interspersed the fighting with periodic negotiations, which were supported by the king's council at Westminster with secret offers of pardons and promises of rewards to all who would desert Oxford. As a result of these tactics, the resolve of the garrison crumbled, and on 15 February 1474 Oxford was forced to surrender St Michael's Mount to Fortescue.[8] Oxford was sent to join Archbishop Neville in Hammes castle in the Calais pale, but his exploits had evidently captured the public imagination, for even in 1477 an impostor pretending to be the earl was stirring up unrest in Cambridgeshire and Huntingdonshire.

THE KING AND HIS FAMILY

The extinction of the Lancastrian main line apart, perhaps the most important consequence of the crisis of 1469–71 had been a thinning of the ranks of the great men about the king. Rivers and Pembroke had been succeeded by their sons, but Devon and Montagu were gone (the former leaving no children and the latter's young son sidelined and eventually deprived of his ducal title), and – crucially – so was Warwick.

The result of the demise of the men who had benefited most from the patronage at Edward's disposal in the first years of the reign allowed, but also necessitated, a full reappraisal not only of royal patronage, but also of the balance of power in the regions. If in 1461 the king had relied in the first instance on the Nevilles, and second on his new friends Hastings, Stafford and Herbert, the settlement of Edward's second reign was heavily focused on members of the immediate royal family, that is, the king's sons and brothers, and the queen's kin. Foremost, however, were Edward's two brothers.

Despite the part that the volatile Clarence had played in bringing about his brother's temporary deposition, Edward was apparently determined that he should not face more than limited consequences of his actions. Thus Clarence's hand in the south-west was even strengthened by a grant of most of the principal estates of the earldom of Devon, and he was also allowed to stake a claim to his wife's share of the dead Earl of Warwick's estates. Characteristically, the duke was not satisfied. To him, nothing less than his father-in-law's entire vast inheritance comprising the estates of his two earldoms of Warwick and Salisbury would do. The only potential stumbling block in his way was Duchess Isabel's younger sister, Anne, who had been briefly married in 1470–71 to the Lancastrian Prince of Wales who died at Tewkesbury. If Clarence was to secure the Warwick inheritance in its entirety, it was imperative that she should not be allowed to marry again, and certainly that she should not be allowed a husband who could successfully mount a challenge to the king's brother. After 1471, there was only one man in England who might do so – the king's other brother, Richard of Gloucester.

By contrast with the shifty Clarence, Richard had displayed conspicuous loyalty throughout the crises of 1469–71. Aged just 9 when Edward ascended the throne, Richard played second fiddle to Clarence for much of the 1460s. Whereas Clarence, as Edward's heir, was made a duke on the eve of the coronation, Richard had to wait until September of that year before in turn being created Duke of Gloucester. Where Clarence had been among Edward's first additions to the ranks of the order of the Garter, the young Richard had to wait for a further five years before he too became a companion of the order.[9] Much of the apanage[10] of lands that Edward provided for Richard early in the reign was subsequently taken from him when domestic policies required a redistribution, and overall the king's youngest brother remained rather less generously endowed than many of Edward's other supporters, and certainly than his brother Clarence.[11] Nevertheless, while Clarence plotted his elder brother's downfall, Richard had kept faith, had gone into exile with Edward in 1470, and had distinguished himself in the military campaign of 1471. With Edward re-established on the throne, Richard could reasonably expect to be rewarded, and so he was. It was to him that Edward granted many of the offices previously held by the Earl of Warwick, and his economic position was also greatly improved by grants of most of the northern estates of the earldom of Salisbury (which had been entailed in the male line of the Neville family), and of the lands in the east and south-east forfeited by the Earl of Oxford and the Lincolnshire rebels of 1470.[12]

From Richard's point of view, a marriage to the 16-year-old Anne Neville and a consequent share in her inheritance represented an attractive prospect, and he readily agreed when the match was proposed. Clarence, however, had no intention of sharing the Warwick lands with his brother. Anne was his ward, and in the first instance he set about keeping her out of Richard's reach, according to one account by concealing her in London disguised as a kitchen maid.[13] Gloucester nevertheless succeeded in locating her, took her to the sanctuary of St Martin's, and in July 1472 made her his wife, without even waiting for the papal dispensation demanded by their close kinship.

This hardly improved relations between the two royal dukes, which were already acrimonious. Even in the winter of 1471 matters had gone so far as to compel Edward to order both of his brothers to appear before his council, where each skilfully argued his case. In February 1472, the king made a fresh attempt at mediation, only to be told bluntly by Clarence that Richard was welcome to the Lady Anne, but he would keep her lands. In March Clarence was finally persuaded to surrender part of the Warwick inheritance to his brother, but in return he had to be compensated by extensive royal guarantees of his tenure of his newly acquired lands in the south-west, a formal grant of the titles of the earldoms of Warwick and Salisbury, and the office of great chamberlain of England, previously held by Duke Richard.

This settlement, however, presented certain difficulties in law. Although Warwick and his brother Montagu had died in battle fighting against an anointed king, they had not been formally attainted of treason. Indeed Edward had refrained from pursuing formal attainder at his brothers' direct request,[14] for it was central to Clarence's and Gloucester's titles to their wives' shares of the Warwick inheritance that this should be so. Had Warwick been attainted, his daughters could not have inherited, and the two royal dukes would have had to claim their lands by a royal grant which could be readily overturned by a parliamentary act of resumption. If, however, the descent of the Neville lands was to follow the rules of the common law, there were other claimants to be considered. In the first instance, much of the Neville patrimony in the north had long been entailed in the male line of the family, and should consequently have fallen to Warwick's heir male, his young nephew George Neville, Duke of Bedford, Montagu's son. Furthermore, the core of the estates of the earldom of Warwick had come to Richard Neville as part of his wife's inheritance from her Beauchamp and Despenser ancestors. With Warwick's death, these lands reverted to the countess's sole possession for the remainder of her life. While she survived, her daughters had no claim to the lands, and – should she remarry and have a son by a further husband – their title might still be superseded. The Countess of Warwick had landed in England on the day of her husband's death at Barnet, and had hurriedly sought sanctuary at Beaulieu Abbey. From there, she had sought to protect her title, appealing in vain to the king, his brothers and other members of the royal family, as well as to parliament when it assembled in October 1472.

By this time, Edward had already been persuaded by his brothers that her claims, as well as those of the young Duke of Bedford, should be set aside, and colluded in an arrangement that has rightly been described as being of 'a high degree of callousness and disregard for the laws of inheritance'.[15] In June 1473 Richard of Gloucester, with Edward's approval, removed the Countess of Warwick from sanctuary and had her taken to the north by his retainer Sir James Tyrell.[16] This move naturally aroused the suspicions of the Duke of Clarence, who was soon even further disgruntled at not having been exempted from the act of resumption passed by parliament. Relations between the king's two brothers were once again deteriorating rapidly. In November 1473 Sir John Paston wrote to his brother that

> the Duke of Clarence makes himself big in whatever he can, showing that he would but deal with the Duke of Gloucester. But the king intends in eschewing all inconveniences to be as big as they both, and to be a stifler between them. And some men think that under this there should be some other thing intended and some treason conspired.[17]

In May 1474 parliament agreed to an act recognising the title of Warwick's two daughters and their husbands to their father's entire estates, and partitioned them between them. The dowager countess was stripped of her paternal inheritance by being declared legally dead. In the event that Gloucester should fail to obtain the papal dispensation necessary to validate his marriage to Anne Neville, he was nevertheless to retain her share of the estates as long as he did not remarry. In February 1475 a further act of parliament disqualified Montagu's male heirs from inheriting any part of the Neville estate, thus securing Gloucester's title to the lands of the earldom of Salisbury.[18]

SECURING THE DYNASTY: THE KING AND HIS CHILDREN

If Edward was forced to expend much time and energy in keeping his squabbling brothers in check, he also had to give some thought to the future. The Prince of Wales, born in the sanctuary of Westminster Abbey on 2 November 1470 during his father's exile in Flanders, had

been the king's fourth child by Elizabeth Wydeville. Between April
1472 and November 1480 the queen gave birth to a further two sons
and four daughters, of whom one boy (Richard, born at Shrewsbury on
17 August 1473) and three daughters (Anne, Katharine and Bridget)
would survive their early years. All these royal children had to be provided for according to their rank, either by marriage or endowment, and
could be expected to play an important political role in a future reign of
their eldest brother, the Prince of Wales. Among them, the position of
Prince Richard of Shrewsbury as his elder brother's next heir was clearly
paramount, and Edward grasped the first opportunity of making a suitable settlement of estates on the boy, who in 1473 had been granted his
grandfather's ducal title, but without a commensurate endowment.

This opportunity arose when the Duke of Norfolk, John Mowbray,
died unexpectedly in January 1476 at the age of just 32, leaving as his
sole heir his infant daughter Anne. Edward's approach to the Mowbray
inheritance was reminiscent of his treatment of the Warwick inheritance
in the high-handed manner in which he overrode the claims of dowagers
and next heirs alike. Within months, Anne Mowbray was betrothed to
Prince Richard, and her lands were settled on the couple, with a provision that the lands should remain to Richard and his heirs even if Anne
should die without issue. This provision meant nothing less than the
disinheritance of the next heirs to the Mowbray lands, William, Lord
Berkeley, and John, Lord Howard, although the dowager duchess,
Elizabeth Mowbray, succeeded in asserting her dower rights.

In 1472, even before Prince Richard had been provided for, Edward's
eldest stepson, Thomas Grey, was created Earl of Huntingdon, and three
years later he was further elevated to the marquessate of Dorset, a title
formerly held by the disgraced Beaufort family. Nor did Edward neglect
his brothers' sons. In 1473 and 1475 respectively Richard of Gloucester
and George of Clarence had fathered legitimate sons called Edward, who
– after the fall of Clarence – were respectively allowed the Neville earldoms of Salisbury and Warwick. In time, Gloucester's son could expect
to inherit his father's vast estates, while Clarence's share of the Warwick
inheritance remained in the king's keeping during his son's minority,
albeit with an expectation that he would in time be allowed to succeed
to it.

Rather more precarious was the position of the king's daughters,
whose principal value lay in their potential use as diplomatic pawns on

the dynastic marriage market of Europe. Elizabeth, the eldest, had been betrothed to George Neville, the son of the Marquess Montagu, during the crisis of 1469–71, but this arrangement was abandoned after Montagu's death at Barnet. In 1475, a rather more prestigious proposal was enshrined in the Treaty of Picquigny, which provided for Elizabeth's marriage to the dauphin, the heir to the French throne. The second daughter, Mary, was named by the same treaty as a reserve in the event of her sister's death, but in 1481 was betrothed in her own right to the King of Denmark, a plan foiled by her death the following May. The third daughter, Cecily, was betrothed to the future James IV of Scotland in October 1474, and – following the outbreak of war with Scotland in 1481 – was proposed as a wife for King James III's brother, Alexander, Duke of Albany, who had laid claim to the Scottish throne. Two of Edward's younger daughters, Anne and Katharine, born in 1475 and 1479, became the subject of negations over possible marriage alliances with the Spanish royal house and the young Philip the Fair, eventual heir to the duchy of Burgundy, but these, like the proposals for their sisters' marriages, came to nothing. At Edward's death, not a single one of his daughters had been married.

EDWARD'S FOREIGN POLICY, 1471–5

The search for suitable matches for his growing family was just one of the concerns of Edward's foreign policy after 1471. Once he had re-established control of his realm, the king could afford to look further afield. The effective extermination of the Lancastrian dynasty in 1471 had freed his foreign policy from the constraints that the existence of a rival for the crown had imposed in the first decade of his reign. In the 1460s the imperative had been the containment of the Lancastrian threat. Any foreign power that might offer succour to Henry VI, his queen and her son needed to be neutralised. There is no reason to doubt that the intention to invade Scotland and France respectively that Edward had expressed to parliament in 1463 and 1468 had been genuine, yet on both occasions the need to deal with domestic rebels had prevented the king from carrying out these plans. The taxes raised for the abortive expeditions had been diverted to other ends, and the consequent popular discontent had, if anything, exacerbated Edward's domestic problems. His throne secure, after 1471 Edward was free to conduct a foreign policy by military, as well as peaceful, means. In the 1460s, the Earl of Warwick had dominated English foreign policy, and it was imperative that the king should recapture the initiative.

Foremost among the concerns of any English foreign policy in the later middle ages were relations with England's neighbour across the Channel, France. Despite the unceremonious expulsion of the English from all their continental possessions except Calais in 1453, Edward IV maintained his claim to the crown of France (first staked by Edward III in the 1330s) in the same way as his predecessors had done. Although not every one of Edward III's successors had successfully waged war on the French, the legacy of Henry V's victories in the second decade of the fifteenth century was one to which the kings who came after him were obliged to aspire, or at least to pay lip service. Even Henry VII and Henry VIII would in their turn lead armies to France, and the English claim to the French crown survived that crown itself. The reconquest of the king's French realm was a staple of late medieval English political discourse, and successive parliaments were willing to vote taxation to this end. Yet in the 1460s none of Edward's proposed expeditions had come to anything.

After 1471, the invasion of France acquired a new and personal urgency for England's restored king, for it was evident that the Lancastrian readeption would have been impossible without the assistance and collusion of the King of France. An understandable desire for revenge aside, Louis XI's potential for mischief-making needed to be curtailed even in the absence of a credible Lancastrian claimant to the English throne. With the domestic threat ostensibly extinguished, Edward decided on a military invasion of France at an early date. In preparation for such an expedition, a network of continental alliances and treaties needed to be put in place, above all with the dukes of Brittany and Burgundy. Anxious not to allow Edward to build such a network of alliances, Louis XI invaded Brittany in the summer of 1472, but with the aid of a force of English archers under Earl Rivers and his brother, Sir Edward Wydeville, Duke Francis of Brittany was able to repel the attack.

Brittany's place on England's side was now guaranteed, and a formal treaty of alliance for an invasion of France was agreed at Chateaugiron on 11 September 1472. At the same time, Edward entered into negotiations with Charles of Burgundy. Here, relations were somewhat strained by Charles's late and hesitant support of his exiled brother-in-law: in September 1471 the Milanese ambassador to the French court reported home that Edward was 'ill content with the savage treatment meted out to him by the Duke of Burgundy, when he was driven out of England'.[19] Nevertheless, if Edward's proposed invasion of France was to proceed, the king needed the support of Burgundy, and Charles the Bold was equally aware that he had little to gain and much to lose from failing to respond to the English king's overtures. In the autumn of 1472 Louis de Gruthuyse, Edward's host in exile, came to England, ostensibly to be rewarded for his services with the earldom of Winchester, but also as an emissary from his ducal master, instructed to outline Charles's conditions for participation in a war against France.

Brittany and Burgundy apart, others also needed to be considered before an invasion of France could proceed. In the first place, there was England's northern neighbour, Scotland. Economically poor and politically unstable, the threat to England's northern border it posed on its own was limited. Yet the shared border gave the Scots a potential for trouble-making whenever England was under attack which meant that they could not be disregarded entirely. In the 1460s Scotland had provided aid to the Lancastrian insurgents in the north – and in return obtained the surrender of the strategic border fortress of Berwick upon Tweed – but had agreed to desist as soon as Louis XI of France had withdrawn his support. After 1471, the threat that Scotland posed in the north needed to be weighed up before any expedition to France could be mounted.

Louis XI of France was not unaware of the importance of the Scots in detaining the King of England at home, and did his best to persuade a hesitant James III either to invade England, or at least to involve himself in an expected rebellion against Edward, which Louis hoped would break out if the King of England once again failed to carry out his planned French campaign. Yet James III displayed little appetite for a costly war against his southern neighbour, and after the birth of his first son, James, in March 1473 showed himself receptive to Edward's proposal of a marriage alliance between his 4-year-old daughter Cecily and the infant heir to the Scottish throne. In October 1473 the two children were formally betrothed, and the accompanying treaty provided for a truce between the two kingdoms until October 1519.[20]

On the sea around England's coasts another conflict threatened trade. In the autumn of 1467 a group of merchants from Boston in Lincolnshire had landed in Iceland, a Danish possession, and had become involved in a violent altercation in the course of which they had killed the Danish governor. King Christian I of Denmark complained indignantly, but failed to receive the compensation he sought, and with the assistance of some of the towns of the Hanseatic league, principally those in the Baltic, seized the ships and goods of English merchants in the Sound. The crisis now escalated rapidly. Hanseatic merchants in England and their goods were placed under arrest, and their headquarters in London, the Steelyard, seized. Among the cities and towns of the league, Cologne had most to lose from a disruption of the trade with England, and the city fathers rapidly came to terms with Edward. As a result, Cologne was excluded from the Hanse, but received confirmation for its citizens alone of the commercial privileges previously extended to all Hanseatic merchants, and was given control of the Steelyard. Yet Hanseatic ships roamed the North and Baltic Seas, and posed a serious threat to English shipping, as Edward himself discovered on his flight to Flanders in October 1470 when his small flotilla came close to falling victim to Hanseatic predators.

While the league – unlike France or Scotland – was unlikely to attempt an invasion of England, it posed a real threat to any attempt to land and supply a large military force in France. As a loose federation of merchant communities the league was – to Edward's benefit – scarcely bound by dynastic considerations: its quarrel was with the kingdom of England, whoever might occupy the throne. Many of the towns of the Hanse did, however, owe allegiance to regional princes: in the case of the towns of Holland and Flanders the Duke of Burgundy. Through his mediation and in return for a promise to restore the Hansards' ancient privileges in England in full, Edward received valuable assistance in his invasion of England in March 1471. Yet once he was again secure on his throne, Edward reneged on the promise he had made to the league only a few months earlier; the privileges enjoyed by alien traders were unpopular among English merchants, who may have exerted pressure on the king, who was once again heavily reliant on their financial support.

Thus in July 1471 Edward once again confirmed the Hanseatic privileges exclusively to the merchants of Cologne. Naval war between England and the league resumed, and it was only once Edward became determined to invade France that negotiations for a settlement began once more. Through the renewed intervention of Charles of Burgundy a formal peace treaty was eventually agreed at Utrecht in February 1474. Its terms fell not far short of a complete surrender on Edward's part. He agreed to reinstate the Hansards' privileges in full, but to exclude the merchants of Cologne from all such privileges until they should have been readmitted by the league. England had to pay £10,000 to the towns of the league in compensation for the goods seized in 1468, and in return got only the limited concession that English merchants should enjoy their former privileges in the territories of the league, but without any exemption from tax.[21] Nevertheless, the North Sea and straits of Calais were once more safe for English ships to cross without fear of attack from the Hanseatic fleets. Not only did the improved conditions allow overseas trade to flourish unimpeded, but the removal of the very real threat posed by the well-armed Hanseatic vessels to English shipping was an important prerequisite for any military action against France.

Such diplomatic success was periodically tempered by setbacks. In the face of the threat of a renewed French invasion, the Duke of Brittany was persuaded within a month of the agreement of Chateaugiron to sign a truce with Louis XI and to exert pressure on Charles the Bold, who (anxious to exploit an opportunity to advance his north-eastern frontier by the acquisition of the duchy of Guelders) agreed a similar truce with the King of France. Negotiations with the Burgundians dragged on into the summer of 1474, while Charles the Bold was preoccupied by a war against the Swiss in Alsace and by the pursuit of a possible election as King of the Romans.

Then, however, Duke Charles suddenly came to terms: the Treaty of London, signed on 25 July 1474, agreed a formal alliance for the invasion of France, and made provision for a partition of Louis XI's kingdom between the allies.[22] Edward now rapidly set about rounding off the system of treaties and alliances he had concluded. In August 1474 an embassy was sent to King Ferdinand I of Naples, a knight of the Garter since 1463, and in the same month the notable condottiere Federico de Montefeltro, Duke of Urbino and commander of the pope's forces, was for his part invested with the order of the Garter. Diplomatic overtures to the Emperor Frederick III and the Hungarian king, Matthias Corvinus, bore no fruit, but by the spring of 1475 treaties of friendship and alliance with King Christian I of Denmark and the King and Queen of

Castile and Aragon had been concluded. In May 1475, finally, Duke Francis of Brittany agreed to conclude a fresh military alliance. The encirclement of Louis XI's France was complete.

THE KING'S GREAT ENTERPRISE

Although the English army was now ready, serious problems arose from the behaviour of Edward's ally, his brother-in-law Charles of Burgundy. Far from making the planned campaign against the French his priority, in the summer of 1474 Duke Charles had laid siege to the heavily fortified city of Neuss in a bid to benefit from a local dispute over control of the archbishopric of Cologne. In November a Burgundian army was routed by Swiss forces at Héricourt, but the siege continued into the early summer of 1475, when a French invasion of Charles's territories on several fronts forced the duke to abandon it.

Burgundy's apparent unwillingness to carry out the agreed plan of invasion necessitated a change of Edward's own strategy. Instead of emulating Henry V by landing in Normandy, as originally intended, the king now decided to land at Calais. Here there was a further delay as Edward awaited the arrival of the Duke of Burgundy. When Charles finally turned up some ten days later, he did not bring the expected army, but came accompanied merely by a small bodyguard. Already there had been heated discussions between Edward and his noble captains, several of whom favoured abandoning the campaign immediately. Yet on this occasion Edward was finely attuned to public opinion in England and was in no doubt how badly it would react were he to abandon his French war once again. Duke Charles himself did much to strengthen the resolve of Edward's followers by taking pains to be heard to declare publicly that the English army was so well-prepared 'that if the men had been his own he would not have wished for more to carry conquest right through France even as far as the gates of Rome'.[23]

Discussions in council were rather more practical, and eventually it was agreed that the English army should advance in a south-easterly direction through Burgundian territory to Péronne and St Quentin, before invading Champagne. There Charles himself would join them with his army once he had completed his own business and crushed the Duke of Lorraine on his south-eastern border. In Champagne, so the duke suggested, Edward could make for Rheims and have himself crowned King of France.

On 18 July the English army set out as planned, but Charles the Bold's conduct continued to cause his allies consternation. Not only did he at one point leave them 'to visit his own cities', he refused the English entry to any of his towns, even leaving them encamped outside the gates of Péronne while he himself entered. None of this served to improve the mood of Edward or his captains who, denied any opportunity for plunder while they were marching through the duke's lands, now found themselves caught between the strongly fortified towns of Champagne ahead, and Louis XI's army, which had moved from Normandy into Picardy and Artois, at their rear.

Duke Charles's departure for his own army in Bar on about 12 August gave Edward his chance. Even before leaving England he had sent Garter King-of-arms to Louis XI, ostensibly to demand the surrender of the kingdom of France and to issue a formal declaration of war, but apparently also with secret instructions to indicate his master's willingness to come to terms after he had satisfied public opinion at home and landed in France. Now a junior French prisoner was released and instructed to give Louis XI certain coded signs, which the shrewd French king interpreted correctly. He promptly sent a valet of his household into Edward's camp to make overtures for the opening of formal negotiations. On 13 August Edward drew up a list of demands which were agreed and witnessed by his senior captains, and on the following day an English delegation consisting of John, Lord Howard, Sir Thomas St Leger, the king's brother-in-law, Dr John Morton, the master of the rolls, and William Dudley, dean of the chapel royal, met French envoys in a village near Amiens. The French readily agreed to the English demands for a financial payoff and a truce guaranteed by a marriage between King Louis's heir, the dauphin, and Edward's eldest daughter, and it was determined that the treaty should be sealed by a personal meeting between the two kings.

The preparations for this encounter were elaborate and designed to facilitate a conference that allowed both monarchs to save face. Between Picquigny and Amiens a stockaded bridge was built over the river Somme. To avoid a repeat of the ugly scene that had seen Duke John of Burgundy, Charles the Bold's grandfather, murdered by the attendants of the Dauphin Charles (the later Charles VII of France, Louis XI's father) during a similar meeting on the bridge at Montereau on 10 September 1419, the two sides were separated in the middle of the bridge by a further stockade, with a section of wooden trelliswork allowing communication between the two monarchs.[24]

The meeting was described in some detail by the Franco-Burgundian agent Philippe de Commynes, who was present. Louis XI was the first to take his place on the bridge, accompanied, as had been previously agreed, by a following of 12 men, including the Duke of Bourbon and his brother, the Cardinal of Bourbon. Commynes recorded the arrival of the English:

> The King of England came along the causeway ... very well attended, and appeared a regal figure. With him was the Duke of Clarence, his brother, the earl of Northumberland and certain other lords, his chamberlain called Lord Hastings, his chancellor and others; and there were not more than three or four dressed in cloth of gold similar to the king. The king had a bonnet of black velvet on his head, and had in it a great fleur de lisle set with precious stones. ... When he had come within four or five feet of the barrier he drew his bonnet and bowed to within half a foot of the ground. The king made him an equally great reverence ... and before embracing him through the holes the king of England made a further great reverence. The king began to speak and said to him 'My lord my cousin, you are very welcome. There is not a man in the world whom I desired to see as much as you, and God be praised that we have come together here for this good purpose.' The King of England replied to this in quite good French. Then the said chancellor of England, a prelate called the Bishop of Ely, began to speak, and began with a prophecy ... which said that in this place of Picquigny a great peace between France and England should be concluded. And afterwards were displayed the letters which the king had sent to the said King of England touching the treaty that had been made. And the said chancellor asked the king whether he was agreed to their content. To which the king answered yes, and also to those which had been sent to him on the part of the King of England. And so a missal was brought and opened, and the two kings placed their hands upon it, and the other two hands on the holy true cross, and both swore to keep what had been promised between them.[25]

The formalities completed, King Louis began to joke with Edward, saying that he ought to come to Paris, and that he would dine him with the ladies, and that he would give him the lord cardinal of Bourbon (who was present) as confessor, who would willingly absolve him of the sin, if he should have committed any. The King of England took this with great pleasure and a cheerful countenance, because he knew well that the said cardinal was good company. When this had gone on for a little while, the King [of France] ... ordered us (who were with him) to retire, and told us that he wished to speak to the King of England alone. Those with the King of England likewise withdrew, without waiting to be told.[26]

The two monarchs spoke privately for a while, and then Louis recalled Commynes, in whose presence they discussed the question of Edward's erstwhile allies, the Dukes of Burgundy and Brittany. Then the attendants of both kings rejoined them, and Louis took his leave of Edward, exchanging a few pleasantries with the lords in his company. Both kings withdrew from the bridge, and Edward returned to his army.

Without question, the terms agreed were highly favourable to the English and their king. In return for Edward's immediate withdrawal from France, he was to receive up front a payment of 75,000 crowns, as well as an annual pension of 50,000 crowns thereafter. There would be a seven-year truce between the two kings and their allies, and a commitment by Edward and Louis not to conclude any leagues with the other's allies without his knowledge. There were to be equal privileged trade conditions for the merchants of either realm in the other, specifically removing the tolls that had been imposed on the English in France during the previous 12 years. As a guarantee of continued good relations between the two kingdoms, Louis's son, the Dauphin Charles, was to marry Edward's eldest daughter Elizabeth as soon as they reached marriageable age, and Louis would provide a jointure of £60,000 per annum.[27]

Nevertheless, there were some who were less than pleased with this outcome. Edward's own brother, Richard of Gloucester, had been conspicuously absent from the meeting of the two kings, and took some time to accept their agreement. He was, however, eventually persuaded to pay his respects to King Louis at Amiens and to accept gifts of horses and plate from him.[28] In this he was not alone: Louis took care to secure the support of Edward's principal captains by generous gifts and pensions. Annual pensions of between 2,000 and 600 crowns went to the Marquess of Dorset, Lords Hastings and Howard, Sir Thomas Montgomery,

Sir Thomas St Leger and Sir John Cheyne, the chancellor, Bishop Rotherham, and the master of the rolls, John Morton. In addition, Hastings, Howard and a number of other English captains received gifts of money and plate worth literally thousands of pounds.[29] But some were not as ready to be bought off, and openly grumbled. In conversation with Philippe de Commynes a member of Edward's retinue, the Gascon Louis de Bretelles, openly mocked the official story that the peace had been brought about by the Holy Ghost which had descended on Edward's tent in the shape of a white dove. Rather, he said, the pigeon in question had been caught up in a rain shower, and had settled on the vantage point of the king's tent to dry out in the sun. All the glory won in the nine victorious battles in which Edward had personally participated, he claimed, could not match the disgrace in which the king would return home from his French expedition.[30] Similarly, Charles the Bold, whose procrastination had played its part in persuading Edward to agree to Louis XI's overtures, was nothing short of furious at the news of the peace treaty, and rushed to confront Edward. According to Philippe de Commynes

> [t]he King of England was very amazed at this sudden coming and asked what brought him, as he could see the duke was furious. ... The duke worked himself up into a fury and spoke in English ... and cited several fine deeds done by English kings who had crossed to France and all the trouble they had taken to acquire honour there; he bitterly inveighed against this truce, saying that he had not sought to bring the English over because he needed them, but to recover what belonged to them. ... And after these words he departed and went back to where he had come from. The King of England and his council took these words badly. Other people who were not satisfied by the peace praised what the duke had said.[31]

Elsewhere in Europe, as well as back in England, the news of the agreement at Picquigny also caused consternation. In early September a Florentine correspondent wrote:

> I feel sure that this agreement will appear very extraordinary, and indeed it seems so to every one, and rather the work of God than of human agents, that so valiant a king should come to France with so great a power and with the support of Burgundy, and then return the enemy of Burgundy and the friend of France, without striking a blow.[32]

A fortnight later the Milanese ambassador at the court of Burgundy reported that word from England was of widespread irritation among the people who had been taxed heavily just to achieve this cowardly accord, and that Edward would not allow his brothers to return to England before him, lest Clarence in particular might use popular discontent to make another bid for the throne.[33] The king was certainly sufficiently worried about public opinion in England to have an article included in the Treaty of Picquigny that provided that in the event that either he or King Louis should face an armed rebellion as the result of their agreement, the other would provide military support. As a further sop to public opinion he waived three-quarters of a fifteenth and tenth, part of the taxes granted by parliament in the spring which had not yet been collected.[34] In the event, fears of a public backlash in England proved unfounded. Before the end of September Edward was back at Westminster. His 'great enterprise' was over, his attentions once more focused on the more mundane duties of ruling his own realm and of keeping the peace between his increasingly fractious nobles.

7

THE FINAL YEARS, 1475–83

THE UNRAVELLING OF EDWARD'S FOREIGN POLICY

The treaty of 1475 gave a new character to Edward's foreign policy. Although both Edward and Louis XI continued to intrigue and conspire against each other, and the possibility of an anti-French alliance continued to be a bargaining chip in Edward's negotiations with other rulers, his French pension was clearly dear to him, and he was prepared to go to considerable lengths to preserve it. At the same time he now began more actively than before to enter into negotiations over alliances with other European powers through the marriages of his growing brood of children. In 1473 Princess Cecily had been betrothed to the heir to the Scottish crown, while Princess Elizabeth was promised to the French dauphin under the terms of Picquigny, and her sister Mary was held in reserve in the event of Elizabeth's premature death. The king's second son, Prince Richard, was provided for by a marriage to Anne Mowbray, negotiated in the wake of the Duke of Norfolk's death in 1476. This still left the young Prince of Wales and his sister Anne (born in November 1475), and subsequently their sisters Katharine (b.1479) and Bridget (b.1480), and temporarily another prince, George (who died in 1479 aged 2), to be considered.

Among them, the question of the Prince of Wales's marriage was clearly of the first importance. When Edward himself had claimed the freedom to chose his own bride, he had done so to the chagrin of many of his councillors, and only after the failure of the various political marriages that had been proposed for him from his childhood. His son and heir, Prince Edward, was to have no such freedom: before the prince was 6 years old, Edward began to scour the ranks of the eligible princesses of Europe for a suitable candidate to be the next Queen of England. In 1476 a proposal was floated for the prince's marriage to Isabella, daughter of Ferdinand and Isabella of Castile and Aragon (the latter had herself once been a candidate to become Edward's wife). At the time, the Infanta Isabella remained her parents' only child and thus the heiress presumptive to their joint crowns. For two years this seemed a promising prospect, but when Queen Isabella gave birth to a son in June 1478, Edward lost interest. Instead, he now floated a proposal for the Prince of Wales's marriage to one of the daughters of the recently murdered Duke Galeazzo Maria of Milan by his wife Bona of Savoy (another former contender for Edward's own hand). This marriage had the advantage of the immense wealth of the bride's family, and the importance of this factor was not lost on the Milanese ambassador at the French court who reported home that the greatest conceivable stumbling block to the match would be

> the great quantity of money which the king of England will want ... for the dowry and for presents, as they say he knows that you have a great treasure, and he proposes in this way to obtain a good share of it. ... They say that the king of England does not desire to make this marriage alliance for any other purpose than to obtain a great quantity of money.[1]

Already, however, another event on the European stage had given a new dimension to the interrelationship of the European powers. On 5 January 1477 Charles the Bold was killed at Nancy in Lorraine in the third of a series of disastrous battles with the Swiss. Charles's marriage to Margaret of York had remained childless, and he left as his only heiress a daughter by his first marriage, Mary, then aged 19.

It was not long before suitors presented themselves to compete for this exceptional prize. The Dowager Duchess Margaret naturally favoured a strengthened alliance with England by a marriage between Mary and her brother, the Duke of Clarence, whose wife, Isabel Neville, had died the previous December. This Edward could not and would not permit, for reasons of both domestic and foreign policy. In the first place, Clarence had shown himself too volatile and too persistently unreliable to be entrusted with the rule of a strategically key state on the European mainland, especially of one that could decisively tip the balance of power against England. Mary of Burgundy herself possessed a viable claim to the English throne through her grandmother, Isabel of Portugal, a granddaughter of John of Gaunt. In the light of Clarence's track record of challenging his brother's title to the crown, Edward was understandably disinclined to allow him a marriage that might encourage him to assert a claim once again. Moreover, it could not be expected that Louis XI would idly sit by while a political entity that technically constituted a fiefdom of his crown was placed in the hands of an English prince and his descendants. Although he had not personally lived through them, Edward must have been aware of the military entanglements on the continent that had arisen during the past century from John of Gaunt's claim to the Castilian throne in the 1380s and Humphrey of Gloucester's marriage to Jacqueline of Hainault. The king was not inclined to risk a similar military commitment in support of a brother who was unlikely to prove a loyal ally.

Yet if Clarence was not to be permitted to wed Mary of Burgundy, England was short of a viable bridegroom. Neither of Edward's sons was old enough, and the king's younger brother Richard was already married. Others, however, also now expressed an interest. Louis XI, with complete disregard of the promises of marriage contained in the Treaty of Picquigny, offered the hand of his son, the dauphin, 16 years Mary's junior. This offer, designed as it was eventually to absorb Burgundy into France, was a direct affront to the English king. Edward offered the best he could, and suggested the queen's brother, Earl Rivers, as a possible husband for Duchess Mary, but he must have known that this proposal would be unacceptable to the Burgundians, even though it was backed up by an offer of an English army should the duchess agree. For all his undoubted qualities, Rivers was only a recently created English earl and no match for the richest heiress in Europe, who in any case had set her heart on a third suitor, the Archduke Maximilian of Austria, son and heir of the Holy Roman Emperor Frederick III. Soon enough Edward accepted the inevitable and agreed to support Maximilian's candidature. This match had first been mooted a few years earlier in Charles the Bold's lifetime, with the added inducement of a possible candidature of Duke

Charles for the elective Imperial crown, and Edward's support now firmly tipped the balance in its favour. On 18 August 1477 Maximilian and Mary were married at Ghent.

In spite of his high birth, Maximilian had few military resources at his disposal. He was, however, prepared to use the wealth of Burgundy to buy military aid from England in the face of French aggression. Louis XI had lost little time in disrupting Burgundian trade and, indeed, in invading the duchy. For the next four years, Edward's diplomacy was thus directed at maintaining a careful balance between lending enough support to Maximilian and Mary to prevent Burgundy's overthrow by Louis XI, and discussing conditions of English neutrality in the event of a full-scale French attack on the duchy with Louis, in order to guarantee the continuation of his French pension and his daughter's marriage to the dauphin. Louis XI had on more than one occasion proven himself to be a masterful diplomat, but towards the end of the 1470s Edward began to become increasingly irritated by his obvious delaying tactics in the face of English demands for the formal betrothal of the dauphin and Princess Elizabeth, and the immediate payment of her jointure of 60,000 crowns per year.

Although outwardly he did everything to maintain good relations with the French king, Edward stepped up his diplomatic activity in Burgundy as a means of applying pressure on Louis XI. In July 1479 he concluded an agreement with Maximilian and Mary for a future marriage of their now 1-year-old heir, Philip, to his daughter Anne. The French position was further weakened by a defeat at the hands of a Burgundian army at Guinegatte that August, and Edward brushed aside the partial concessions that Louis XI was prepared to make in its wake. The Milanese ambassador to the French court sent home regular reports on the diplomatic wrangling and commented on the French king's delaying tactics, but in January 1480 he observed:

> I doubt, however, whether the King of England does not quite well see through this plan, and for that reason he has sent his ambassadors here to press this question as much as possible, while the king here stands in the fear of the King of England.[2]

Edward was indeed losing patience with Louis's prevarication, and by the summer of 1480 was moving towards a renewal of his old anti-

French alliances with Brittany and Burgundy. Through the mediation of Edward's sister, the Dowager Duchess Margaret, a treaty between England and Burgundy was agreed in August 1480. Its terms were highly favourable to the English. Maximilian not only agreed to replace Edward's French pension, should he lose it as a consequence of their alliance, he also agreed to his son's marriage to the Princess Anne without payment of the dowry of 200,000 crowns which he had originally demanded. All Edward offered in return was to forgo in lieu of his daughter's dowry the first year's instalment of the pension he was to receive from Maximilian, and permission to recruit 6,000 archers in England.

At the same time, the king opened negotiations with Duke Francis of Brittany over a marriage alliance. The proposal for the marriage of the Prince of Wales to a daughter of the Duke of Milan was abandoned, and by the end of 1480 firm plans for his union with the heiress to the Duchy of Brittany had taken its place. Once again, Edward was able to dictate profitable terms: Anne (or, in the event of her premature death, her sister Isabella) was to receive a dowry of 100,000 crowns, which was to double if Duke Francis had a son and heir before the marriage took place. If such a son was born after the marriage, he was to marry one of Edward's daughters, whose dowry of 100,000 crowns was to be found by the Duke of Brittany, rather than by her father. To this Duke Francis eventually agreed, and in the early summer of 1481 the marriage treaty and a treaty of mutual military aid were concluded. Furthermore, Edward now also encouraged direct negotiations between Maximilian and Francis, as a result of which an alliance between the two dukes was signed on 16 April 1482.[3]

Further afield, King Ferdinand of Aragon and Castile and the Este Duke of Ferrara and Modena were elected to the order of the Garter in 1480, and King João II of Portugal was added in 1482. Edward seemed to have successfully recreated the system of alliances he had established on the eve of his invasion of France in 1475. Already, however, troubles were brewing that would within a short time throw Edward's carefully crafted continental foreign policy into disarray. Louis XI had been observing Edward's diplomatic activities with increasing alarm. Although he continued the charade of negotiating over the dauphin's marriage to Princess Elizabeth for some time, he was under no illusion that he would be able to hoodwink Edward for any length of time. He, like other continental observers, realized the value that Edward attached to his annual pension, and sought to exploit to the utmost his reluctance to forfeit it, but he also realized that it had lost its value as a diplomatic bargaining chip once Maximilian committed himself to replace it if necessary. In the wake of the Anglo-Burgundian treaty of August 1480 he failed to pay the instalment of the pension due two months later. Already, he had been stirring up trouble in another theatre.

WAR WITH SCOTLAND, 1480–82

Ever since the marriage treaty of 1473 relations between England and Scotland had been amicable, so much so that in 1478 James III had offered to forge a further bond between the two royal houses by a marriage of his sister Margaret to the English queen's widowed brother, Earl Rivers. This was agreed, but before long preparations were thrown into disarray by a series of skirmishes on the Anglo-Scottish border in open breach of the truce between the two kingdoms. James III sought to blame the disturbances on the English, but Edward – perhaps encouraged by his brother, Richard of Gloucester, the warden of the West Marches – responded with uncharacteristic sharpness. Early in 1480 he issued James III with an ultimatum. The King of Scots was to ensure that full reparations for his subjects' incursions were paid, he was to surrender Berwick, and to hand over his son and heir into English care as a guarantee for his marriage to Cecily of York. Should James fail to comply, Edward threatened war. To back up these threats, on 12 May 1480 the Duke of Gloucester was appointed lieutenant-general and empowered to call out the levies of the northern counties if necessary. James III responded with an offer of a peace conference but Edward, further angered by the burning of Bamborough in the course of a raid into the English East March by the Earl of Angus in August, now announced that he would personally lead a punitive expedition against the Scots the following spring.

Throughout the winter of 1480–1 supplies and armaments for an invasion by both land and sea were assembled, and funds were raised both by means of a fresh benevolence and by calling in parts of the parliamentary grant of war taxation of 1475 which the king had remitted at the time. Yet, in spite of these preparations, Edward delayed his departure for the north, and only the English fleet under Lord Howard conducted a few raids into the Firth of Forth. While the bulk of Edward's army remained in the south waiting for the king, James III for his part conducted a series of damaging forays into English territory, which the Duke of Gloucester and the Earl of Northumberland were left to fend off as best they could with what resources were at their disposal. Edward himself did not leave the south-east until September, and never moved any further north than Nottingham, from where he returned to London in mid-October. Differing reasons for Edward's dithering have been put forward. Continental commentators naturally sought to place an unfavourable spin on the king's irresolution, and suggested that he had come to prefer the bed and banqueting table to the battlefield and the tent. However, as Charles Ross has argued, it is more probable that the desire to keep in direct control of the complex negotiations with France, Brittany and Burgundy caused Edward to delay in the south.[4]

What the king apparently failed to foresee was the impact that the decision to go to war against Scotland would have on his continental diplomacy. Maximilian of Burgundy, under military pressure from the French, was anxious for an English invasion of France, or at least a further contingent of English archers. By early 1481 Edward was unable to agree to either, as he had committed his full resources to a campaign in the north. Moreover he now also needed to cover his back, and consequently sent envoys to Louis XI to explain that he had no hostile intentions towards France, and that the troops he had provided to Maximilian were merely intended to assist the duke in putting down a rebellion in the duchy of Guelders. As long as Louis was prepared to resume payment of the annual pension and the negotiations over arrangements for the dauphin's marriage to Princess Elizabeth, Edward would continue to respect the truce with France. Louis lost little time in agreeing to Edward's offer, and in August 1481 resumed payment of the English king's pension.

Intermittent warfare on the Scottish border continued inconclusively through the winter of 1481–2, and if the requirements of his continental negotiations might have inclined Edward towards seeking a settlement with the king of Scots, public opinion at home forbade such a course of action. In April 1482 the policy of war against Scotland was given fresh vigour by the agreement of James III's brother, Alexander, Duke of

Albany, to stake a claim to the Scottish throne with English support. In return for a promise to surrender Berwick to the English and to do homage and fealty to their king, Edward agreed that Alexander might marry his nephew's intended bride, Princess Cecily, provided that he could procure an annulment of his recent marriage to a daughter of the French Count of Boulogne. A formal treaty between Edward and Alexander was signed at Fotheringhay on 11 June 1482, but immediately afterwards the English king entrusted the further conduct of the campaign to Richard of Gloucester and returned south.

Gloucester carried out his commission without delay and by mid-July had assembled a sizeable army near the Scottish border. The threat posed by this army proved enough not only to cause the town of Berwick to surrender to the English but also to throw Scotland into political turmoil. As James III's army marched south to meet the invader, a number of his barons openly rebelled, seized their king, and placed him under arrest in Edinburgh castle. Within days, Gloucester's army entered the Scottish capital unopposed. Although the Duke of Albany now renounced his claim to his brother's throne, the Scottish leadership was anxious for a peace treaty and readily agreed to the surrender of Berwick and the repayment of any monies that Edward had already paid towards Princess Cecily's dower, should the agreement for her marriage to James III's heir not be renewed. Although Gloucester declared himself unable to conclude a peace treaty without express instructions from his brother, he now withdrew to Berwick, where he began to disband his army even before the castle finally surrendered on 24 August 1482.

It is uncertain to what extent Gloucester's decision was sanctioned by the king. Before returning south, Edward had established a courier system to keep him personally informed of events in the north, a measure which should have enabled him to issue fresh instructions to his brother with minimal delay. The usually well-informed Crowland continuator indicated that Edward was annoyed by the limited results of the expensive campaign, and this in itself may account for the king's decision to resume the war. In October he formally called off the marriages between Princess Cecily and the Duke of Rothsay, and between Earl Rivers and Margaret of Scotland, and demanded the repayment of Cecily's dowry. In November writs were issued summoning a parliament to Westminster for the following January, expressly to find money for 'the hasty defence of the realm'.[5]

Events on the continent now began to turn against Edward. While England's resources had been concentrated on the conduct of the war with Scotland, Maximilian of Burgundy had continued to press for an English invasion of France. In January 1482 Edward had all but admitted to his ally that he was unable to do so in the short term, and had advised Maximilian to conclude a truce with Louis XI. Ostensibly, this was sound advice, for time appeared to be on the side of France's opponents. In the course of 1481 Louis had suffered two successive strokes, and it was unlikely that he would survive for many years. His heir, the Dauphin Charles, was aged only 12, offering the prospect of a regency of some years.

Now, however, Maximilian's own position was complicated further by the death on 27 March 1482 of Duchess Mary of Burgundy as the result of a riding accident. Maximilian, acting as guardian of his young son Philip, was significantly weakened by the determination of the estates of Flanders and Brabant to use the minority of their young duke to strengthen their autonomy, which they had already asserted during the period of dynastic uncertainty after the death of Charles the Bold. Before long, the estates took control of Philip and his sister Margaret, and against Maximilian's opposition opened negotiations with Louis XI.

In September the French king administered a final blow to Maximilian's hopes of maintaining an anti-French alliance with the English by publishing the secret truce that Edward had concluded with him a year earlier. Franco-Burgundian negotiations now progressed swiftly, and on 23 December the two sides' representatives at the peace conference of Arras concluded a bilateral agreement, expressly excluding England and Brittany from the peace. The cessation of hostilities was to be sealed by a marriage between the French dauphin and Maximilian's daughter Margaret, who was to receive as her dowry the counties of Artois and Burgundy.

This agreement left Edward's foreign policy since 1475 in ruins. Although, as has been suggested, the recovery of Berwick represented a more significant achievement than has sometimes been allowed, in that it provided a boost to the morale of the inhabitants of the northern border counties of England, Edward's diplomacy on the continent had failed completely. He had lost his French pension and the proposed marriage alliance with the next king of France, and in addition had seen the collapse of his cautious policy, conducted since the early years of the reign, of keeping Burgundy on his side without actively committing greater numbers of troops or money than was absolutely necessary. There was now a real possibility that the marriage of Margaret of Burgundy to the dauphin might bring Artois, the strategically vital hinterland of the English-held Calais Pale, into French hands. Edward was understandably furious. He vowed revenge, and in the final months of his reign renewed active preparations for an eventual attack on France.[6] In time, the king might have recovered some ground. He had overcome diplomatic set-backs before, and the Treaty of Arras did not remain the final word in the ongoing conflict between France, Brittany and Burgundy. Fresh negotiations might yet have produced a renewed anti-French alliance and resulted in a different course of political events on the continent. Time, however, was not on Edward's side, and in the event it was he, rather than Louis XI, who died first.

THE FALL OF THE DUKE OF CLARENCE

Both of Edward's brothers had every reason to be content with the arrangements for the partition of the Warwick inheritance between them. Yet, characteristically, Clarence was soon plotting again. The thought that he more than anyone else owed his brother gratitude for his forgiveness of repeated past disloyalty (see Chapter 5) was lost on the arrogant young duke. If Edward had expected popular discontent at the Treaty of Picquigny, Clarence may positively have hoped for renewed disturbances that he might use to his advantage. In late September 1475 the Milanese ambassador to the Burgundian court reported home that 'Edward did not want his brothers to proceed to England before him, as he feared some disturbance, especially as the Duke of Clarence, on a previous occasion, aspired to make himself king'.[7] In the event, however, the disturbances that Edward had feared, and his brother perhaps hoped for, failed to materialize.

Still, Clarence doggedly refused to settle down and continued to look for further advancement. The deaths in quick succession of his duchess, Warwick's daughter, (probably in childbirth) at the end of December 1476, and of Charles the Bold at the siege of Nancy in January 1477 seemed to open up a renewed possibility of his ascent to the Burgundian throne as husband of Charles's daughter and heiress, Mary. Clarence had expressed previous desires for a Burgundian match, and on this occasion his suit was supported by his sister, the Dowager Duchess Margaret of Burgundy. Edward, however, was not prepared to allow this match (as discussed earlier in this chapter). A second marriage proposal also came to nothing. Within months, James III of Scotland proposed that ties between his royal house and that of England (which would in the course of time be cemented by the marriage of the heir to the Scottish crown to Edward's daughter Cecily) should be strengthened further by parallel marriages between his brother, the Duke of Albany, and Edward's now widowed sister, the Dowager Duchess of Burgundy, on the one hand, and between Clarence and James's sister Margaret on the other. Edward's reply was evasive: while he thanked James for his offer, he claimed that it was not customary for a woman to remarry quite so soon after being widowed and asked that the negotiations be delayed by at least a year.

Clarence was nothing short of furious at his brother's refusal to allow him a marriage equal to his station and his ambition, but his subsequent behaviour gave Edward even less reason to look favourably on any marriage that might increase his influence either at home or abroad. After it became apparent that Edward would not support either a Burgundian or a Scottish marriage for him, Clarence absented himself from the court and council and holed himself up in Warwick Castle to sulk. Relations between the brothers were hardly helped by some of their clients who used their connexions with both to pass between them, reporting any disparaging remarks made by one about the other. Yet, whereas the king's comments about Clarence might be hurtful to his brother, anything the duke said could viably be construed as nothing short of treason.

What brought matters to a head, however, was a private act of revenge of extraordinary highhandedness and disregard for the law on which Clarence embarked in the spring of 1477. On 12 April two of the duke's servants broke into the house of Ankarette Twynyho, a former servant of Duchess Isabel, at Keyford. They dragged Ankarette off to Warwick, where she was brought to trial before the justices of the peace on charges of having poisoned her mistress. Convicted by a jury under coercion in a trial that lasted less than three hours, she and an associate, John Thuresby, were executed forthwith, while a third purported accomplice, Roger Tocotes, managed to escape.[8] Historians have struggled to explain Clarence's motives for this baffling act of judicial murder. J.R. Lander maintained that Clarence had genuinely believed in Ankarette's guilt, but more recently Michael Hicks has pointed to the lack of obvious connexions between her and her associates, and suggested that the victims of the duke's private revenge in April 1477 were the very individuals who had been guilty of carrying tales about him to the king.[9]

Edward could not tolerate such behaviour on the part of his brother, but ostensibly all the forms of the common law had been observed, and other grounds to proceed against Clarence were needed. These were soon found as the result of the arrest and trial of an Oxford astronomer, Dr John Stacy, a fellow of Merton College with connexions to the king himself. Questioned under torture over allegations that he had practised black magic for evil purposes, Stacy incriminated one of the chaplains of his college, Thomas Blake, and one of Clarence's servants, the Warwickshire esquire Thomas Burdett of Arrow. On the strength of Stacy's confession, Edward appointed a powerful judicial commission, comprising no fewer than five earls, twelve barons and six justices. Central to the indictments were the charges against Burdett. At his explicit request, it was claimed, Stacy and Blake had predicted the early deaths of the king and the Prince of Wales, and had made their predictions public with the intention of making the prophecy self-fulfilling by shortening the king's life through the grief that the knowledge of his impending fate would cause him. Furthermore, and in the immediate term more seriously, Burdett was said to have sought the destruction of the king and the Prince of Wales 'by exciting war and discord between the king and his lieges' and to this end had in the spring of 1477 disseminated

> divers seditious and treasonable bills, rhymes and ballads, containing complaints, seditions and treasonable arguments, to the intent that the people should withdraw their cordial love from the king and abandon him, and rise and make war against the king, to the final destruction of the king and prince.[10]

The accused were found guilty, and sentenced to death. Blake received a last-minute pardon, but Burdett and Stacy were hanged at Tyburn on 20 May, still protesting their innocence.

The implications of the charges against Burdett were not lost on many, least of all on the Duke of Clarence, who appears to have lost his head. Within days of Burdett's execution, the duke appeared in a meeting of the king's council at Westminster (Edward himself was at

Windsor) accompanied by a distinguished Franciscan preacher, Dr William Goddard, who at Clarence's bidding read out Burdett's and Stacy's declarations of innocence. Then Clarence and Goddard departed, leaving the members of the council stunned. This performance only served to annoy the king further. He angrily summoned his brother to appear before him, and in the presence of the mayor and aldermen of London charged him with 'conduct ... derogatory to the laws of the realm and most dangerous to judges and juries throughout the kingdom', the latter charge perhaps a reference to the part Clarence had played in the judicial murder of Ankarette Twynyho.[11] Then Clarence was despatched to the Tower to await further proceedings. On 16 January 1478 a parliament assembled, principally for the purpose of trying the Duke of Clarence. Edward took no chances: the Commons were liberally packed with royal retainers, and the king himself took the lead in proceedings. The well-informed Crowland continuator, who was probably present, described the scene:

> No-one argued against the duke except the king; no-one answered the king except the duke. Some persons, however, were introduced concerning whom many people wondered whether they performed the offices of accusers or witnesses. ... The duke swept aside all charges with a disclaimer offering, if it were acceptable, to uphold his case by personal combat. ... Those in Parliament, believing the information they had heard to be well-founded, formally condemned him; the sentence was pronounced by the mouth of Henry, duke of Buckingham, newly created steward of England for the occasion.[12]

Clarence was returned to the Tower to await execution. Now, however, Edward recoiled from taking the final step and having his own brother executed. Probably, members of his family also pleaded with him for mercy: his mother, Cecily, Duchess of York, was said to have made 'great prayer and request'. As a result, the customary penalty for high treason, hanging, drawing and quartering, was commuted. More than likely, she had pleaded for her son's life.[13] The part played by the other brother, Richard of Gloucester, is uncertain. The events of the preceding six years had given him little reason to regard Clarence with fondness, but if evidence dating from after his later usurpation of the throne can be believed, he may nevertheless have shied away from seeking his brother's death and may have intervened on his behalf.[14]

Edward himself seems to have been not disinclined to give in to the sustained pleas for Clarence's life to be spared. Certainly, it seems, he soon regretted the determined steps he had taken. The Tudor historian Polydore Vergil, who claimed to have questioned some of Edward's surviving councillors on the matter, maintained that ever after Clarence's execution 'whensoever anyone sued to save a man's life, he was wont to cry out in a rage: "O unfortunate brother, for whose life no man in this world would once make request".'[15] From an early date, the king took all necessary steps to ensure the smooth passage of his brother's soul into the afterlife. Yet Edward was a king and not merely a brother. For some days he dithered, and refused to give the order for the execution. Perhaps he even contemplated a pardon. Eventually the Speaker of the Commons, William Allington, appeared before the Lords and asked that the matter be brought to a conclusion. This left the king with no choice. Within a fortnight, Clarence was put to death privately in the Tower, possibly, as was believed within a few years, by drowning in a barrel of malmsey wine.

If Richard of Gloucester had initially opposed his brother's execution, he soon reaped benefits that may have gone some way to reconcile him with the course events had taken. Already his control of the lands of the earldom of Salisbury and other important estates, and a collection of northern offices including the wardenship of the West March towards Scotland and the life shrievalty of Cumberland, had made him the most powerful magnate in the north of England. Clarence's fall not only gave the king's sole surviving brother even greater political importance throughout the realm, it also left him the wealthiest landowner after the king himself. Edward, for his part, placed considerable trust in his youngest brother, who had displayed nothing but loyalty to him, and rewarded him generously for his acquiescence in Duke George's removal. Before the end of February 1478 he had received back the office of great chamberlain of England, which he had relinquished in Clarence's favour six years earlier. A series of acts of parliament gave him a free hand in the reorganisation of his estates. Even greater rewards were to follow. In 1480 Edward delegated to Richard overall control of the war against Scotland, and in January 1483 he bestowed on him a newly created hereditary palatinate to be constituted of the counties of Cumberland and Westmoreland and any lands that should henceforth be taken from the Scots.[16]

8

EDWARDIAN GOVERNMENT

EDWARD'S KINGSHIP

Edward's accession was made possible above all by the crisis of Henry VI's kingship. One of the first tasks the young king had to grapple with was the restoration of the monarchical authority now vested in his person. Yet the monarchy that the king bequeathed to his successors was more than just an operational version of that of the Lancastrian kings, or indeed of that of Richard II. Undeniably, as J.R. Green recognised even in the 1870s, some of the foundations of the 'new monarchy' – as Green termed it – of the Tudors were laid in Edward's reign. Certainly, Edward's rule was different from that of his Lancastrian predecessors. At no other point in English history since the Norman conquest did more members of the nobility owe their advancement directly to the ruling monarch. The king's relations with, and use of, the assembly of his lesser as well as his greater subjects, parliament, differed sharply from what they had been under previous monarchs. The crown's finances were for the first time in several generations placed on a sound footing, at last rendering the crown solvent. Above all, the monarch once more established his place as the pinnacle of the English polity. Moreover, an emphasis was now placed on the visual manifestation of the king's exalted position that had not been seen since the days of Richard II.

In many respects, the developments of Edward's reign were an unavoidable consequence of the circumstances of his accession and reign. Thus the civil wars which initiated Edward's reign and continued both during and after it resulted in profound change to the makeup of the English nobility. While the battles and subsequent executions claimed the lives of peers in their dozens, the king was more active in creating new peers or elevating existing ones than any monarch since Richard II. Over the course of his reign, Edward created some 45 new titles, more than two-thirds of them between 1461 and 1470. In this, Edward at least initially had little choice. In the 1460s, his relations with his secular nobility were, above all, determined by the interconnected needs to replenish the ranks of the peerage depleted by the aristocratic bloodletting of the previous decade, to place the rule of the English regions on a new footing, to reward supporters and to give the new dynasty's rule a broad base by, wherever possible, reconciling former Lancastrians. The outset of the reign saw the creation or recognition of 13 new barons, two earls and two dukes, and in the years up to 1470 to these were added a further six barons, seven earls, a marquess and a duke (see above, p. 61).

By contrast, after Edward's return in 1471 the pattern of creations changed both qualitatively and quantitatively. Not only were there only isolated new peerage creations, but they were in their majority reserved for members of the king's immediate family, principally his sons, stepsons and nephews. Outside the ranks of Edward's blood relatives, just four new barons, an earl and a viscount were created or recognised between 1472 and 1482, and two of these creations were directly necessitated by the provision for Edward's sons.[1] While there were rewards for those who, like Louis de Gruthuyse (created Earl of Winchester in 1472), had stood by Edward in exile, there were no further concessions to former Lancastrian lords. Those who had escaped death in battle or execution in the aftermath of Barnet and Tewkesbury either spent the remainder of the reign in prison or in continental exile, always in danger of becoming mere pawns in the diplomatic negotiations of their hosts with the English crown.

Rather more stable were the ranks of the lords spiritual, who (their ecclesiastical functions aside) were also great landowners and tenants-in-chief called upon to exercise secular authority within their dioceses. They were summoned to parliament and to the king's council, and several of the great offices of state, such as the chancellorship and the keepership of the privy seal, still remained their near-exclusive preserve. The two Archbishops of Canterbury and York aside, two other diocesans stood out among their peers: the incumbent of the bishopric of Winchester, which was reckoned the wealthiest in western Christendom, and the Bishop of Durham, who exercised extensive palatine authority in his diocese, exempt from the direct intervention of the king's officers. Although the bishops and archbishops were in theory elected by their cathedral chapters and confirmed by the Pope, in reality their preferment had long been effectively in the gift of the King of England, and thus subject to the vagaries of the politics of the day. Notoriously, during the Duke of York's protectorate in 1456 the Exeter cathedral chapter's election of its dean, John Hals, scion of a local gentry family, had been overturned in favour of the Earl of Salisbury's younger son George Neville, aged just 24 and deemed too young for consecration for a further two years, while Hals had to wait for a further three years before being preferred to the see of Coventry and Lichfield when the queen's party was once more in the ascendant following the Yorkist rout at Ludford.

The example of George Neville proved a case in point: once a man had been consecrated to a bishopric, he could not simply be removed, however hostile he had shown himself to the ruling monarch and his partisans. Henry IV had found this to his cost in 1403, when the execution of the rebellious Archbishop of York, Richard Scrope, had not only fostered an entire saint's cult but had also cast a shadow over his kingship that had continued to dog him for the remainder of his reign. Mindful of this example, Edward avoided executing even the shifty George Neville in spite of his open support for Henry VI in the crisis of 1470–1 and subsequent plotting, although Neville, by then Archbishop of York, spent much of his final years in prison in Hammes Castle in the Calais marches.[2] Although Edward probably made overtures to Rome to have Neville deprived of his see, these came to nothing and the only member of the English and Welsh episcopate to lose his bishopric during the reign was the insignificant Thomas Bird, Bishop of St Asaph, who was deprived in 1463.

In the 22 years of his reign, Edward had to fill vacancies created by the death of one or other of his prelates on 21 occasions. This did not always entail merely the elevation of a single individual to the episcopate.

A vacancy in one of the archbishoprics or in one of the wealthier sees could set in motion an entire carousel of preferment, as bishops were promoted to more important sees and others provided to their former dioceses. In total, Edward thus appointed four men each to the bishoprics of Carlisle and Rochester, three to the archbishopric of York, and two to Bath and Wells, Exeter, Lincoln and Llandaff. The bishoprics of Bangor, Chichester, Durham, Ely, Hereford, Norwich, Salisbury, St Asaph, St Davids and Worcester each had to be filled once. The sees of Canterbury, London, Winchester and Coventry and Lichfield never fell vacant during the reign.

Just nine of Edward's episcopal appointments fell within the first decade of the reign: three bishops of Carlisle died in quick succession in 1462, 1464 and 1468; the deaths of Bishop Beckington of Bath and his short-lived replacement, John Phreas, in 1465 and that of Bishop Lowe of Rochester in 1468 allowed for the promotion of two former keepers of the privy seal, Robert Stillington and Thomas Rotherham. Only after 1471 was Edward able to shape the English episcopate according to his own wishes. Among his new creations, men of aristocratic birth were in a minority. Just three of the 17 bishops created or promoted after Edward's restoration were of noble birth, joining William Grey and Richard Scrope, two younger sons of peers consecrated respectively in 1454 and 1464. Rather, Edward's bishops were highly educated men, mostly holding university degrees, many of whom had proved their ability as administrators in royal service.

Three of the men so promoted (John Booth, James Goldwell and Oliver King) had served as Edward's secretaries, one (John Russell) as keeper of the privy seal, and two (John Alcock and John Morton) as masters of the rolls of Chancery. There is no better indication of the value the king placed on such administrative skills than his readiness to prefer Peter Courtenay, a member of the disgraced Duke of Clarence's circle who had served as Henry VI's secretary during the readeption, to the see of Exeter in 1478. Two bishops (William Dudley and Richard Martin) were provided from among the ranks of Edward's personal chaplains. Two others had been heads of religious houses: Richard Redman, Abbot of Shap and Visitor-general of the Premonstratensian order in England, who was consecrated to St Asaph in 1471, and Thomas Milling, the Abbot of Westminster, who had stood godfather to Prince Edward in the sanctuary of his abbey during the king's exile and had subsequently been appointed as the prince's chancellor, who was preferred to the see of Hereford in 1474. The services they had rendered prior to their elevation aside, many of Edward's bishops went on to serve him in a variety of ways, as councillors, ambassadors and in the senior administrative offices of England and of the royal earldoms, duchies and lands.

For the most part, then, Edward's bishops were men distinguished by ability, who paid for their advancement by many years of service. There seems little to support the grumble of the Crowland chronicle's continuator (a royal servant perhaps himself disappointed in his quest for preferment) that the king was prone to sell his bishoprics to the highest bidder.[3]

THE KING AND HIS ADVISORS

One of the central organs of late medieval government was the king's council. It was accepted political doctrine that the magnates of England had a right, indeed a duty, to advise the king. This right to provide counsel had been asserted by Richard of York in the 1450s, and again by Warwick in 1469: in its terms alone was opposition to an anointed king possible. The council was personal to the monarch and its functions largely determined by his abilities and character. At times when the king was a minor or incapacitated by illness or absence abroad, the council might collectively exercise some degree of royal authority. This had been the case during Henry VI's long minority, and also to a greater or lesser extent during the remainder of his troubled reign. By contrast, the council of a vigorous king in command of his faculties could expect to play a largely advisory rather than an executive role.

While it was an accepted premise that the great lords, particularly those 'of the king's blood', were the monarch's 'natural councillors', the council had no fixed membership. The principal officers of state (chancellor, keeper of the privy seal and treasurer, the former two of whom were normally senior clerics) usually attended meetings as a matter of course, and as well as other lay lords and bishops the king could from time to time appoint men of lesser status, both lay and clerical, on the basis of their abilities. Although as many as 105 individuals served as councillors at some stage in Edward's reign, only about 9 to 12 men normally attended a meeting of the council at any one time.

In striking contrast to Henry VI's council in the 1450s, the higher nobility remained in a minority among Edward's advisors. When he came to the throne as a young and inexperienced king, it was natural that Edward should include among his councillors not only his Neville and Bourgchier relatives but also a number of men who had been members of his father's council: J.R. Lander identified among the membership of Edward's council no fewer than 11 men who had served York in a similar capacity after 1455. Even then, however, the numbers of magnates were balanced by a range of men chosen for their administrative expertise. After 1471, this emphasis on experts among the councillors became even more marked. The removal of the Nevilles and their allies such as John, Lord Wenlock, aside, lay officials and men of gentry origins as well as imaginative clerical administrators now became increasingly more prominent. Alongside men who had proved their abilities in long careers in one of the departments of state or the royal household, the council now also included men of constitutional vision, not afraid to promote their ideas of how the governance of the realm might be reformed. The observations and thinking of these men are exemplified by the anonymous Crowland continuator, whose chronicle conveys a unique perspective from within Edward's council chamber, and Bishop John Russell (sometimes identified with the former), the last keeper of Edward's privy seal, whose draft parliamentary sermons of 1483 give an impression of rapidly evolving political thinking in the midst of a political crisis. There were undoubtedly others whose thoughts were not recorded for posterity.[4]

The result was that while Edward had competent advice at his disposal, his will carried the day without opposition. By contrast with his Tudor successors Edward showed no marked predilection for lawyers among his council: law officers such as the attorney general or solicitor general (the latter an office created by Edward shortly after his accession) were often in attendance, but they were outnumbered among the king's councillors by the officers of the household. Nevertheless, the king's council played its part in dispensing an equitable justice in the same way as the councils of individual magnates did in the regions. Although the evolution of formal courts from the legal element of the king's council did not occur until after 1483, it seems that the council was already dealing with an increasing amount of legal business initiated by petitions.[5]

Overall, Edward's choice of advisors was judicious; he recognised a man's abilities, and was happy to use them in full. Much as he intended to rule himself, he was prepared to be advised by his councillors and there can be little doubt that many of the governmental innovations of his reign, such as they were, owed something to the influence of the experienced administrators with whom he surrounded himself. There can be no clearer indication of the degree to which Edward's councillors were chosen for their ability than the high proportion of their number who went on to serve as councillors to his successors – to Richard III, but above all to Henry VII, in whose reign the reforms that had begun under Edward's rule gathered pace.

EDWARD AND PARLIAMENT

Parliaments were a distinctive feature of late medieval English political life, noticed and commented upon by foreign visitors, often with some degree of bemusement. The scope they had for elaborate debate astonished and amused such observers. Thus, in November 1472 an Italian described to the Duke of Milan how

> [t]hey are now engaged at London upon the great parliament of the three estates of England, to reform the kingdom; but so far they have done nothing but talk. They devote every moment to gormandising.[6]

In parliament, the king would, in the terms of the standard writ of summons, consult with the nobles and prelates and the community of his realm over urgent matters concerning the governance and defence of the kingdom and of the English Church; he would put to them requests for supply, that is, taxation in support of his duty to defend the realm, and he would hear and provide redress for their grievances. Yet, parliament did not meet of right; it was summoned only when the monarch chose to do so.

The fifteenth-century English parliament was bicameral. The Lords and Commons normally met separately, although both houses would come together for occasions such as the chancellor's opening sermons, and delegations from the two could periodically meet to discuss their response to questions that concerned both. In Edward's reign, parliament's deliberations took place almost without exception at Westminster. In 1464 Lords and Commons were on several occasions asked to come together at York, since the king was expected to be detained in the north by the need to besiege the remaining Lancastrian strongholds there, and in 1467 and 1468 parliament twice assembled at Reading for a day, but on none of these occasions was any business transacted. When parliament, as was normal, deliberated at Westminster, the Lords would assemble in the White Hall of the Palace of Westminster, while the Commons would gather in the refectory of nearby Westminster Abbey. This arrangement itself illustrated the temporary nature of parliament: the Commons were forced to interrupt their deliberations several times a day to make room for the monks' meals.[7]

Just six parliaments met in the 22 years of Edward's reign. (A further parliament was scheduled to meet at York in September 1469 during Edward's captivity, but was abandoned when the king regained his liberty.) Four of these parliaments sat for between 30 and 58 days; those of 1463 and 1472 were exceptional in that they respectively deliberated for a total of 121 and 312. Parliament did not sit continuously; there were regular prorogations for the harvest and for the great feasts of Christmas and Easter, and at other times also exceptional circumstances could necessitate a postponement of further deliberations. In July 1467 the Lords and Commons were sent home after meeting for less than a month because the plague had struck London and had already claimed the life of at least one member of the Commons.

Compared with the previous decades, in Edward's reign parliament sat infrequently. Under Henry VI, the sessions had averaged between 45 and 57 sitting days per year; under Edward this figure halved to between 23 and 29 days per year. In the 1460s parliament met at intervals of approximately two years, comparable to those that had been customary in the second half of Henry VI's reign. After 1475, however, the gaps between parliaments grew longer, as the king became increasingly less reliant on financial grants by the Commons. Parliament was not yet an organ of government *per se*; it was principally a means of securing grants of money, in return for which the king would hear petitions and redress grievances. Where, however, the means of redress took the form of a statute which could be pleaded at common law, parliament provided at least the forum for legislative activity, even if it had not yet assumed the character of a formal legislature outside which no laws could be created. On occasion, the quasi-legislative activity of Edward's parliaments even fell outside the framework of statute law. In 1472–5 parliament heard a host of complaints from members of the Cornish gentry, some of which were answered with legal remedies outside the scope of the common law.

Beyond this, parliament provided an occasion for the king to address a representative gathering of his subjects, or more specifically, of the Commons of his realm, in his own person. Thus, on 21 December 1461 Speaker Strangways appeared before the king in the parliament chamber to present the bill of attainder agreed by the Commons. It is not clear whether he came alone or was accompanied by a delegation from the Commons, or whether the entire house had been summoned, but whichever the case, the king addressed them directly:

> James Strangways, and you who have come for the commons of this my land, for the true hearts and sympathetic consideration that you have had for the right and title that I and my ancestors have had to the crown of this realm, which has been long withheld from us; and now, thanks be to Almighty God, from whose grace comes all victory, by your true hearts and great assistance, I am restored to that which is my right and title; wherefore I thank you as heartily as I can. Also for the tender and true hearts that you have shown me, in that you have sympathetically given thought to the punishment of the horrible murder and cruel death of my lord my father, my brother Rutland and my cousin Salisbury, and others, I thank you most heartily: and I shall be to you, with the grace of Almighty God, as good and gracious a sovereign lord as ever was any of my noble progenitors to their subjects and liegemen. And for the faithful and loving hearts, and also the great labours that you have borne and sustained on my behalf, in the recovery of my said right and title which I now possess, I thank you with all my heart. And if I had any better thing to reward you with than my body, you should have it, which will always be ready for your defence, never sparing or holding back for any danger; praying you all of your hearty assistance and good continuance, as I shall be to you your most righteous and loving liege lord.[8]

Similarly, in 1467, after the Commons had presented John Say as their Speaker, and Edward had signified his assent to the Speaker's customary protestation through the medium of the Treasurer, Earl Rivers, the king turned directly to the Commons gathered at the far end of the Parliament Chamber, where the lords met, and addressed them:

John Say, and you, sirs, who have come to this my court of parliament for the commons of this my land. The reason why I have called and summoned this my present parliament is that I intend to live upon my own resources, and not charge my subjects except for important and urgent reasons which more concern their own well-being, and also their defence and that of this my realm, than my own pleasure, as has previously been done and borne by the commons of this realm for my progenitors in time of need; in which matter I trust that you, sirs, and all the commons of this my land will be as sympathetic and kind to me in such matters as any commons have been to any of my said progenitors in the past. And for the goodwill, kindness and the true affection that you have always borne, maintained and showed towards me in the past I thank you as sincerely as I can, and so I trust you will continue in future; for which, by the grace of God, I shall be as good and gracious a king to you, and reign as righteously over you, as ever did any of my progenitors over the commons of this my realm in the past; and I shall also, in time of need, devote my person for your weal and defence and that of this my realm, not sparing my body or life because of any danger that might befall them.[9]

These were fine words indeed, and much appreciated by the flattered Commons, whose speaker declared 'how very pleasing it had been to [them] that the lord king had announced at the beginning of the said parliament, with his own lips, that he intended to live of his own'.[10] Yet at many times Edward's attitude to his parliaments, and especially the Commons, left much to be desired. Under Henry VI parliamentary elections had occurred almost annually, the Commons had been pressed for ever fresh grants of taxation in support of the increasingly disastrous war in France, and more than once the Commons were dismissed for Christmas or the harvest season, only to be instructed to reassemble again, sometimes in provincial backwaters like Coventry or Bury St Edmunds. But reassemble they did, and parliamentary business continued. Only in the crisis of November 1453, while the council decided what was to be done in the face of the king's incapacity were the Commons dismissed on the day of their reassembly at Reading, and instructed to return to Westminster the following February.

In the 1460s, futile gatherings became the norm rather than the exception for Edward's long-suffering Commons. In December 1461, Chancellor Neville informed parliament that the business for which it had been summoned had not yet been completed, and instructed the

Lords and Commons to return to Westminster on 6 May. When they reassembled, they were met by the Archbishop of Canterbury and the chancellor, Bishop Neville, who conveyed to them the king's thanks for their efforts and dismissed them to their homes on the same day.[11] A new parliament, summoned for 5 February 1463 was unceremoniously cancelled, and the communities were ordered to conduct new elections. Parliament eventually met on 29 April and sat until 17 June, when it was prorogued for the summer. On 4 November the Lords and Commons reconvened, only to be informed that the king was urgently needed in the north to crush Lancastrian resistance, and that he would meet them on 20 February 1464 at York. On that day and on two subsequent occasions (on 5 May and 26 November) the parliament reassembled at York in vain, and only on 21 January 1465 did the Lords and Commons meet for a final session of two months at Westminster. The next parliament, which began in June 1467 at Westminster, was moved to Reading in July on account of the plague in London, but only continued to transact any business in May 1468 at Westminster, after the members and peers had twice travelled to Reading for a day to hear the Chancellor's prorogation addresses. A parliament was summoned for 22 September 1469 to York, and many members of the Commons travelled there, only to discover that it had been abandoned altogether.

In the later fifteenth century, the Lords were still unquestionably the more important house of parliament. It was here that the king might from time to time preside over a session, and it was here that he came to open parliament, to hear the chancellor's sermon setting out the reasons for the summons of parliament, and to receive the Commons' nomination of a speaker. In theory, the Lords represented an extended version of the king's council, but in reality their composition varied considerably from the latter. The membership of the House of Lords at any given time was, like that of the council, determined directly by the monarch, although he would interfere in the routine administrative task of summoning the lords only in exceptional cases. The lay peers who could routinely expect a summons were the dukes, marquesses, earls, viscounts and barons of England; whereas the higher ranks of the peerage were subject to a formal creation ceremony, the rank of baron was so inextricably connected with a seat among the lords in parliament that receipt of a writ of summons was accepted as equal to a formal royal grant under the great seal in elevating a man to the ranks of the peerage.

Alongside the lay lords, the two archbishops of Canterbury and York, the 19 English and Welsh diocesan bishops, some 26 heads of religious houses, and the Prior of the order of St John in England were summoned to parliament. In attendance upon the lords were a number of law officers: the judges of the Westminster courts of King's Bench, common pleas and Exchequer, and a number of senior barristers, the king's serjeants-at-law. It has in the past been assumed that the personal attendance of the lords was erratic, and that the abbots in particular preferred to be represented in the house by proxies, but more recent work has emphasised that attendance among the bishops was very often determined by an individual prelate's personal circumstances,[12] and what little evidence we have for the presence of the lay magnates does point to the attendance of even those lords normally charged with the rule of the further-flung regions: among those who can be shown to have been present during the final session of the parliament of 1463–5 were not only the Welsh peers lords Herbert and Ferrers, but also John Neville, Earl of Northumberland.[13]

Thirty-seven shires and 107 cities and boroughs sent members to Edward's first parliament. Most counties in England sent two representatives; the exception were the palatinates of Chester and Durham, which were unrepresented. The choice of the urban constituencies which were ordered to send members to parliament was governed by custom. There was no official list of parliamentary boroughs; sheriffs followed precedent in determining which cities and towns would receive precepts instructing them to make a return, and the list of towns represented in the Commons was thus subject to some variation. Thus for instance, Ashburton in Devon had returned MPs to only a single fifteenth-century parliament in 1407, and Farnham made an isolated election in 1460. The reign of Henry VI had seen an innovation in the formal creation of 12 new boroughs by explicit clauses in new royal charters granted to them. In Edward's reign, just four new parliamentary boroughs were created; three of these creations (Grantham, Ludlow and Stamford, incorporated between 1461 and 1463) were boroughs held by the king himself as parcel of the duchy of York and earldom of March, while the fourth, Much Wenlock, received its charter of incorporation granting it the right to send a single representative to parliament at the instance of John, Lord Wenlock.

The procedure to be observed in parliamentary elections was regulated by a series of electoral statutes passed between 1406 and 1445.

These governed not only aspects of the electoral procedure, the time and venue of the election, but also the franchise and even the required social standing of the prospective members of parliament. Yet statutes could be, and were, broken, and above all, whereas the regulation of the election of the knights of the shire grew ever tighter, that of the election of the city and borough members remained comparatively general and allowed room for varying local customs. In many prosperous merchant communities ruling oligarchies controlled and increasingly narrowed the electoral franchise, while elsewhere regional magnates exerted their influence to impose their retainers on the borough electorates: at Great Yarmouth Bishop Lyhert of Norwich attempted unsuccessfully to have one of his men returned in 1463,[14] at Grimsby Ralph Neville, Earl of Westmoreland, sought to charm the burgesses into accepting his nominees by pointing to the financial savings they could make, while Anthony Wydeville, Earl Rivers, as tutor to the king's sons, was able to issue sweeping instructions to his servants as to the candidates to be suggested to the authorities of the boroughs within the spheres of influence of the Prince of Wales and of Prince Richard as Duke of Norfolk. There was nothing new in such practices: horse-trading over parliamentary seats had taken place both in East Anglia and at Grismby in the 1450s, and the process which increasingly saw outsiders with no connexions within a town returned by the smaller English boroughs had been well under way even by the end of the fourteenth century.[15]

Rather more interesting is Edward's apparent personal intervention in the elections to the 1463 parliament: the assembly, originally summoned on 22 December 1462 to meet at York on the following 5 February, was twice postponed and its venue changed. In late January 1463 Margaret Paston wrote to her husband John that she had received a visit from the ageing soldier Sir Robert Conyers, who had shown her a letter from the king, asking him to attend upon the Duke of Suffolk at the shire elections a few days later, and had told her that 'every gentleman of Norfolk and Suffolk of any reputation' had received a similar missive.[16] Whatever influence the duke and his counterparts in other shires had been expected to bring to bear (probably to secure a pliant House of Commons) clearly failed to achieve the desired result, for on 25 February the election results were unceremoniously quashed, ostensibly on the grounds that the elections had been held not 'by the order of his laws but contrary thereunto',[17] and fresh elections ordered. If this was indeed an attempt at securing a pliant House of Commons, it was evidently unsuccessful, and was not directly repeated. Nevertheless, the parliament summoned in 1478 for the attainder of the Duke of Clarence was heavily dominated by royal servants who offered no opposition to the king's all-out attack on his brother.

Much of the business transacted by Edward's parliaments was in its nature routine and differed little from the matters that had occupied parliament under the Lancastrian kings. As before, a range of private grievances put forward by individuals and communities alike received some consideration. On occasion, parliament could be called upon to provide judicial remedies outside the framework of the common law. The long parliament of 1472–5 heard a large number of petitions, many of them originating from the south-west of England, concerned with instances of murder and other serious breaches of the law, and in many instances answered by special acts of parliament providing for speedy remedies over and above the normal process of the common law. Other measures augmented the common law. So acts were passed regulating various aspects of the conduct of the sheriff's office, prohibiting the giving and receiving of liveries by and from others than the king and Prince of Wales, and ordering the observation of existing statute legislation. Successive parliaments inconclusively discussed the power of justices of the peace to grant bail and the question of whether the theft of pyxes should constitute high treason, while the protection from arrest enjoyed by members of parliament, peers and their servants while parliament was in session was in 1478 extended to protect them also from being indicted. Perhaps representative of the new king's own interests was the weight given to commercial affairs in the parliaments of 1463–5 and 1467–8 (see Chapter 3). A peculiar feature of Edward's parliaments which resulted directly from the circumstances of his accession was the part they were asked to play in sanctioning the change of dynasty and the condemnation of the house of Lancaster and its adherents, with successive parliaments passing acts of attainder, exempting individuals from their provisions or restoring the previously attainted.[18] Similarly, the change of dynasty resulted in a string of acts in favour of the members of the wider royal family, including the queen, her children and the king's siblings.

RESUMPTION AND TAXATION

A central factor that defined Edward's relations with parliament in his later years was his relative independence from communal grants of taxation. From the crown's point of view, parliament's most important function had long been to provide such grants. The Commons jealously guarded the principles that governed parliamentary grants of taxation: the money should be used for the defence of the realm, and wherever possible should follow the time-honoured scheme of assessment established since 1334, which required the payment of a tenth on land and a fifteenth on moveable goods. Innovative taxes were frowned upon, and steps were taken wherever possible to prevent the establishment of a precedent.

One of the most serious challenges to the stability of the rule of the Lancastrian kings had been the almost permanent financial crisis they faced. When Henry V's initial French campaigns were successful, the Commons readily provided money, but as the wars continued year after year, and as under Henry VI the English position in France deteriorated, they were increasingly less happy to do so. Moreover, it was the Commons' express position that while they accepted a responsibility to provide money for the defence of the king's French possessions, it was not for them to meet the routine costs of the royal household. Where this was concerned, it was claimed, the king should live of his own, that is, of the fee farms of the shires, cities and boroughs of his realm and the revenues of the crown estates.

At Henry VI's accession these estates had included not only the lands of the duchy of Cornwall and earldom of Chester, traditionally assigned to the reigning monarch's eldest son and heir, but also the Lancastrian king's patrimony, the duchy of Lancaster. Yet, from the outset of Henry's reign, the crown's finances had been in crisis. The deaths of Henry IV and Henry V in comparatively rapid succession had placed them under considerable pressure: the widows of two kings had to be provided with a landed endowment for their dower, and the provisions of the two monarchs' wills required that further parts of the crown lands be withdrawn at least temporarily from the day-to-day control of the reigning king. If this were not bad enough, Henry V had borrowed heavily in the last years of his life to finance what should have been the final stages of his conquest of France, and these loans needed to be repaid. Much of the lands and offices that remained in the king's hands, and such estates as came into his hands temporarily on the death of a tenant-in-chief, needed to be parcelled out to crown officials and magnates by way of reward for good and loyal service. With this, however, the parliamentary Commons disagreed. From their point of view, the alienation of the crown estates was undesirable and needed to be checked at regular intervals by parliamentary acts of resumption which cancelled all royal grants except for those specifically exempted from its provisions.

Still groaning under the tax burden imposed under Henry V, the Commons were parsimonious in their grants of taxation to Henry VI from the outset. Wherever possible, the payment dates of any tax were spread over a long period and the crown's pleas for funds for the prosecution of the French war were repeatedly met with endorsements of loans which anticipated future taxation that in practice failed to materialise. Only in the wake of the complete loss of France in 1453 did the Commons agree to a grant of customs and subsidies imposed on imports and exports by alien merchants for the remainder of Henry VI's life that gave the king some degree of financial independence at last.

When he came to the throne, Edward was in a very different position: the royal duchies and earldoms of York, Lancaster, Cornwall, Chester and March aside, the forfeitures of the early months of the reign had brought estates worth as much as £30,000 *per annum* into his hands. Yet within three years most of these lands had been granted away to new supporters or restored former enemies, and in 1463 Edward for the first time faced the need to turn to parliament for taxation. Over the course of the reign, the Commons agreed to the payment of six and three-quarters fifteenths and tenths.[19] In 1463 Edward asked parliament for an aid of £37,000 for a campaign against the Scots. This was granted under the condition that it should be used for a Scottish war, but in the event this never came about and the money was instead used to pay the Calais garrison, and in the second session of parliament the grant was formally converted into a normal fifteenth and tenth of £31,000.[20] In 1468 Edward, who just months earlier at the opening of parliament had announced his intention to live off his own, declared his desire to invade France, and was consequently granted two full fifteenths and tenths. The proposed invasion never came about as England descended into renewed civil war, and the tax, although only partially collected, caused considerable resentment.[21]

Once Edward was securely re-established on his throne after 1471, the question of an invasion of France which would put an end to Louis XI's mischief-making once more came to the fore. The protracted parliament of 1472–5 proved one of the most munificent of the fifteenth century. Once again, its grants were ring-fenced with conditions, including a deadline for the king's departure to France, but its total tax grants amounted to more than £118,000, and the Commons took steps to ensure that the king should receive the entire sum. In November 1472 they agreed to an unusual income tax of 10 per cent, which was to raise a total of £118,625, the equivalent of almost four fifteenths and tenths. This grant was calculated on the basis of the wages of an army of 13,000 archers for one year, and had its sole precedent in a similar grant to Henry VI in 1453, which had never been levied. When it became apparent that the money raised by this subsidy fell far short of the intended total, the Commons agreed to the levy of a string of additional subsidies to make up the shortfall, most of them raised as, or converted into, traditional fifteenths and tenths. In July 1475 Edward finally sailed for France, but the anticipated campaign of conquest never occurred, and after less than two months the king made peace with the French and returned to England, politically remitting the collection of three-quarters of a fifteenth and tenth that were still outstanding. He nevertheless reactivated the grant in 1480, when war with Scotland loomed, and received over £20,000. A fifteenth and tenth agreed by Edward's final parliament of January 1483 was never collected on account of the king's death.

In every instance, the Commons' grants of taxation had been preceded by lengthy and painstaking negotiations. Parliament successfully insisted that taxes should be an exception, rather than the regular basis of the crown's funding. This was nothing new. Throughout the later middle ages, English kings had found their subjects' tax grants insufficient to meet their needs and had been forced to find money by other means. Edward III had borrowed heavily from commercial bankers, and had at one stage been forced to pawn his great crown to the merchants of Cologne.

The Lancastrians had adopted a different approach: commissioners were dispatched to the shires to negotiate loans from the inhabitants of the county and its boroughs, and under Henry VI these loans were notionally underwritten by the parliamentary Commons, who authorised borrowing up to specified levels on the security of future taxation which, often enough, was never granted. As Henry VI's reign progressed and his financial situation became ever more precarious, the crown's appeals for further loans from his subjects increasingly fell on deaf ears.

A new approach was needed. In March 1464 Edward was in need of funds for the continued siege of the Northumbrian castles still held by Lancastrian insurgents. The decision to use the previous year's tax earmarked for a campaign against the Scots to pay the wages of the Calais garrison had caused considerable resentment and no further grants from parliament could be hoped for. Edward decided to reap the rewards of the extensive patronage he had exercised over the preceding three years by imposing a special 25 per cent levy on all those holding lands, fees, annuities or offices worth ten marks per year or more.[22]

In 1474, when Edward's grip on his kingdom was more secure, he was able to take an altogether more daring step. By the end of 1474 preparations for the invasion of France were well underway, and in spite of the taxes granted by parliament, Edward was still in need of ready money. The king and council now decided to impose a new kind of levy, a 'benevolence', a free gift offered in lieu of military service leviable by royal prerogative for the defence of the realm, and based on the fourteenth-century precedent of the scutage. In theory, the benevolence was given voluntarily and without compulsion, but Edward's commissioners did not hesitate to point out to anyone reluctant to pay that the alternative could be to perform war-service in person. The king himself played his part in cajoling his subjects into paying. Like Henry V, who in the spring of 1421 had used a progress through his realm to collect loans from his subjects, Edward now also set out into the shires, and proved more successful than Henry had ever been. In March 1475 an Italian observer reported admiringly:

> The last four months in particular [King Edward] has been very active, and has discovered an excellent device to raise money. He has plucked out the feathers of his magpies without making them cry out. This autumn the king went into the country, from place to place, and took information of how much each place could pay. He sent for them all, one by one, and told them that he wished to cross to conquer France and deluded them with other words. Finally, he has so contrived that he obtained money from everyone who had the value of 40*l.* sterling and upwards. Everyone seemed to give willingly. I

have frequently seen our neighbours here who were summoned before the king, and when they went they looked as if they were going to the gallows; when they returned they were joyful, saying that they had spoken to the king and he had spoken to them so benignly that they did not regret the money they had paid. From what I have heard some say, the king adopted this method. When anyone went before him he gave him a welcome as if he had known him always. After some time he asked him what he could pay of his free will towards this expedition. If the man offered something proper he had his notary ready, who took down the name and the amount. If the king thought otherwise he told him, Such a one, who is poorer than you, has paid so much; you who are richer can easily pay more, and thus by fair words he brought him up to the mark and in this way it is argued that he has extracted a very large amount of money.[23]

There is no question that the levy was successful: it raised over £21,000, and moreover it bypassed the exchequer completely. The money was collected by the keeper of the king's wardrobe, John Elrington, and the sealed bills recording the sums that any given individual had promised to contribute were expressly not to be handed in to the exchequer or any other court of record.[24] In the light of the success of the benevolence in raising money, it was only natural that Edward should adopt the practice again in 1480, when he required money for his proposed campaign against the Scots. Once again, reluctant contributors were threatened with a personal summons for war service, and once again this threat proved remarkably successful: the benevolence raised as much as £30,000, but also fomented popular resentment, which caused the practice to be banned by parliament just three years later.[25]

9

EDWARD: MAN AND MONARCHY

In writing about the life of any medieval monarch, particularly one as dramatic as Edward IV, there is a temptation to concentrate on the political events of the reign, losing sight of the living, thinking individual they so often obscure from view. This is in part a result of the absorption of the records which might be personal to a private individual – his correspondence, the details of his expenditure – into the records of the monarch's government. In Edward's case we are fortunate that, quite apart from being able to filter some personal details of his life from the records of the English government, we have records of the private impressions of individuals who had met or at least observed him.

Many of them commented on his striking appearance. He retained his good looks into his thirties, and even the waspish Philippe de Commynes had to admit that when he saw the 33-year-old Edward at Picquigny in 1475 the king

> appeared a truly regal figure. ... He was a very good-looking, tall prince, but he was beginning to get fat and I had seen him on previous occasions looking more handsome. Indeed I do not recall ever having seen such a fine-looking man as he was when my lord of Warwick forced him to flee from England.[1]

Shortly after Edward's death Dominic Mancini was told of the dead king's 'fine stature', and that originally he had been 'not only tall but rather lean', but by his immoderate eating and drinking 'had grown fat in the loins'.[2] Polydore Vergil heard that Edward had been 'very tall of personage, exceeding the stature almost of all others, of comely visage, pleasant look, broad chested, the remainder proportionate even to his feet',[3] and Thomas More's informants likewise described him as 'a goodly personage and very princely to behold ... of visage lovely; of body mighty, strong and clean made; howbeit in his latter days, with over liberal diet, somewhat corpulent and burly but nevertheless not uncomely'.[4]

Along with Edward's attractive physique went an easy manner and a common touch. While he slotted effortlessly into the rigid courtly ceremonial observed and described by a Bohemian visitor in 1466 (below, p. 190), he was also ready to break out of its corset when the opportunity presented itself. A monastic chronicler at Crowland Abbey remarked how on a visit in 1469 Edward had been

> honourably received as befitted the royal dignity and passed the night a well-pleased guest. On the morrow, being greatly delighted with the quietude of the place and the courtesy shown to him he walked on foot through the streets to the western outlet of the vill, and after praising in high terms of commendation the plan of the stone bridge and houses, there embarked together with his attendants.[5]

Similarly, one of Edward's heralds, Bluemantle Pursuivant, described the easy familiarity with which the restored king and his family welcomed his former Burgundian host, Louis de Gruthuyse, in the autumn of 1472, drawing their guest into the royal family's semi-private life wherever the ceremonial of the court permitted. Having been greeted in the quadrangle of Windsor Castle by Lord Hastings and other members of the king's household, Gruthuyse was brought into the king's presence and warmly welcomed by Edward and Queen Elizabeth. The guest then dined in his own chambers before Lord Hastings came to take him once more to his host. Edward personally conducted him to the queen's chamber, where Elizabeth and her ladies were engaged in a variety of games, and the king himself danced with his eldest daughter. On the following day, the visitor attended the sung Lady mass with the king, and after breakfast was introduced to the 2-year-old Prince of Wales. The day was spent hunting in Windsor park, and in the evening before darkness fell the king showed his guest his pleasure garden and vineyard. That evening the queen gave a banquet in Gruthuyse's honour. When dinner had ended, there was dancing before Edward, the queen and her ladies conducted the guest to a set of chambers richly decked out for him. The royal party then withdrew to their own apartments, leaving Lord Hastings to undress the visitor and to share his bath.[6]

Edward's easy manner continued to be commented on after his death. So, the Italian visitor Dominic Mancini heard that

> Edward was of a gentle nature and cheerful aspect: nevertheless should he assume an angry countenance he could appear very terrible to beholders. He was easy of access to his friends and to others, even the least notable. Frequently he called to his side complete strangers, when he thought that they had come with the intention of addressing or beholding him more closely. ... He was so genial in his greeting, that if he saw a newcomer bewildered at his appearance and royal magnificence, he would give him courage to speak by laying a kindly hand upon his shoulder.[7]

Some, however, believed that Edward's familiarity with his subjects went rather too far. Partly because of his abandonment to bodily lust, Polydore Vergil recorded, and partly 'of humanity which was abundantly bred in him, he would conduct himself more familiarly among private persons than the honour of his majesty required'. This easy access to the king's person, Vergil noted after his death, led to 'a great rumour that he was poisoned'.[8]

EDWARD'S PRIVATE LIFE

Edward IV came to the throne as a young man, and was still relatively young when he died some weeks short of his forty-first birthday. It is thus not surprising that he was given to enjoying himself in the manner of a young nobleman of the time, in hunting and jousting. To this end, he surrounded himself with young nobles. The first generation of young Yorkist aristocrats, many ennobled by Edward himself, was decimated during the crisis years of 1469–71: the Earl of Devon was executed at

Warwick's behest in 1469, Viscount Lisle was killed at Nibley Green, and lords Cromwell and Say and the Marquess of Montagu died fighting at Barnet. Their places were soon taken by other young men. These young aristocrats provided the king with congenial companionship in his distractions. No more than companionship, though. Far from satisfying an all-encompassing sexual appetite in their young sovereign, they played their part in satisfying his entirely orthodox needs. When Edward had grown weary of any given woman he was prone to pass her on to one or other of his courtiers. Chief among his accomplices in his dalliances, so Mancini heard shortly after the king's death, were the queen's two sons, the Marquess of Dorset and Sir Richard Grey, and her brother, Sir Edward Wydeville.[9] Thomas More believed that Hastings had also played his part, and that the queen had disliked him because 'she thought him secretly familiar with the king in wanton company'.[10] Certainly, in the autumn of 1483 Dorset, who was then in rebellion against Richard III, was publicly denounced for his adultery with Edward's former mistress Elizabeth Shore,[11] and not long after Shore was forced to do public penance for 'the life that she led with the ... Lord Hastings and other great men'.[12]

The king and his companions hunted other game too; hunting continued to be the aristocracy's sport of choice, and Edward's enjoyment of it is well documented. A hunting expedition provided the pretext for the king's journey to Northamptonshire at the time of his clandestine marriage to Elizabeth Wydeville; in the spring of 1472 Edward was hunting at Windsor in the company of Archbishop Neville, and at the time of the prelate's arrest that April he was expecting the king to join him at his Hertfordshire manor of the Moor for further similar sport. Visits to the royal parks and hunting lodges represented an important part of the king's annual itinerary. So he visited the old royal palace and park at Woodstock in the autumn or winter (usually in September) of 1464, 1466, 1467, 1471, 1474, 1476 and 1481; sojourns at Windsor provided opportunities for hunting in the great and little parks, sometimes staying at the manor in the park, or the hunting lodge known as the 'Tower on the Heath'; and for much of the reign Greenwich remained one of Edward's most favoured residences.[13]

Along with his indulgence of these appetites, Edward also enjoyed his food and drink: in the opinion of some, overly so. In 1483 Mancini heard that the king had been 'most immoderate' in his eating and drinking. Indeed, so the Italian recorded: 'it was his habit … to take an emetic for the delight of gorging his stomach once more.'[14] Thomas More too was told of Edward's 'over liberal diet',[15] and the Crowland continuator who had observed both Edward and many of his subjects at close hand remarked more even more critically that

> men of every rank, condition and degree of experience in the kingdom mar-
> velled that such a gross man so addicted to conviviality, vanity, drunkenness,
> extravagance and passion could have such a wide memory that the names
> and circumstances of almost all men, scattered over the counties of the king-
> dom, were known to him just as if they were daily within his sight even if, in
> the districts where they operated, they were reckoned of somewhat inferior
> status.[16]

There was, however, also another side to Edward's character. Not only had he married for love, he was something of a family man. In the summer of 1460 he had paid regular visits to his younger brothers and sister, then respectively aged 8, 11 and 14. After 1471 it is occasionally possible to catch glimpses of the family life of the Yorkist royal family. In 1472 the heraldic observer of the festivities that accompanied the creation of Louis de Gruthuyse as Earl of Winchester watched as the king danced with his 6-year-old daughter, Elizabeth, who was beginning to play her part in the life of the court,[17] and it was probably a similar observance of Edward's family that prompted the clerical continuator of the Crowland chronicle to comment on the royal couple's 'handsome and most delightful children'.[18]

EDWARD'S RELIGIOUS LIFE

To men and women throughout the late medieval west, their Christian faith was a given. The life of the universal Church and its doctrine tran-scended and permeated all aspects of life. Kings ruled by the grace of God and had a duty to use the power with which they had been entrusted for the defence of the Church of Christ. Beyond this public duty, even a monarch was nevertheless an individual, who had to find a way of recon-ciling his private devotions with their more public display which his office required of him. A degree of pragmatism was acceptable, even

desirable. Thus one of Edward's clerical councillors was able to comment
with approval that in 1471 Edward had decided to lead his army against
Warwick in spite of the approach of Easter, 'behaving rather in response
to immediate necessity than foolish propriety'.[19] The same commentator
observed of Edward after his death:

> This prince, although in his own day he was thought to have indulged too
> intemperately his own passions and desire for luxury, was nevertheless a
> catholic of the strongest faith, the sternest enemy of heretics, the kindliest
> patron of wise and learned men and of clerics, the most devoted venerator of
> the Church's sacraments, the most penitent of men for all his sins.[20]

Edward IV's attitude to religion has been compared unfavourably to
that of his mother and siblings. For all his love of ostentatious display,
Edward was not given to making a show of his piety beyond the utterly
conventional. He appears to have been entirely free from any devotional extremes, and comfortable in the pursuit of the established
rites.[21] Not for him the religious fervour of the feeble-minded Henry
VI, nor the reforming zeal of the impressionable young Edward VI.
His principal religious foundation at Windsor owed more to sound
reason of state than a particular desire to glorify the Virgin Mary or St
George, and characteristically, his own preparation for the afterlife, his
chantry at Windsor, was left incomplete at his death, never to be
finished according to his plans.

To a large extent, the devotions of an English monarch were, in any
case, predetermined. It was expected that the king would regularly hear
mass and other offices, make his offerings and listen to sermons. Apart
from England's military patron, St George, it could be expected that a
King of England would demonstrate some dedication to the Virgin and
England's royal saints, St Edward the confessor and St Edmund the
martyr. Perhaps the most striking aspect of Edward's religious practice
and devotion is the very sparseness of evidence for it, which by contemporary standards seems to suggest almost a lack of interest in religion.
To suggest that Edward was an agnostic would be profoundly anachro-
nistic, for Edward, and indeed his century, knew no such concept.
It may be closer to the truth to suggest that the king was perhaps akin
to many of his subjects (and many of the English since) in being
comfortable with the religious beliefs of the age and happy to conform

to its devotional practices, but disinclined to go to any particular lengths in the pursuit of his faith. This trait of his character cannot fail to stand out, perhaps more so than is necessarily justified, by its contrast with the saintly image posthumously created for Henry VI.

Edward and his queen extended some patronage to the charterhouse at Sheen, founded by Henry V in 1414, and in 1479 obtained a special papal licence to attend divine services in a chapel separate from the main body of the monastic church.[22] Wider patronage of the Carthusian order remained limited, although a number of houses received gifts of wine from the royal household, as did the Dominican nunnery at Dartford, which Edward's youngest daughter Bridget would eventually enter as a nun.[23] Probably under the influence of his more profoundly religious sister, Margaret of Burgundy, Edward founded the first house of Observant Franciscans in England on a site adjacent to Greenwich palace in the final years of his reign.[24] Similarly, the influence of the queen may have played its part in influencing Edward's patronage of religious houses on other occasions. Thus, an exemption of the house of Minoresses outside London's Aldgate from the provisions of the 1465 act of resumption was signed by the king and delivered to the clerk of the parliament by the queen's sewer, accompanied by the token of a ring from the king.[25]

If Edward himself had any particular devotion to an individual saint, it may have been to St Anne, the mother of the Virgin Mary. Yet, there is little indication whether this was a life-long devotion, or whether it developed in the peculiar circumstances of the king's troubles of 1470–71. The official account of Edward's restoration was at pains to record that

> the king, being out of his realm, in great trouble, thought, and heaviness, for the misfortune and adversity that had befallen him, full often, and, especially upon the sea, prayed to God, our Lady, and St. George, and, among other saints, he specially prayed to St. Anne to help him, whereas he promised, that, at the next time that he should happen to see any image of St. Anne, he should make his prayers thereto, and give his offering, in the honour and worship of that blessed saint.[26]

Otherwise, it is rare to see the king at his private devotions, other than on set-piece occasions. In May 1469 Edward undertook pilgrimages to the shrines of St Edmund the martyr at Bury and of Our Lady at Walsingham.[27] Characteristically, he did not make a special journey, he merely arranged to pass through the monasteries on his progress north to deal with Robin of Redesdale's rebels. Edward's return from exile in 1471 provided the occasion for a number of, probably heart-felt, public thanksgivings. On 7 April Edward kept Palm Sunday at Daventry, entering the parish church in the procession of the people and participating in the office, and witnessed a miracle of St Anne:

[W]hen the procession had come into the church and by order of the service had come to the place where the veil should be raised before the rood, that all the people might honour the rood, with the anthem, *Ave*, three times begun, in a pillar of the church, directly before the place where the king knelt, and devoutly honoured the rood, was a little image of St. Anne, made of alabaster, standing fixed to the pillar, closed and clasped together with four boards, small, painted, and going round about the image, in the manner of a compass, like as it is to be seen commonly. ... And this image was thus shut, closed and clasped, according to the rules that, in all the churches of England, are observed, all images to be hidden from Ash Wednesday to the morning of Easter Day. And so the said image had been from Ash Wednesday to that time. And even suddenly at that season of the service, the boards encompassing the image gave a great crack and opened a little, which the king and all the people about him perceived well. And anon, after, the boards drew and closed together again without any man's hand or touching, and, as though it had been a thing done with a violence, with a greater might it opened all abroad, and so the image stood open and uncovered in the sight of all the people being there. The king, seeing this, thanked and honoured God, and St. Anne, taking it for a good sign and token of good and prosperous adventure that God would send him in what he had to do, and, remembering his promise, he honoured God and St. Anne in that same place and gave his offerings.[28]

Similarly, Edward was careful to stop and give thanks at the major religious sites of his realm at every opportunity during subsequent weeks. On his entry into London, he rode straight to St Paul's Cathedral, and only after making his devotions there rode on to the bishop's palace to secure the person of Henry VI. He then rode to Westminster Abbey, where he stopped to venerate the abbey's patron, St Peter, and its royal saint, Edward the Confessor, before making his way to the sanctuary, where he saw his son for the first time.

If to the modern mind these public thanksgivings seem like almost cynical political demonstrations, it is nevertheless likely that to Edward they were entirely sincere, indeed, that to him the political and personal dimensions of his piety were inseparable. In another area, too, it seems that the overtly political coincided neatly with the king's personal piety: the king showed a keen concern for the commemoration not only of his immediate family, but also of the lesser servants who had given their lives in his cause.

In February and March 1461, as soon as reasonably practical, Edward had obsequies for his father celebrated in St Paul's Cathedral, and in subsequent years provisions were made for prayers to be said for the souls of Richard of York and Edward's brother Edmund of Rutland, as well as the king's ancestors, in Fotheringhay college, the college of St Julian at Southampton, Henry V's chantry in Westminster Abbey, Syon Abbey and the collegiate church of Westbury in Gloucestershire. Probably delayed by the political crisis of the late 1460s as much as by the slow progress of the re-glazing of the nave of the church of Fotheringhay, it was not until July 1476 that Edward had the bodies of his father and brother exhumed from their initial resting place at Pontefract and removed to the Yorkist foundation of Fotheringhay in an elaborate ceremony.[29] Yet, there was more than simply filial or fraternal piety to this. Even in 1467 Edward had agreed to rebuild and enlarge the partly derelict chapel near the battlefield of Towton where many of the victims of the bloody engagement on Palm Sunday 1461 had been interred, and to this end had procured a special papal grant of indulgences to all who would contribute to the cost of the rebuilding.[30]

However limited his interest in ostentatious displays of piety, Edward was not a stupid man, and distinguished theologians were summoned to preach before him and his family in the chapels royal, as they had previously done before Henry VI. Among these preachers were men like Dr William Wolflete, the chancellor of Cambridge university, Dr Thomas Eborall and Dr William Ive, two successive masters of Whittington College, and several other learned men who had taken a leading part in the condemnation of the opinions of the controversial bishop Reginald Pecock in the 1450s. In the last years of Henry VI, Ive in particular had complained openly of the censorship exercised over the sermons preached before the monarch by William Say, dean of the chapel royal, and had been penalized for speaking out. Yet after Edward's accession Say remained in post and Ive returned to preach: is it too much to suggest that Say knew better than to attempt to censor what was preached before the new and intellectually more vigorous king?[31]

More importantly, Say's continuation in the post of dean of the chapel royal may have provided continuity in what was perhaps the most important liturgical development of the period, the evolution of polyphonic church music where plainsong had previously been the norm. The music of Edward's court was widely admired, and recent research has indicated that Edward's reign saw a number of musicians of note gathered not only in the chapel royal, but more poignantly also at the king's favoured foundation of St George's, Windsor. We may draw inferences as to the importance that the king himself placed on the music performed in his presence from the fact that the second half of his reign not only saw the incorporation of the chapel of the household including a body of 'gentlemen-clerks', selected on the basis of their musical ability, but also a dramatic increase of the number of choristers at Windsor from the six provided for by Edward III to 19.[32]

BUILDING ACTIVITIES

The enhancement of the musical provision at Windsor was part of Edward's wider plans for the rebuilding and enlargement of the college of St George in Windsor Castle and the chapel which was to provide the setting for the annual St George's day celebrations of the Order of the Garter, and which the king eventually decided to turn into his dynasty's mausoleum. In February 1473 one of Edward's confidants, Richard Beauchamp, Bishop of Salisbury, who had extensive experience of such matters from the earlier remodelling of his own cathedral church, was appointed master and surveyor of the king's works in Windsor Castle, and over the following two years a grand scheme was drawn up which entailed the wholesale reconstruction of the castle's lower ward, with a splendid new chapel at its heart. By the time the building work began in the summer of 1475, Edward had determined that he himself would be buried in his new chapel.[33] The building works aside, the king extended more generous patronage to the college of St George than to any other individual institution, religious or educational. The college was formally incorporated, and – the increased choir aside – the size of its clerical membership substantially increased. The king also made personal additions to the chapel's apparatus. Images of St George and the dragon, St Edward the Confessor, and Christ on the cross with the Virgin Mary and St John the evangelist were acquired at his expense.[34] In 1478 an embroiderer was paid £40 as part of a greater sum for the making of copes and vestments depicting the life of St George,[35] and in the same year Edward commissioned a richly jewelled gold head of St George, standing on white enamelled lions and bearing the Prince of Wales's badge of the ostrich feather, at a cost of over £80.[36]

The works at Windsor formed the centrepiece of a wider programme of building focused on Edward's principal residences. Especially in the second decade of his reign Edward favoured the royal palaces of the Thames valley – Windsor, Sheen, Eltham, Greenwich and Westminster – and it was on improving these residences for his comfort that the king spent considerable sums. A new hall was built at Eltham in the years after 1475, while major improvements were made particularly at Westminster and Greenwich. Edward's preferred residences on his increasingly rare forays into the northern parts of his kingdom were the castles of Nottingham and Fotheringhay, and substantial sums were spent on extensive building works, including the construction of new latrines, chambers and a kitchen at Fotheringhay and of a polygonal tower at Nottingham, which was much admired even by near-contemporaries.[37]

TRADING ACTIVITIES

Another thing Edward knew about was money. In his early years, he had experienced a lack of it. When he had learnt of his father's death, one of his first thoughts, according to one contemporary chronicler, had been of the cost of raising an army to defeat Queen Margaret. His gravest concern was 'that he was so poor, for he had no money'.[38] Nor was this situation alleviated after the accession. Time and time again, friends, supporters and courtiers, not least the useful (and well-heeled) John Dynham whose money had already procured shipping to Calais after the debacle of Ludford bridge, had to put their hands into their pockets and advance sums of ready money to their young monarch. Even more crucial were the very substantial sums advanced by the City of London and the merchants of the Calais staple, but these creditors were hard-nosed businessmen who expected repayment either in cash or in the form of mercantile advantage, and – as the Lancastrians had found – were quite prepared to withhold credit from a regime they regarded as financially or politically bankrupt.[39]

Nor was it viable simply to tax the community of the realm. The Commons were prepared in principle to abide by the ancient convention that while it was the king's duty to defend the realm, the community was obliged to provide him with the necessary funding. Edward soon discovered, however, that the country was not prepared to stand by idly as taxes granted for war were diverted to other purposes, such as the payment of the king's creditors. His first attempt to do so in 1463 caused enough of an outcry to force him to remit part of the taxation that had been granted to him, and his renewed failure to put the tax granted in 1467 to the specified purpose of an invasion of France caused widespread discontent and made many of his subjects all too ready to listen to the blandishments of Warwick and Clarence.

Clearly an alternative remedy had to be found. Although the crown lands had been augmented substantially at the beginning of Edward's reign by the addition of Edward's own duchy of York and earldom of March, their value to the monarch was diminished by the endowments of Cecily, Duchess of York and Queen Elizabeth, and after 1471 the settlement of the duchy of Cornwall and the earldoms of March and Chester on the Prince of Wales. Consequently, their revenues alone were insufficient to meet more than the routine expenditure of the royal household.

Parliament had already recognised the insufficiency of the crown estates for the sustenance of the royal household in 1453 when it had granted the revenues of the customs collected in the English ports to Henry VI for his life. From 1461 to 1465 Edward IV had collected the customs by authority of this grant (with dubious legitimacy); that year, parliament granted them to him personally. Edward did what he could to maximise their returns to his coffers. In each customs district survey-ors of the customs were appointed to oversee the activities of collectors and controllers, and the king was not above making use of common informers to ensure that no one evaded due payment. So, for instance, in 1476 a major inquiry took place at Exeter on possibly malicious infor-mation arising from a private dispute, and was personally overseen by

Edward's secretary, William Hatcliff. In addition to the roll of charges openly supplied, the commissioners were instructed also to investigate other charges that the informer should verbally make before them.[40]

But Edward was not content merely to take a slice of his increasingly prosperous merchants' winnings in the form of customs revenue; he wanted a larger piece of the cake. Unlike his Lancastrian predecessors, Edward took a keen personal interest in mercantile affairs. As we have seen, this interest stood him in good stead when determining commercial policy, but he took it a step further. Through a string of factors, most of them Italians, Edward himself engaged actively in trade. Contemporary reaction was, as far as we can tell, one of surprise rather than outrage that the King of England might choose to make money by buying and selling 'like a man who earns his living by trade',[41] and the Italian observer Dominic Mancini recorded with approval that Edward 'was more favourable than other princes to foreigners, who visited his realm for trade or any other reason'.[42]

From time to time, Edward's coffers were swollen by extraordinary sources of revenue. He made efficient use of the lands that temporarily came into his hands by feudal incidents, he was diligent in pursuing the perquisites of the administration of the law in the government's records, and from 1475 to 1482 he received his annual pension of 50,000 crowns from Louis XI under the terms of the Treaty of Picquigny. As the reign wore on, guaranteeing a steady flow of income that would allow him to maintain an increasingly lavish court may have become something of an obsession with Edward. Observers of his foreign diplomacy were scathing about the bargains he drove in order to avoid paying dowries commensurate to his daughters' rank and to maximise the dowry that potential brides for his son and heir might offer. To them and other contemporaries this made him guilty of the cardinal sin of avarice.

'A little before the end of his life,' Polydore Vergil wrote, 'we have said, that he began to slide little by little into avarice, who before had used towards all men great liberality',[43] and Mancini, to whom the principles of English parliamentary taxation were alien, heard that 'though not rapacious for other men's goods, [Edward] was yet so eager for money, that in pursuing it he acquired a reputation for avarice.'[44] This view arose from the incoherence of medieval taxpayers' attitude to their monarchs' financial position. If kings were unable to make ends meet, chroniclers complained of their profligacy. Where monarchs, one might say prudently, amassed treasure, they complained of their avarice. Both Edward IV and after him Henry VII built up considerable reserves in the second half of their reigns, and were duly chastised for it. Yet Vergil's comments were somewhat unfair to Edward. Unlike Henry VII with his dogged determination to amass and retain wealth, Edward to the end used the resources at his disposal for the maintenance of his splendid court. What reserves he had were depleted by the Scottish wars of 1480–82, and at his death he left barely enough to pay for his funeral. The short-lived administration of the young Edward V immediately found itself in serious financial trouble.[45]

THE EDWARDIAN COURT

Edward's stabilising of the crown's finances was an important prerequisite for a central dimension of his kingship: the visual manifestation of the English king's renewed royal majesty. If Edward was Richard II's true successor in any one respect, it was surely in his sense for the theatre of monarchy. Although it is now accepted that the court of the Lancastrian kings was a far cry from being the pale reflection of earlier or later courts as which it was once seen,[46] the Edwardian court excited comment from more than one observer for its magnificence. In 1466 the Bohemian visitor Gabriel Tetzel recorded the ceremonial dinner held following the churching of Queen Elizabeth after the birth of her first daughter:

> The Queen sat alone at table on a costly golden chair. The Queen's mother and the king's sister had to stand some distance away. When the Queen spoke with her mother or the King's sister, they knelt down before her until she had drunk water. Not until the first dish was set before the Queen could the Queen's mother and the King's sister be seated. The ladies and maidens and all who served the Queen at table were all of noble birth and had to kneel so long as the queen was eating.[47]

By contrast, Edward's own conduct had been far less formal:

> We saw with what extraordinary reverence [the King] was treated by his servants. Even mighty counts had to kneel to him. But the King offered his hand to my lord and to his honourable attendants. ... Then the King admitted my

lord and all his attendants to his fellowship. The knights received a gold [badge], and those who were not knights a silver one, which he himself hung about our necks.[48]

Edward's involuntary sojourn in the house of Louis de Gruthuyse in 1470–71 gave him an opportunity to study at first hand the splendours of Burgundian courtly life, and to develop a taste for the refined material objects produced by the skilled artisans of the low countries. After his restoration, and particularly as his wealth grew in the second half of the 1470s, Edward became active as a collector of luxury items, many, but not all of them, imported from the continent. Although there is no evidence that he became any more interested in reading books as he matured, he was evidently able to appreciate artistic beauty, and began to acquire illuminated manuscripts (which became the foundation of the English royal library). The evolving splendour of the English court, combining continental influences with home-grown craftsmanship, was such that after Edward's death a clerical observer could comment that in the final years of the reign it had been 'such as befitted a mighty kingdom, filled with riches and men from almost every nation'.[49]

Set-piece occasions provided important opportunities for the court to display its full glories. To this end, the elaborate spectacles of the chapters of the order of the Garter and the feast of St George were played out, and important occasions in the life of the court were invariably accompanied by tournaments and jousting. Thus, at Pentecost 1463 the king held a tournament so that the Duke of Somerset, newly taken into his allegiance, might 'see some manner sport of chivalry after his great labour and heaviness';[50] Queen Elizabeth's coronation in May 1465 was celebrated with a tournament in which knights from the entourage of the new queen's maternal uncle, Jacques de Luxemburg, took part;[51] and even more lavish celebrations surrounded a long-planned tournament between Elizabeth's brother, Anthony, Lord Scales, and the Bastard of Burgundy in June 1467.[52] Similarly, in January 1478 the tense parliamentary proceedings of the Duke of Clarence's trial were lightened by jousts held to celebrate the marriage of Edward's younger son, Richard, to the heiress of the last Mowbray Duke of Norfolk.[53] On occasion, Edward himself took to the lists, something no English king since Edward III had done. In April 1467 John Paston wrote to his brother, Sir John:

My hand was hurt at the tourney at Eltham on Wednesday last, I would that you had been there and seen it, for it was the goodliest sight that was seen in England this forty years of so few men. There was on the one side within the King, my lord Scales, myself and St Leger, and without my lord Chamberlain, Sir John Woodville, Sir Thomas Montgomery and John Parre etc.[54]

Other set pieces were provided by occasions such as the creation of Louis de Gruthuyse as Earl of Winchester in 1472, or even seemingly informal hunting parties, such as one in Waltham forest in 1482 to which the king invited the mayor and other leading Londoners.[55]

To all of this, the king himself was pivotal. What Edward grasped, perhaps better than many of his contemporaries, was the visual dimension of kingship. He had understood that while it was important that the northern and western rebel strongholds should be reduced, there was little to be gained from his personal presence in the war camp. Rather, this tiresome and muddy task could be carried out by trusted lieutenants, while the king himself remained in the heartlands of his realm, doing 'kingly' things, and being seen to do them. Nothing could have confirmed this view better than the dispiriting impact on all observers of Henry VI's final, and deeply uninspiring, public showing in London in April 1471, wearing an old blue gown.

Edward, by contrast, knew how to offset his already considerable physical attributes to best effect by splendid clothing. The quantities of clothes provided for the king fell hardly short of what was acquired by his Tudor successors: among the garments purchased for Edward's use in the 18 months between June 1471 and December 1472 were 22 doublets of satin, seven of velvet, six of damask, four of chamlet and two of cloth of gold; ten long gowns of velvet, one of them lined with satin and one with damask, three of chamlet, two of them lined with velvet and one with satin, three of satin, two of them lined with cloth of gold, and two entirely of cloth of gold, one lined with velvet; eight short gowns of velvet, four of cloth of gold, two of damask, one of them lined with buckram, and one of chamlet lined with velvet; seven gowns of middling or unspecified length, two of them of chamlet and satin lined with cloth of gold, and five of velvet, one of them lined with sarsenet; ten jackets, four of them of cloth of gold, one of these lined with sarsenet, four of velvet, one of them 'pointed' with cloth of gold, and one each of chamlet and damask; as well as three cloaks and a number of hoods and other items, some richly furred. At the same time, an array of doublets, gowns and bonnets was also provided for the infant Prince of Wales and the king's bastard son.[56] Even the normally sober Crowland continuator remarked admiringly how at his last Christmas Edward had appeared

> dressed in a variety of the costliest clothes very different in style from what used to be seen hitherto in our time. The sleeves of the robes hung full in the fashion of the monastic frock and the insides were lined with such sumptuous fur that, when turned back over the shoulders, they displayed the prince (who always stood out because of his elegant figure) like a new and incomparable spectacle set before the onlookers.[57]

Above all, Edward understood that it was important that the king should be seen. In the weeks after the king's death the Italian visitor Mancini was told how Edward had

> called to his side complete strangers, when he thought that they had come with the intention of ... beholding him more closely. He was wont to show himself to those who wished to watch him, and he seized any opportunity that the occasion offered of revealing his fine stature more protractedly and more evidently to on-lookers.[58]

Just how far Edward's grasp of the uses of the imagery of kingship went is hinted at by the Crowland continuator, who suggests that even Edward's renewal of the coinage in 1464–5 had a propagandistic dimension, in that he sought to remove from circulation the coinage with the image and name of the three Henrys. This, however, also illustrates the limitations of Edward's use of the royal image. His coins, like his seal, bore the stylised images of the monarch that had been in use unchanged for centuries. It was left to Henry VII to bring into circulation a new coinage and new seals displaying recognisable images of the monarch personal to each individual ruler.

A PERSONAL MONARCHY – A NEW MONARCHY?

As more than one commentator has argued, by the reign of Edward IV the older medieval ideal of a constitutional arrangement in which kings and nobles co-operated for the common weal had become obscured by an unseemly scrabble for profit of those about the king. This was the political framework in which Edward had grown up, and in which his self-indulgent character was not completely out of place. Regrettably, Edward did not think to commit his political philosophy to paper, and we have to hazard a guess at what he thought he was doing on the basis of other evidence. Above all, we may point to his upbringing. He had been raised as heir to the greatest private estate in England, and, as others have argued, it is surely instructive that the language he used with regard to his acquisition of the crown of England was that of the land market. He spoke of taking 'possession' and 'seisin' of his realm: a proprietary notion of kingship, which perceived the kingdom as the monarch's personal possession descended to him from his ancestors in the same way as the duchy of York and the earldom of March.

Edward was in no doubt that he should rule in person. Medieval political philosophy expected the king to rule himself, albeit within the limitations imposed by the law and with the advice of his magnates, and the contortions into which the minority and subsequently the repeated incapacity of Henry VI thrust the governance of the realm served only to emphasise this point. The body politic needed a single head, hence the recourse in 1422, 1453 and 1455, and again in 1483, to the appointment of a protector to preside over the conciliar government *loco regis*. On account of its hierarchical structure the heavily bureaucratic machine of government was able to operate even in the absence of an effective king. When, however, the king was able to rule in person, the demands on him were considerable. Along with the weightier matters of foreign policy and the dispensation of justice, he was expected to give personal attention to a vast array of individual concerns and petitions for grace or pardon. The king's sign manual on many such documents bears ample evidence to the literally hundreds of decisions that Edward was expected to make on a daily basis. Happily, he was personally well-suited to this task. We have seen earlier how the Crowland continuator was amazed that despite his 'conviviality, vanity, drunkenness, extravagance and passion' the king had a comprehensive knowledge of even the less important gentry 'scattered over the counties of the kingdom'.[39]

Edward's policies were unquestionably personal in so far as they reflected his desire to conciliate. The king had an almost pathological need to be loved and admired, perhaps rooted in the sudden loss of his father and the brother with whom he had shared his childhood and youth. Here, as much as in any *raison d'état*, lay the origins of his readiness to show favour far beyond their deserts to seemingly reconciled former Lancastrians, like the Duke of Somerset in 1463. Here too, far beyond sober judgement of the evidence, originated his stubborn refusal to believe in the treason of Clarence and Warwick in the crisis of 1469–71 until it was too late.

One way in which the extent of Edward's personal rule becomes manifest is the increased use of the king's signature, the royal sign manual, to authenticate official documents. The authorisation of late medieval government documents, like so many other aspects of government, followed a rigid hierarchy. The king would issue an order which his secretary would seal with the royal signet, and send to the keeper of the privy seal. The clerks of the privy seal office would then make out a warrant under the privy seal which instructed the chancellor, who was custodian of the great seal, to issue letters patent or close under the king's great seal. Although there was a traditional understanding of which instruments should be issued under what seal, this was gradually being eroded. Whereas royal writs and grants required the authority of the great seal, warrants for payments from the exchequer, for instance, were normally issued under the privy seal, but could increasingly also bear the king's signet. After 1471, there was a marked increase in Edward's use of the sign manual in addition to, or instead of, the signet.

This is not to say that the king or his predecessors had not scrutinised government documents. Some documents which were personal to the monarch or authorised when his secretary might not be at hand, for instance provisos to successive acts of resumption, had always been signed with the king's cypher. When in possession of his faculties, Henry VI had done so, and Edward equally did so during his first reign.[60] Yet by the reign of Henry VIII, the sign manual evolved so far into an institution as to be executed by a wooden stamp, and the records of Henry VII's reign stand out by the sheer proliferation of the king's signature. One possible explanation is that by 1471 the signet had become effectively institutionalised. The signet, in the custody of the king's secretary, no longer accompanied the monarch everywhere and a separate means of authorisation was required. Hand in hand with this theory runs the possibility that during the crisis of 1470–1, when there were two monarchs with identical signets, only the sign manual could indicate which side had issued a particular order.

Nor was even the young and inexperienced Edward ever entirely another man's tool. He might be prepared to delegate substantial authority in a particular field or region to a trusted lieutenant, but he did so at his own pleasure, and was prepared to change his mind and override an appointment when it suited his plans. Nowhere is this more apparent than in the king's early clashes with the Earl of Warwick. Warwick had developed detailed ideas of his own place in a Yorkist settlement at an early date, and these did not always fit in with Edward's evolving plans for the rule of his realm. So, for instance, although he was initially persuaded to grant the executed Duke of Buckingham's southern Welsh lordships to Warwick, within days he transferred control to William, Lord Herbert, who was to serve as his principal lieutenant in the region. Similarly, the decision to make William, Lord Hastings, responsible for the rule of the midlands made it necessary to transfer offices like that of steward of the duchy of Lancaster in the honour of Leicester from Warwick to Hastings, and Edward did not hesitate to do so.[61]

It was J.R. Green, writing in the 1870s, who first suggested that Edward had presided over the creation of a 'new monarchy', on which the rule of the Tudors had been founded. Initially he believed that this reform had taken place after Edward's restoration in 1471, but he went on to revise this view and to suggest that the 'new monarchy' had begun to evolve even in the 1460s. Yet, Charles Ross among others questioned the extent to which Edward's administrative reforms represented a considered and systematic restructuring of royal government. Indeed, when he came to the throne Edward was in no position to make dramatic changes to the time-honoured forms of government. He was a young usurper with little experience of the running of a great noble estate, let alone of the rule of a kingdom, who had replaced a king to whom England had got used over almost four decades. He thus needed to restate his claim to be the true heir of Edward III and his predecessors by governing in the fashion prescribed by long-established precedent and through the established institutions of government.

In terms of its administration, England was a deeply conservative country. Term after term the cumbersome mechanisms of the monolithic institutions of government chugged on, following their rigid, century-old rules and producing their unwieldy records. If there was to be administrative reform it had to bypass these established institutions, but without challenging their primacy, and operating within their framework. The king could (and did) largely remove royal expenditure from the control of the exchequer and put it into the hands of the treasurer of his chamber, but the required funds needed to be transferred to the chamber from the exchequer, and accounted for in the latter's records. The slow and inefficient common law courts at Westminster could be bypassed by the evolving and burgeoning equity courts, such as the Chancery, or even by direct petitions to the king, parliament or the prince's council, but the primacy of the common law could not be challenged. Edward himself had emphatically restated this by himself sitting in judgement in the King's Bench, and any suitor who sought redress in the equity courts had to be careful to couch his request in terms which explained why he could find no remedy at common law. Similarly, the administrative experts on whom Edward had to rely had been trained within the machinery of the Chancery, Exchequer and common law courts. What appetite they had for administrative reform was necessarily focused on structural changes to improve the workings of the institutions of government, rather than their wholesale disbandment or replacement. Edward's was less of a new monarchy than a renewed monarchy.

10

THE END OF
THE REIGN

THE KING'S DEATH

In the aftermath of the expedition of 1475, Edward's increasingly self-indulgent lifestyle visibly began to take a toll on his health. Even at Picquigny, Philippe de Commynes had noticed that he was beginning to grow somewhat portly, and in subsequent years there were periodic concerns for his well-being. In April 1477 Louis XI heard rumours (which Lord Hastings was quick to deny) that Edward was suffering from a severe illness, and in the early 1480s there was renewed speculation about the king's state of health.[1]

Whether or not any of the earlier rumours of Edward's failing health were true, it is certain that around Easter 1483 he was forced to retire to his bed with a serious ailment. The nature of this illness has been the subject of some degree of speculation; contemporary observers were, not surprisingly, vague, even baffled. The Italian Dominic Mancini believed that he had caught a cold while out fishing in a small boat.[2] Philippe de Commynes maintained that he had died of apoplexy.[3] Polydore Vergil only knew that he had died 'of an unknown disease'.[4] Several observers hinted at some form of depression or mental stress that played its part in Edward's death: Mancini reported rumours that Edward had been cast 'into the greatest melancholy' by the news of the Treaty of Arras, a frame of mind which he had been unable to hide in spite of his supreme show-manship,[5] and Commynes likewise suggested that Edward's dismay at the marriage of Margaret of Austria to the French dauphin was the direct cause of his final illness.[6] Polydore Vergil alone reported a 'great rumour' that the king had been poisoned.[7]

Whatever the truth of the matter, Edward's illness was brief, but evidently severe, and his decline rapid. By 6 April the city of York believed the king to be dead and had a requiem celebrated for his soul. Edward himself also realised that death was approaching. He had made a will on the eve of his departure for France in 1475, but now hastily began to revise his provisions by adding a number of codicils. As the inevitability of the king's end became increasingly apparent, the coming and going in Edward's bed chamber became ever more hectic. Among those who assembled to hear the final additions to his will were the queen, Archbishop Rotherham of York and Bishop Morton of Ely.[8] Two days before his death, Edward summoned his old friend Lord Hastings, and his stepson, Dorset. At the dying man's entreaties the two men agreed to put aside their long-standing mutual hostility.[9]

Yet there were also notable absences from the king's death bed. Edward's sole surviving brother, Richard of Gloucester, designated to act as protector to the young Prince Edward, was in the north. The prince himself remained at Ludlow and could not be returned to Westminster in time for a final paternal blessing, nor, it would appear, was any attempt made to summon him. With him was Earl Rivers, who was serving as his tutor. Also missing were many of the king's early friends and contemporaries. Humphrey Stafford and William Herbert, Humphrey Bourgchier, Lord Cromwell, and John Stafford, Earl of Wiltshire, were dead, as were Warwick and Montagu. John Dynham was serving across the Channel at the head of Calais garrison as Lord Hastings' deputy. There remained the two ageing Bourgchiers, Henry, Earl of Essex, and Thomas, Archbishop of Canterbury, both of whom had first held high office during the Duke of York's protectorates in the 1450s.

On 9 April 1483, King Edward IV died, probably in the small hours of the morning.[10] He was still some weeks short of his forty-first birthday. Throughout that day, the king's body was put on display in Westminster palace, perhaps in the Great Hall, naked except for a covering from the navel to the knees. That evening, the body was taken to be embalmed and placed in its coffin, and the following morning the coffin was placed in the king's private chapel of St Stephen's, where it remained for a period of eight days while masses and other offices and prayers for the dead were sung and said over it, and nightly vigils kept.

On 17 April four knights and 11 esquires of the body carried the coffin, covered with a cloth of gold, from the palace across to Westminster abbey. Four knights of the household bore a canopy of imperial purple fringed with blue and gold over it, and it was surrounded by other members of Edward's household carrying banners of the various heraldic and devotional devices associated with their dead master: the Holy Trinity, Our Lady, St George, St Edmund the martyr and St Edward the Confessor, and the arms of the King of England, the earldoms of March and Ulster, and the white hind. The coffin was preceded on this short journey by a procession of the senior clergy of the realm, including the abbots of Bermondsey and Abingdon, the bishops of London, Coventry and Lichfield, Bath and Wells, Chichester, Carlisle, Norwich, Durham, Lincoln, Ely, Rochester, Exeter and Salisbury, and rounded off by Archbishop Rotherham of York. The ancient Archbishop Bourgchier of Canterbury was too frail to attend the funeral.

Behind the coffin processed the lay peerage of England, probably led by Edward's eldest nephew, John de la Pole, Earl of Lincoln, the dead king's nearest blood relative present. Among them were Queen Elizabeth's son, the Marquess of Dorset; William Herbert, Earl of Huntingdon; William, Viscount Berkeley; Lord Hastings, the great chamberlain; Lord Stanley, the steward of the household; and at least nine other barons. The king's wider family was represented by three of his Bourgchier cousins (Sir John Bourgchier and Sir Thomas Bourgchier the elder and the younger), and the queen's brothers, Sir Richard and Sir Edward Wydeville.

In the abbey, the coffin was placed inside a great hearse, a specially constructed wooden pavilion supported by carved pillars and surmounted by smaller pillars crowned with branched candelabra bearing thousands of burning candles. Above the coffin was placed an effigy of the king, royally attired, holding a sceptre and an orb, and wearing the crown on its head. During the service, celebrated by the Archbishop of York, the lords knelt within the hearse, while the abbey church was crowded by the members of the king's household, the judges, barons of the exchequer, the mayor and aldermen of London and their attendants, mostly dressed in black robes specially procured for the occasion.

The mass ended, the coffin with its cloth of gold and effigy was transferred to a royal chariot, and preceded by Lord Howard bearing the
king's personal banner and followed by the other lords, all on horseback,
the bishops in their pontificals and representatives of the four orders of
friars, it began its journey to its ultimate resting place at Windsor. At
Charing Cross the procession halted and the bishops censed the coffin,
before continuing to Syon Abbey where it rested for the night, after
further offices had been celebrated by Bishop Dudley of Durham.

Early on the next morning the procession set out once more, probably met along the way by processions of mourners from the villages and
townships it passed, as well as from other neighbouring communities.
Outside Eton, it was received by the members of the college and bishops
Russell of Lincoln and Morton of Ely, who had gone ahead. All those
who had ridden thus far now dismounted and the entire funeral procession continued on foot across the bridge and up the castle hill. At the
castle gates the body was met by processions of the dean and canons of
St George's and of the members of the king's own chapel, and was censed
once more by the Archbishop of York and Bishop Waynflete of
Winchester, assisted by other bishops, before being carried into the new
chapel that Edward had himself commissioned.

The building was only partly completed, but it was roofed and the
choir stalls were in place, and much could be disguised by the black
cloth with which it was hung and floored, as was the custom. In the
choir, a spectacular hearse that excited the comment of contemporaries
had been built, and it was in this that the coffin was now placed. Further
services and prayers followed, and throughout the night a vigil was kept.
Nine lords and two knights stood within the hearse and 34 other knights,
esquires and gentlemen of Edward's household, as well as six kings-of-
arms, heralds and pursuivants, were gathered around.

On the morning of 19 April the actual burial began. The customary
masses of Our Lady and the Holy Trinity were followed by the requiem
mass, during which the dead king's knightly achievements were offered.
A richly embroidered and jewelled coat of arms was brought to the altar
by the Earl of Huntingdon and the Marquess of Dorset, and then held
by Garter King-of-arms to the left of the altar until the end of mass. The
king's shield was to be presented by Lord Maltravers and Viscount
Berkeley, but at this point the rivalries of Edward's lords which so far
had been kept in check by the solemnity of the occasion suddenly broke

out into the open, when the two men began to jostle for the position of precedence on the right: Maltravers, one of Edward's young companions, created a baron in his own right by the king himself in 1465, was heir to the ageing Earl of Arundel, but was also close in blood to the royal house both through his mother, Joan Neville, Edward's first cousin, and through his marriage to the queen's sister Margaret. Berkeley, almost a quarter of a century older than his rival, was a man deeply conscious of his rank (acquired less than two years earlier) and felt that as a viscount he should take precedence over a mere baron. The other lords present were at least taken aback, if not outraged, by the untimely quibble over protocol, and curtly decided that Maltravers would walk on the right, 'because he was the eldest son of an earl'.

After Edward's shield had finally been presented, the two elder Bourgchiers, Sir John and Sir Thomas senior, offered the king's sword to the archbishop, and Lords Hastings and Stanley brought the helmet with its splendid crown. Then all those heralds who were not yet holding one or other of the achievements around the altar processed to the church door to receive the king's champion, Sir William Parr, riding Edward's own charger, fully armed and bearing a battle-axe, although bare-headed, representing the king himself. Lords Audley and Ferrers received the man-at-arms at the choir door, where he dismounted, and conducted him to the altar, where he made his offering on behalf of the dead monarch. All the achievements that had been offered were then removed to the sacristy, where they would remain until the tomb had been completed and they could be hung above it.

Then it was the turn of the lords, knights and other members of the royal household to make their offerings, before the lords individually returned once more to the hearse to place pieces of cloth of gold on the coffin, in strict order of precedence according to rank and closeness to the deceased, the least important going first. The choir of the chapel was now getting so crowded with onlookers trying to catch a glimpse of the proceedings that even those directly involved were experiencing difficulty in following what was going on.

The funeral had, in any case, reached its final stages, as the lords, knights and esquires of the body raised the coffin once more, and with the aid of the officers of arms placed it in its grave on the north side of the choir, the bishops celebrating the customary liturgy. Then the great officers of Edward's household, the steward, chamberlain, treasurer and controller, threw their staves of office into the open grave, to indicate that their service had come to an end with the final passing of their master, and the heralds all threw in their heraldic tabards, before donning new ones, also of the arms of England, and proclaiming the unbroken succession to the crown by crying 'The king lives!', and saying the Lord's prayer and an Ave Maria for the deceased. This brought an end to the formal ceremonies in the chapel, and in their majority the lords probably repaired to the castle's upper ward for a funeral feast.[11]

However hastily they had been arranged, these ceremonies followed the usual practices for a royal funeral, last rehearsed seven years earlier at the quasi-royal reburial of Edward's father, and the ceremonies for the king's children who died in infancy in 1479 and 1482. Nevertheless, in spite of the repeated concerns for his health, Edward's death had been sudden and unexpected. Certainly, it was premature; so much so, that his tomb at Windsor was only half complete when he was laid to rest. It was a mark of the security that Edward had achieved that he died in his bed. He was and would remain the only male member of his immediate family to die of natural causes. His father and grandfather, his three brothers who survived into adulthood and possibly also his two sons all died violently; at more than one time in his turbulent career it had seemed likely that he would suffer a similar fate.

EPILOGUE

Edward's reign was over. It had seen many successes. He had defeated and eliminated any opposition worth the name to his family's rule: any who still dreamt of a Lancastrian restoration now had to look to the young Henry Tudor, a refugee in France who had spent most of his life on the run. Few in England preferred the uncertainty of an unknown pretender and the certainty of renewed civil war to the succession of the dead king's 12-year-old eldest son.

The aftermath of Edward's death is too well documented to need rehearsing in detail. Within three months the young Edward V had been removed to the Tower and his throne occupied by his uncle, Richard of Gloucester. Within three years both of Edward's sons had disappeared, and Gloucester himself lost his life to the unknown pretender on the battlefield of Bosworth. Ironically, it was left to this very pretender to build his and his son's rule on the foundations that Edward had laid. Yet the same pretender and his descendants also had a vested interest in emphasising their ties with the dynasty defeated by Edward and its legitimacy, and consequently needed to play down Edward's achievements and place in history. Within a century of his death, when William Shakespeare wrote, Edward had become little more than a secondary character in plays about Henry VI and Richard III.

This did not mean that Edward was simply forgotten: if anything, the troubles that befell those of his servants who transferred their loyalty to his young son caused Edward's reign to be remembered as something of a golden age. Before long, laments began to circulate, listing his achievements:

> Where is this Prince that conquered his right
> Within England, master of all his foes;
> And afterwards France, by sheer force and might,
> Without a stroke, and afterwards came home;
> Made Scotland yield, and Berwick he won from [it];
> Riding hunting, to disport himself and play?
> All men of England are bound for him to pray.[12]

and:

> Edward the Fourth, King of England, ornament of the world.
> Taken from us is the Rose of the World and the Sun of Triumph,
> In looks like Absalom, in habit like Solomon, almost like Christ,
> Founder of the church, and new restorer of the castle.[13]

The fate of Edward's sons after their father's death continues to excite considerable debate, but all that can be known for certain is that they were last seen alive towards the end of 1483.[14] Rumours that at least the younger prince, Richard, Duke of York, had escaped from imprisonment in the Tower persisted during the reign of Henry VII, when successive challengers to the Tudor king's rule adopted his guise.

Edward's five surviving daughters were all unmarried at their father's death, a number of proposals for foreign matches having failed. Richard of Gloucester, following his accession as Richard III, sought to find them husbands among his supporters, but succeeded in doing so only in the case of the second oldest, Cecily, who was married to Ralph Scrope, the brother of John, Lord Scrope of Masham, and subsequently (after this marriage had been annulled) to John, Viscount Welles, and the Lincolnshire landowner Thomas Kyme. Richard himself was reputed to have contemplated a marriage to his eldest niece, Princess Elizabeth, but denied such plans before a specially convened council meeting in the spring of 1485. Already, the pretender Henry Tudor had taken a public oath promising to marry Elizabeth, and he did so in January 1486 following his accession as Henry VII. Only in the mid-1490s were Edward's younger daughters Anne and Katharine married, respectively to Thomas Howard, Earl of Surrey, and William Courtenay, Earl of Devon. The youngest daughter, Bridget, never married and became a nun at Dartford Priory. Edward's queen sought sanctuary at Westminster when Gloucester seized the throne, but eventually came to an accommodation with her erstwhile son-in-law. Although her eldest daughter became Queen of England by her marriage to Henry VII, the widowed Elizabeth – in striking contrast with her husband's mother, Lady Margaret Beaufort – ended her days in comparative poverty in Bermondsey Abbey, where she died on 8 June 1492.

Edward himself lay in his tomb undisturbed for over a century and a half. Throughout these years, his tomb lay partly unfinished. Richard of Gloucester, the ostensibly loyal brother, found time and money to atone for some perceived offence by moving the body of Henry VI to the chapel that the first Yorkist monarch had envisaged as his dynasty's mausoleum. His brother's memorial, however, remained incomplete and bereft of the effigy that had crowned the tomb of every other English king since the eleventh century. It was left to a commoner, Reynold Bray, one of Henry VII's administrator-servants, to complete the rebuilding of St George's chapel. By this time, Edward had been joined in his grave by his queen, who was interred at Windsor two days after her death on 10 June 1492. The completion of Edward's tomb formed no part of Bray's scheme.

Above the tomb hung Edward's gilt harness with its coat of arms, richly embroidered with pearls and rubies, his jewelled sword, a cap of maintenance and his banner. These achievements survived the upheavals of the sixteenth century unscathed, but were eventually plundered by parliamentary soldiers on 23 October 1642.[15]

Edward's body was allowed to remain undisturbed, and with time the exact location of his burial vault underneath the tomb was forgotten. It was accidentally discovered on 13 March 1789 by a group of workmen in the course of alterations to the east end of the chapel begun seven years earlier. The grave's discovery caused a good deal of antiquarian excitement, and the coffin was opened on the same day in the presence of the president of the Royal Society, the member of parliament for the borough of Windsor, and 'other gentlemen'. Eventually, the body was laid to rest once more, but not before a quantity of the hair that remained on the skeleton's head and other scraps of the remains had been extracted. As a final indignity, these relics became sought-after collectors' items which are today scattered throughout the world.[16]

11

CONCLUSION

Edward's sudden death and the renewed political turmoil that followed it left little room for posthumous apotheosis. Within three months of the king's death, his son and heir had been displaced by an uncle who had a vested interest in calling into question not merely the validity of Edward's marriage, and thus the legitimacy of his offspring, but also the king's own paternity, and consequently his and his line's claim to the crown.

Two years later, Edward's brother was himself violently deprived of the throne by an invader who – despite seeking to bolster his tenuous title by a marriage to Edward's daughter and eldest surviving heir – traced this title from the house of Lancaster, and could thus not be seen to condone Henry VI's deposition at Edward's hands. Under these circumstances it is not surprising that Edward IV was not commemorated by contemporary (or near-contemporary) adulatory works similar to those that were written about other fifteenth-century monarchs: John Capgrave's *Liber de Illustribus Henricis*, John Blacman's hagiographical memoir of Henry VI, and the *Gesta Henrici Quinti*, compiled by an anonymous royal chaplain after Henry V's death.[1] The closest Edward came to similar apotheosis was in the works of Polydore Vergil and Thomas More, which used him as a counterfoil to the villain of their stories, Richard III.

Where, though, does Edward fit into the pantheon of English kings? Even if we dismiss Bishop Stubbs's view of the cruel, self-indulgent and lazy monarch as prejudiced and ill-informed,[2] opinions of modern scholars still differ. Was he, as one recent commentator has suggested, one of England's greatest kings? Or was he, as others have maintained, guilty of establishing an unsustainable political construct that – not surprisingly – collapsed within months of his death?

Unquestionably, Edward IV did much to stabilise the English polity. He successfully saw off a series of challenges to his rule and eliminated all who could credibly mount such a challenge. He sought to come to an accommodation with the established nobility wherever possible, while at the same time creating a new Yorkist peerage who owed their wealth and titles to him alone. There was in 1483 no immediate doubt that his young son, Prince Edward should succeed him.

In other ways, also, Edward had learnt the lessons of Henry VI's failure. By his personal conduct of frequent judicial progresses through the kingdom, he re-established the rule of law and order as far as could be reasonably expected of any medieval English king. The crown's finances were placed on a new footing. No longer was the king to be constantly reliant on occasional grants of money by parliament or the convocation of the clergy. The merger of the royal duchies of Lancaster and Cornwall with the vast estates of the house of York gave the king and his immediate family a secure endowment. Still more was gained by Edward's promotion of commercial activity. Not only did the burgeoning cross-channel trade vastly increase the customs revenues that found their way into the king's coffers, Edward saw nothing wrong in actively having goods bought and sold for his own profit. Reforms of administrative practice further strengthened the king's control of his finances. Specially appointed surveyors oversaw the collection and recording of the customs revenues in the ports, while at the centre the increased channelling of royal expenditure through the king's chamber bypassed the cumbersome and inefficient, if time-honoured, accounting practices of the exchequer. On the foreign stage, Edward conducted an invasion of France which, while it did not repeat Henry V's triumphs or restore even an acre of French land to the English crown, brought the English king a valuable annual pension (or tribute, as the English liked to call it) from the King of France.

Yet, in other respects, Edward's policies were less than successful. His – as some perceived it – excessive generosity to defeated Lancastrians led to repeated setbacks in the establishment of control over the outlying parts of England; his failure to use taxation raised for its stated purpose of waging war on France or Scotland undermined his rule by fomenting popular discontent; at his death, he barely left enough money to pay for his funeral; the aftermath of his death saw the nobility tear itself apart in renewed civil war, and his son and heir deprived of his throne within months of his accession. On the foreign stage, many resented the peaceful conclusion of the French war in 1475; the advantages that should have arisen from the successful invasion of Scotland in 1481 were squandered by Richard of Gloucester's untimely withdrawal from Edinburgh; the complete collapse of Edward's foreign policy in 1482 saw England isolated and its traditional continental allies in league with the French.

There can be no doubt that Edward personally earned many of his successes. When he led his troops in person, he showed himself an able general, and even his detractors had to acknowledge the renown that nine victorious battles had won him by 1475. He took a strong personal interest in trade and the restoration of law and order, which found reflection in his economic policies and the resultant boost to commerce, and his energetic enforcement of the law. Above all, he possessed a profound understanding of the importance of the theatre of monarchy in an age that was susceptible to visual stimulation, and played his role within it to perfection. He knew that a king did not merely need to be an effective administrator and dispenser of justice, he also needed to be seen to act and look like a king. In this Edward excelled: he possessed a profound sense of occasion. He was aware of his fine physique, and relished the opportunity of showing it off enhanced by fine clothes. He knew that he could charm others, and mischievously enjoyed using this ability, enhanced to even better advantage by his exalted station, to his advantage.

If, however, Edward's successes were his personal achievement, so were the failures of his policy. Some of Edward's contemporaries were in no doubt about the flaws in his character. They pointed to his self-indulgence, his womanising, his perceived avarice, even his personal laziness. Modern historians have added to this a criticism of the king's judgement in showing himself over-ready to accept former Lancastrians into his grace, and his blatant disregard for the rules of inheritance in making provision for his family in the 1470s. Yet these were not in themselves fatal faults. Edward's lieutenants in the north and west proved as capable of taking the remaining Lancastrian strongholds as the king himself might have been; the evidence of Edward's own signature on a plethora of official documents does not suggest that the king neglected the business of government; the king's impetuous marriage to

Elizabeth Wydeville was only indirectly to blame for his disagreement with Warwick; Edward's perceived avarice was in fact an essential prerequisite for the stabilisation of the crown's finances.

Yet there was one trait at the centre of Edward's character that for better or worse profoundly influenced all aspects of his policy – a profound need to be loved and admired. This found its expression in what some contemporaries perceived as excessive generosity to defeated enemies, but also in Edward's petulant abandoning in 1471 of his earlier policy of sparing the common people, who had refused to adore him as he felt was appropriate. It also found an expression in the king's almost narcissistic levels of self-confidence, his belief that his personal influence was enough to keep the peace between his quarrelling magnates, as well as to outwit the scheming Louis XI of France in a complex continental diplomacy. In some respects, his self-belief was justified. It was not until after his death that the quarrels among his nobles, which he had sought to settle with an appeal to their loyalty to his person even on his death bed, became destructive once more. In many other respects, this central tenet of Edwardian policy proved disastrous. Edward's total faith in his ability to win over opponents led to his undoing when faced by able and calculating politicians like Warwick or Louis XI.

Edward's legacy was, above all, determined by his early death. It is unlikely that Richard III would ever have been in a position to usurp the throne had his brother lived until his son and heir had reached adulthood. Had Edward outlived Louis XI, it is more than likely that he could have resurrected a successful foreign policy during the long minority of the new French king, Charles VIII. Like Henry V before him, Edward died before his love affair with his people could turn entirely sour. But for the circumstances of the Tudors' acquisition of the crown and the shaky title that led them to emphasise their Lancastrian roots, Edward IV might have been hailed as the re-founder of the dynasty.

It is tempting to wonder how much like his grandson, Henry VIII, the elderly Edward IV might have been. Certainly there are some intriguing parallels. Henry, like Edward, came to the throne as a handsome and athletic youth, contrasting sharply with his predecessor. Henry like Edward had an insatiable taste for women, and the course of both their reigns was profoundly shaped by their marital choices. Henry VIII was unquestionably his grandfather's grandson. Yet we should not take the parallels too far. Where Henry VIII was an exceptional figure in an exceptional age, Edward was as conventional as he could possibly be. He was not a stupid man – by the standards of the age, he was very well educated – but he was no scholar. He had none of his grandson's cultural accomplishments. He had undoubted gifts as a soldier and as a commander in the field, not least on account of his physical qualities, which allowed him to lead by example, but he allowed these advantages to be tempered by a devotion to his own comfort and leisure.

Indeed if Henry VIII shaped his age by his exceptional qualities, Edward's relative success owed much to his very conventionality: it is hard not to recognise him in Gerald Harriss's definition of the ageless characteristics of the English gentleman, 'his ... courage, stoicism, fidelity, courtesy and honesty', or, for that matter, also in Colin Richmond's more cynical additions to the list, 'his arrogance, bloody-mindedness, cruelty (to animals), disdain (for the deserving poor), and his ignorance'.[3] Yet, in his very conventionality, and in the apparent contradictions of his character, Edward was perhaps England's most human king of the Middle Ages, or at least the one whose humanity is most readily apparent to the modern observer. Where historians have endlessly pored over the limited evidence for Henry VII's gambling losses and employment of fools and court jesters, the evidence for Edward's 'joie de vivre' is overwhelming. It is hard not to have some sympathy with a monarch of genial character and some devotion to his family who sought to temper the rigours of the daily business of actively ruling a kingdom and the boredom of an endless stream of ambassadors, councillors and petitioners by congenial companionship and a recourse to the athletic pursuits appropriate to his rank.

In many ways, Edward's legacy was symbolised by his great edifice, the chapel of St George in Windsor Castle. Like the business of the reign, it was left unfinished when Edward died, to be completed in the reign of his son-in-law. In removing some of the functions of government from the time-honoured institutions of the Westminster bureaucracy into his own household or chamber, Edward had done vital groundwork for the eventual evolution of the strengthened monarchy of the Tudors, but it was left to his more serious-minded successors to bring this process to a conclusion. Just how far Edward had already travelled down this road is, as one recent commentator has pointed out, evident from the disaster that befell his heir. By the end of his life, the process of strengthening the monarch's grip on his kingdom had advanced far enough to allow a usurper to take control of it by a simple coup at the centre directed at the person of the king.[4] Yet the centralisation of royal power around the person of the king still had some way to go. Edward's constitutional achievements, like his tomb at Windsor, could serve their purpose, but they fell short of a completed edifice. Much had been done over the course of Edward's reign, but much still remained to do.

CHRONOLOGY

Date	Personal	Political	General
1442			
28 Apr.	Birth of Edward IV at Rouen		
1443 17 May	Birth of Edward's next surviving brother, Edmund		
1444	Birth of Edward's second surviving sister, Elizabeth		
1445 by Sep.	Edward recognised as Earl of March		
1446	Birth of Edward's third surviving sister, Margaret		
1447	Marriage of Edward's eldest sister Anne (*b.*1439) to Henry Holland, Duke of Exeter		
1449	Edward and his brother Edmund established at Ludlow Castle		

Date	Personal	Political	General
21 Oct.	Birth of Edward's second surviving brother, George		
1450 July			Loss of Normandy; Jack Cade's Uprising
1451 Apr.			Thomas Young demands the Duke of York be recognised as King Henry VI's heir
1452 Mar.		Richard, Duke of York's abortive coup at Dartford. Edward rumoured to be marching on London with 10,000 men	
1452 2 Oct.	Birth of Edward's youngest brother, Richard		
1453 17 July			Battle of Castillon
c. Aug.			Henry VI falls ill
19 Oct.			Capitulation of Bordeaux; loss of Gascony
1454 Jan.		Edward accompanies his father to London for parliament for the first time	York's first protectorate
1454 Dec.			Henry VI recovers
1455	Birth of Edward's youngest sister, Ursula		End of York's first protectorate
22 May			First battle of St Albans
1455 Nov.– 1456 Feb.			York's second protectorate
1458 25 Mar.			'Love-day' at St Paul's

Date	Personal	Political	General
1459 23 Sep.			Battle of Blore Heath
12–13 Oct.		Rout at Ludford bridge; Edward flees to Calais	
2 Nov.		Edward reaches Calais	
20 Nov. – 20 Dec.		Parliament at Coventry; Edward, his father, brother and supporters are attainted	
1460 15 Jan.			John Dynham's first raid on Sandwich. Capture of Lords Rivers and Scales
23 Apr.			Battle of Newnham Bridge
June			Dynham's second raid on Sandwich
26 June		Edward, Warwick and Salisbury land at Sandwich	
10 July		Battle of Northampton	
Sept./Oct.		York lands at Chester, makes his way to London and stakes his claim to the throne	
30 Dec.	Death of Edward's father, brother Edmund and uncle at the battle of Wakefield		
1461 2/3 Feb.		Battle of Mortimer's Cross	
17 Feb.			2nd Battle of St Albans
4 Mar.		Edward proclaimed King	
29 Mar.		Battle of Towton; decisive defeat of the Lancastrians	

Date	Personal	Political	General
1 May		Execution of the Earl of Wiltshire in Edward's presence	
June			Scottish–Lancastrian raid on Carlisle repelled Henry VI dislodged from Brancepeth Castle
28 June		Coronation of Edward IV at Westminster	
9 Sept.		Execution of Sir Baldwin Fulford in Edward's presence	
30 Sept.			Surrender of Pembroke Castle
Oct.			Battle of Twt Hill
24 Oct.			Surrender of Guisnes Castle
1462 May			Surrender of Careg Cennen Castle
Oct.		Edward sits in judgement in the court of King's Bench	
Dec.	Edward detained at Durham by the measles		
1463 June			Henry VI and Queen Margaret invade Co. Durham with a Scottish army
Dec.			Duke of Somerset defects to the Lancastrian cause
1464 Apr.			Battle of Hedgeley Moor
1464 1 May	Clandestine marriage to Elizabeth Wydeville		
15 May			Battle of Hexham

Date	Personal	Political	General
23/24 June			Surrender of Alnwick and Dunstanborough castles
Sept.		Edward's marriage to Elizabeth Wydeville made public	
1465 27 May		Coronation of Queen Elizabeth	
13 July			Capture of Henry VI
Sep.			Enthronement of George Neville as Archbishop of York
1466 11 Feb.	Birth of Edward's first daughter, Princess Elizabeth		
1467 8 June		Archbishop Neville dismissed as chancellor	
15 June			Death of Philip the Good, Duke of Burgundy
Aug.	Birth of a second daughter, Princess Mary		
1468 Jan./Feb.		First rumours of rebel gatherings in Yorkshire under a leader called Robin	
June			Arrest of the agent Cornelius; treason trial of Sir Thomas Cook
3 July	Marriage of Margaret of York to Charles the Bold of Burgundy		
Aug.			Surrender of Harlech Castle

Date	Personal	Political	General
1469 Jan.		Execution of the Hungerford and Courtenay heirs at Salisbury	
1469 20 Mar.	Birth of a third daughter, Princess Cecily		
Apr.–June			Northern risings under 'Robin of Redesdale' and 'Robin of Holderness'
7–26 June	Edward goes on pilgrimage to Bury St Edmunds and Walsingham		
11 July			Marriage of the Duke of Clarence to Warwick's daughter Isabel
16 July			Warwick and Clarence land in Kent
25 July			Battle of Edgecote; execution of the Earl of Pembroke
29 July	Edward arrested by Archbishop Neville, and subsequently held captive in Warwick and Middleham castles		
12 Aug.			Execution of Earl Rivers and Sir John Wydeville at Coventry
17 Aug.			Execution of the Earl of Devon at Bridgwater
c. 10 Sep.	Edward regains his liberty		

Date	Personal	Political	General
29 Sep.		Execution of Sir Humphrey and Charles Neville at York	
1470 12 Mar.			Battle of Empingham ('Lose-Cote field')
20 Mar.			Battle of Nibley Green
25 Mar.			Restoration of the Earl of Northumberland
9 Apr.			Warwick and Clarence sail for Calais
22 July			Reconciliation of Warwick and Queen Margaret
13 Sep.			Warwick's fleet lands in Devon
2 Oct.	Edward sails for Flanders		
3 Oct.	Edward lands on the Dutch island of Texel		
6 Oct.			Henry VI released from the Tower and formally restored; beginning of the 'readeption'
11 Oct.	Edward's party reaches The Hague		
2 Nov.	Birth of Edward's first son, Prince Edward, in the sanctuary of Westminster Abbey		
1471 2–4 Jan.		Meeting between Edward and Charles the Bold of Burgundy at Aire	
11 Mar.		Edward sets sail from Flushing	

Date	Personal	Political	General
14 Mar.		Edward lands at Ravenspur	
3 Apr.		Reconciliation between Edward and Clarence	
11 Apr.		Edward enters London; end of Henry VI's readeption	
14 Apr.		Battle of Barnet; death of the Earl of Warwick	
2 May			Bastard of Fauconberg lands in Kent
4 May		Battle of Tewkesbury	
12 May			Fauconberg attacks London Bridge
21 May		Edward enters London in triumph	Death of Henry VI in the Tower of London
26 May			Submission of the Bastard of Fauconberg
1472 10 Apr.	Birth of a fourth daughter, Princess Margaret		
25 Apr.		Arrest of Archbishop Neville	
12 July	Marriage of the Duke of Gloucester to Warwick's daughter Anne		
11 Sept.		Treaty of Chateaugiron (alliance with Brittany)	
11 Dec.	Death of Princess Margaret		
1473	Birth of Gloucester's son, Richard		
28 May			Attempted landing of the Earl of Oxford at St Osyth

Date	Personal	Political	General
Aug.	Birth of Clarence's daughter, Margaret		
17 Aug.	Birth of a second son, Prince Richard, at Shrewsbury		
30 Sep.			Earl of Oxford seizes St Michael's Mount
1474 15 Feb.			Surrender of the Earl of Oxford
28 Feb.		Peace Treaty of Utrecht with the Hanseatic league	
25 July		Treaty of London (alliance with Burgundy)	
1475 21 Feb.	Birth of Clarence's first son, Edward		
4 July		Edward invades France	
29 Aug.		Meeting between Edward and Louis XI of France at Picquigny; peace treaty of Picquigny	
2 Nov.	Birth of a fifth daughter, Princess Anne		
1476 21–30 July	Reburial of the Duke of York and Earl of Rutland at Fotheringhay		
Nov.	Birth of Clarence's second son, Richard		
22 Dec.	Death of Clarence's wife, Duchess Isabel		
1477	Birth of a third son, Prince George		
1 Jan.	Death of Clarence's second son, Richard		

Date	Personal	Political	General
5 Jan.			Battle of Nancy; death of Charles the Bold
Apr.	Edward rumoured to be ill		
18 Aug.			Marriage of Maximilian of Austria to Mary of Burgundy
1478 15 Jan.	Marriage of Richard, Duke of York, to Anne Mowbray		
16 Jan.		Opening of parliament; trial of the Duke of Clarence	
18 Feb.		Execution of the Duke of Clarence	
1479	Birth of a sixth daughter, Princess Katharine		
Mar.	Death of Prince George		
7 Aug.			Burgundian victory over the French at Guinegatte
1480 Aug.		Scottish raid into the East March; burning of Bamborough. Edward declares war on Scotland	
10 Nov.	Birth of a seventh daughter, Princess Bridget		
1482 27 Mar.			Death of Mary of Burgundy
23 May	Death of Princess Mary		
24 Aug.		Berwick-upon-Tweed surrendered by the Scots	
23 Dec.			Treaty of Arras between Burgundy and France

Date	Personal	Political	General
1483 Jan.		Duke of Gloucester created hereditary warden of the West March and given palatine powers in Cumberland	
late Mar.	Edward falls ill		
6 Apr.	Rumour of Edward's death reaches York		
9 Apr.	Death of Edward IV		
17–19 Apr.	Edward IV's funeral		
26 June		Edward's son, Edward V, deposed by Richard of Gloucester who succeeds as Richard III	

FURTHER READING

SOURCES

Extracts from many of the principal sources for Edward's reign are collected in modern English translation in *Edward IV: A Sourcebook*, ed. Keith Dockray (Stroud, 1999). Full editions of most of the chronicles and newsletters of the period have been available in print for a number of years, several of them providing a translation parallel to the original text. Among the more important are 'Warkworth's Chronicle', recently newly edited in *Death and Dissent: Two Fifteenth Century Chronicles*, ed. L.M. Matheson (Woodbridge, 1999); *The Historie of the Arrivall of King Edward IV A.D. 1471*, ed. J. Bruce (London, Camden Society original series 1, 1838); *The Crowland Chronicle Continuations*, ed. Nicholas Pronay and John Cox (London, 1986); *Ingulph's Chronicle of the Abbey of Croyland*, ed. H.T. Riley (London, 1854); *Great Chronicle of London*, ed. A.H. Thomas and I.D. Thornley (London, 1938).

A colourful personal take on many of the events of the reign is provided by various collections of correspondence from the period. The best known of these are the letters of the East Anglian Paston family, now available in a new and expanded edition as *Paston Letters and Papers of the Fifteenth Century*, ed. N. Davis, R. Beadle and C. Richmond (3 vols, Oxford, 2004–5). Less expansive, but nevertheless useful are the letters of the Plumpton and Stonor families, respectively based in Yorkshire and Oxfordshire: *The Plumpton Letters and Papers*, ed. Joan Kirby (Cambridge, 1996) and *Kingsford's Stonor Letters and Papers, 1290–1483*, ed. C. Carpenter (Cambridge, 1996).

A useful, if at times confused, continental perspective is provided by the correspondence of various Italian and German ambassadors and merchants based in England, France and the Low Countries. Much of the relevant Italian correspondence is available calendared in modern English as *Calendar of State Papers and Manuscripts Existing in the Archives and Collections of Milan*, Vol. 1, 1385–1618, ed. A.B. Hinds (London, 1912) and *Calendar of State Papers and Manuscripts Existing in the Archives and Collections of Venice*, Vol. 1, 1202–1509, ed. R. Brown, (London 1864). Of the German letters only the most important has been published in English translation, most recently as Hannes Kleineke, 'Gerhard von Wesel's Newsletter from England, 17 April 1471', *The Ricardian*, 16 (2006), pp. 66–83, but other relevant material is printed in its original language in *Hanserecesse von 1431–1476*, ed. G. von der Ropp and D. Schäfer (7 vols, Leipzig, 1876–92) and *Hanserecesse von 1477–1530*, ed. D. Schäfer and F. Techen (9 vols, Leipzig, 1881–1913). The memoirs of the Franco-Burgundian agent Philippe de Commynes have recently been re-edited in French by Joël Blanchard, as *Philippe de Commynes: Mémoires* (2 vols, Geneva, 2007); there are a number of English translations, the most accessible (if incomplete) of which is *Memoirs of Philippe de Commynes: The Reign of Louis XI, 1461–83*, ed. Michael Jones (Harmondsworth, 1972). The standard edition of Jean de Wavrin's chronicles is still *Recueil des croniques et anciennes istories de la Grant Bretaigne, a present nomme Engleterre par Jehan de Waurin, Seigneur Du Forestel*, ed. W. Hardy and E. L.C.P. Hardy (5 vols, London, Rolls Series 39, 1864–91); some interesting supplementary documents are printed in the older edition *Anchiennes Croniques d'Engleterre par Jehan de Wavrin*, ed. L.M.E. Dupont (3 vols, Paris, 1858–63).

GENERAL

To date the best concise modern account of Edward's reign remains Charles Ross, *Edward IV* (London, 1974). Rather fuller, and unsurpassed in its use of the original sources, is Cora Scofield, *The Life and Reign of*

Edward the Fourth (London, 1923), although in minor points this work has over the years been subject to correction by other authors. An idiosyncratic study of the king is Jonathan Hughes, *Arthurian Myths and Alchemy: The Kingship of Edward IV* (Stroud, 2002), which seeks to explain Edward's reign against the background of its contemporary world of thought.

THE WARS OF THE ROSES

Context for Edward's reign is provided by a number of broad discussions of the Wars of the Roses, most notably John Gillingham, *The Wars of the Roses* (London, 1981), A.J. Pollard, *Late Medieval England 1399–1509* (Harlow, 2000) and the essays collected in *The Wars of the Roses*, ed. A.J. Pollard (Basingstoke, 1995). For a detailed account of the events of Henry VI's troubled reign that led up to Edward's accession Ralph Griffiths's magisterial *The Reign of Henry VI* (London, 1981) remains unsurpassed, but Bertram Wolffe's shorter *Henry VI* (London, 1981) and J.L. Watts's more recent analysis of the politics of the reign, *Henry VI and the Politics of Kingship* (Cambridge, 1996) are also worth consulting.

Several other works look at the wars from a specific angle. A constitutionalist perspective is provided by Christine Carpenter, *The Wars of the Roses: Politics and the Constitution in England, c. 1437–1509* (Cambridge, 1997), while P.A. Haigh, *The Military Campaigns of the Wars of the Roses* (Stroud, 1995), Anthony Goodman, *The Wars of the Roses: Military Activity and English Society, 1452–97* (London, 1981) and the same author's *The Wars of the Roses: The Soldiers' Experience* (Stroud, 2005) are concerned with the details of the individual battles and the impact of the civil wars.

Several of Edward's more important contemporaries have in recent years been the subject of book-length studies, among them Charles Ross's account of the career of Richard of Gloucester, *Richard III* (Yale, 1981); A.J. Pollard's new study of Edward's early ally and erstwhile nemesis, *Warwick the Kingmaker* (London, 2007); and Michael Hicks's series of biographical works, including *False, Fleeting, Perjur'd Clarence: George, Duke of Clarence, 1449–1478* (Gloucester, 1980), *Warwick the Kingmaker* (Oxford, 1998), and (of particular interest for the end of Edward's reign) *Edward V* (Stroud, 2003).

EDWARD'S MARRIAGE AND THE RISE OF THE WYDEVILLES

The role of the Wydevilles was comprehensively reassessed by J.R. Lander, *Crown and Nobility 1450–1509* (London, 1976), esp. pp. 104–25. Lander's views have since been challenged by Michael Hicks, 'The Changing Role of the Wydevilles in Yorkist Politics to 1483', in *Patronage, Pedigree and Power*, ed. C.D. Ross (Gloucester, 1979), pp. 60–86. Edward's queen herself has become the subject of scrutiny. The evolution of her image is discussed by A.J. Pollard, 'Elizabeth Woodville and her Historians', in *Traditions and Transformations in Late Medieval England*, ed. D. Biggs, A.C. Reeves and S. Michalove (Leiden, 2001), pp. 145–58; a study of Elizabeth's career and queenship may be found in J.L. Laynesmith, *The Last Medieval Queens: English Queenship 1445–1503* (Oxford, 2004).

THE CRISIS OF 1468–71

The atmosphere of suspicion that prevailed in 1468 is exemplified by the case of Sir Thomas Cook, which is discussed by A.F. Sutton, 'Sir Thomas Cook and his Troubles: An Investigation', *Guildhall Studies in London History* 3, No. 2, April 1978, pp. 85–108, and M.A. Hicks, 'The Case of Sir Thomas Cook', *English Historical Review*, 93 (1978), pp. 82–96. Perhaps the best modern account of the confused events of 1469–70 is found in Michael Hicks, *Warwick the Kingmaker* (see above). Edward's exile in the Low Countries is explored by Maaike Lulofs, 'King Edward IV in Exile', *The Ricardian*, 3 (1974), pp. 9–11; Rosemary Horrox, 'Preparation for Edward IV's Return from Exile', *The Ricardian*, 6 (1978), pp. 124–27; Livia Visser-Fuchs, '"Il n'a pas lion ne lieppart, qui voeulle tenir de sa part": Edouard IV in Exile, October 1470 to March 1471', in *L'Angleterre et les pays bourguignons: relations et comparaisons (XVe-XVIe s.)*, ed. Jean-Marie Cauchies (Neuchâtel, 1995), pp. 91–106. A detailed narrative of Edward's recovery of his kingdom in 1471 is provided by P.W. Hammond, *The Battles of Barnet and Tewkesbury* (Gloucester, 1990).

YORKIST GOVERNMENT AND ADMINISTRATION

The most important work on Edward's government and administration is still that done by Jack Lander in the 1960s and 1970s. Many of his seminal essays are gathered in J.R. Lander, *Crown and Nobility, 1450–1509* (London, 1976). Rather less attention has been given to Edward IV's parliaments. The biographies of the members of the Commons for the reign published by J.C. Wedgwood and A.D. Holt, *The History of Parliament: Biographies of the Members of the Commons House, 1439–1509* (London, 1936) will shortly be superseded by new ones in *The History of Parliament: The Commons 1461–1504*, ed. L.S. Clark (forthcoming). Aspects of the workings of parliament are discussed, *inter alia*, by M.A. Hicks, 'King in Lords and Commons: Three Insights into Late-Fifteenth-Century Parliaments 1461–85', in *People, Places and Perspectives*, ed. K. Dockray and P. Fleming (Stroud, 2005), pp. 131–53, and Colin Richmond, 'The Nobility and the Wars of the Roses: The Parliamentary Session of January 1461', *Parliamentary History*, 18 (1999), pp. 261–9.

EDWARDIAN COURT LIFE AND CULTURE

Much work has been done in recent years on the culture of Edward's court, its music and display and the king's royal library. Some examples include R. Rastall, 'The Minstrels and Trumpeters of Edward IV: Some Further Thoughts', *Plainsong & Medieval Music*, 13 (2004), pp. 163–9; J. Backhouse, 'Memorials and Manuscripts of a Yorkist Elite', in *St. George's Chapel, Windsor, in the Late Middle Ages*, ed. C. Richmond and E. Scarff (Windsor, 2001), pp. 151–60; A.F. Sutton and L. Visser-Fuchs, 'The Cult of Angels in Late Fifteenth Century England: An Hours of the Guardian Angel Presented to Queen Elizabeth Woodville', in *Women and the Book*: *Assessing the Visual Evidence*, ed. J.H.M. Taylor and L. Smith, (London, 1996), pp. 230–65; '"Chevalerie ... in som partie is worthi forto be comendid, and in some part to ben amendid": Chivalry and the Yorkist Kings', in *St. George's Chapel, Windsor, in the Late Middle Ages*, ed. C. Richmond and E. Scarff (Windsor, 2001), pp. 107–33; A.F. Sutton, L. Visser-Fuchs and P.W. Hammond, *The Reburial of Richard, Duke of York, 21–30 July 1476* (London, 1996); A.F. Sutton and L. Visser-Fuchs with R.A. Griffiths, *The Royal Funerals of the House of York at Windsor* (London, 2005).

Notes

1 INTRODUCTION

1 Sean Cunningham, *Richard III: a Royal Enigma*, Kew: TNA, 2003; Sean Cunningham, *Henry VII*, London: Routledge, 2007, p. 3.

2 Jane Austen, *Juvenilia*, ed. Peter Sabor, Cambridge: Cambridge University Press, 2006, p. 178.

3 John Farman, *The Very Boring History of Britain without the Boring Bits*, London: Piccadilly Press, 1990, p. 52.

4 Keith Dockray, 'Edward IV: Playboy or Politician?', *The Ricardian*, 10, 1995, pp. 306–25; A.J. Pollard, 'Elizabeth Woodville and her Historians', in *Traditions and Transformations in Late Medieval England*, ed. D. Biggs, A.C. Reeves and S. Michalove, Leiden: Brill, 2001, pp. 145–58.

5 *The Usurpation of Richard the Third*, ed. C.A.J. Armstrong, Gloucester: Alan Sutton, 1989, pp. 59, 61, 67.

6 *The Crowland Chronicle Continuations: 1459–1486*, ed. Nicholas Pronay and John Cox, London: Richard III and Yorkist History Trust, 1986, pp. 143, 147, 151.

7 Sir Thomas More, 'History of King Richard III', in *Richard III: The Great Debate*, ed. Paul Kendall, London: Folio Society, 1965, p. 32.

8 Charles Ross, *Edward IV*, London: Eyre Methuen, 1974, pp. 434–5.

9 *Polydore Vergil's English History*, ed. Henry Ellis, London: Camden Society original series 29, 1844, p. 172.

10 Ibid.; More, 'Richard III', p. 32.

11 P. de Rapin-Thoyras, *The History of England*, transl. N. Tindal, 15 vols, London, 1725–31, Vol. 6, pp. 148–51.

12 Ross, *Edward IV*, pp. 418–19; Rapin-Thoyras, *History of England*, p. 150.

13 D. Hume, *The History of England*, 6 vols, Boston: Philipps, Sampson & Co., 1858, Vol. 2, p. 483.

14 Ross, *Edward IV*, p. 419.

15 J.R. Green, *History of the English People*, 4 vols, London: Macmillan, 1877–80, Vol. 2, pp. 27–8, 51.

16 K.B. McFarlane, 'The Wars of the Roses', in K. B. McFarlane, *England in the Fifteenth Century*, London: Hambledon, 1981, p. 256.

17 Ross, *Edward IV*, pp. 420, 426.

18 J. Hughes, *Arthurian Myths and Alchemy: The Kingship of Edward IV*, Stroud: Sutton, 2002, pp. 192–3.

19 M.K. Jones, *Bosworth 1485: Psychology of a Battle*, Stroud: Tempus, 2002, pp. 67–70.

20 For examples, see the suggestions for further reading provided on page 228.

21 P. Johnson, *Duke Richard of York*, Oxford: Clarendon Press, 1988; M.A. Hicks, '*False, Fleeting, Perjur'd Clarence': George, Duke of Clarence, 1449–1478*, 2nd, revised, edn, Bangor: Headstart History, 1992; C.D. Ross, *Richard III*, London: Eyre Methuen, 1981; M.A. Hicks, *Edward V*, Stroud: Tempus, 2003; M.A. Hicks, *Warwick the Kingmaker*, Oxford: Blackwell, 1998.

22 Dockray, 'Edward IV: Playboy or Politician?' pp. 306–25.

23 Christine Carpenter, *The Wars of the Roses: Politics and the Constitution in England c. 1437–1509*, Cambridge: Cambridge University Press, 1997, p. 205.

24 Hicks, *Edward IV*, pp. 94, 230.

25 A.J. Pollard, *Late Medieval England 1399–1509*, Harlow: Longman, 2000, pp. 319–20.

26 Colin Richmond, 'Edward's Second Reign', in *The Politics of Fifteenth Century England: John Vale's Book*, ed. M.L. Kekewich, Colin Richmond, A.F. Sutton, Livia Visser-Fuchs and J.L. Watts, Stroud: Alan Sutton, 1995, pp. 43–4, 67, 71–2.

27 J.P. Cooper, 'Introduction', in K.B. McFarlane, *The Nobility of Later Medieval England*, Oxford: Clarendon Press, 1973, p. xxxvii.

28 Ibid.

29 For the debate over the chronicler's identity see *Crowland Chronicle Continuations: 1459–1486*, ed. N. Pronay and J. Cox, pp. 78–98, A.J. Pollard, 'Memoirs of a Yorkist Civil Servant', *The Ricardian*, 7, 1987, pp. 380–5 and the responses, ibid. pp. 498–524, and most recently M.A. Hicks, 'The Second Anonymous Continuation of the Crowland Abbey Chronicle 1459–86 Revisited', *English Historical Review*, 122, 2007, pp. 349–70 and the literature cited there.

30 *Recueil des croniques et anchiennes Istories de la Grant Bretaigne, a present nomme Engleterre, par Jehan de Waurin, seigneur du Forestel*, ed. W. Hardy and E.L.C.P. Hardy, 5 vols, London: HMSO, 1864–91; *Philippe de Commynes: Mémoires*, ed. Joël Blanchard, 2 vols, Geneva: Droz, 2007.

31 *The Great Chronicle of London*, ed. A.H. Thomas and I.D. Thornley, London, 1938; *Historical Collections of a Citizen of London in the Fifteenth Century*, ed. J. Gairdner, London: Camden Society new series 17, 1876.

32 *The Maire of Bristowe is Kalendar*, ed. L. Toulmin Smith, London: Camden Society new series 5, 1872; *Six Town Chronicles*, ed. R. Flenley, Oxford, 1911; *Records of Early English Drama: Coventry*, ed. R.W. Ingram, Manchester, 1981, pp. xxxvii, xli; *The Description of the Citie of Excester*, ed. W.J. Harte, J.W. Schopp and H. Tapley-Soper, 3 vols, Exeter: Devon and Cornwall Record Society, 1919–47.

33 *The Historie of the Arrivall of King Edward IV A.D. 1471*, ed. J. Bruce, London: Camden Society original series 1, 1838; R.F. Green, 'The Short Version of The Arrival of Edward IV', *Speculum*, 56, 1981, pp. 324–36; 'Chronicle of the Rebellion in Lincolnshire, in 1470', ed. J.G. Nichols, *Camden Miscellany I*, London: Camden Society, 1847; Livia Visser-Fuchs, 'Edward IV's Memoir on Paper to Charles, Duke of Burgundy: The So-called "Short Version of the Arrivall"', *Nottingham Medieval Studies*, 36, 1992, pp. 167–227; Lina Visser-Fuchs, 'Jean de Wavrin and the English newsletters: The *Chronicle of the Rebellion in Lincolnshire*', *Nottingham Mediaeval Studies*, 47, 2003, 217–35.

34 *Calendar of State Papers and Manuscripts Existing in the Archives and Collections of Venice*, Vol. 1, 1202–1509, ed. R. Brown, London: HMSO, 1864; *Calendar of State Papers and Manuscripts Existing in the Archives and Collections of Milan*, Vol. 1, 1385–1618, ed. A.B. Hinds, London: HMSO, 1912; *Paston Letters and Papers of the Fifteenth Century*, ed. N. Davis, R. Beadle and C. Richmond, 3 vols, Oxford: Oxford University Press, 2004–5; *Kingsford's Stonor Letters and Papers, 1290–1483*, ed. C. Carpenter, Cambridge: Cambridge University Press, 1996; *The Plumpton Letters and Papers*, ed. Joan Kirby, Cambridge: Cambridge University Press, 1996; H. Kleineke, 'Gerhard von Wesel's Newsletter from England, 17 April 1471', *The Ricardian*, 16, 2006, pp. 66–83.

35 The case for the active Henry VI is made above all by R.A. Griffiths, *The Reign of King Henry VI*, London: Ernest Benn, 1981; that for the cipher by J.L. Watts, *Henry VI and the Politics of Kingship*, Cambridge: Cambridge University Press, 1996.

36 R.A. Griffiths, 'The Sense of Dynasty in the Reign of Henry VI', in *Patronage, Pedigree and Power in Later Medieval England*, ed. C. Ross, Gloucester: Alan Sutton, 1979, pp. 13–36, esp. pp. 17–21.

37 Griffiths, *Henry VI*, pp. 515–22.

38 Ibid., pp. 610–49; R.L. Storey, *The End of the House of Lancaster*, 2nd edn, Gloucester: Alan Sutton, 1986, pp. 61–8.

39 Carpenter, *Wars of the Roses*, pp. 116–20.

40 Griffiths, *Henry VI*, p. 674.

41 Griffiths, 'Sense of Dynasty', pp. 20–2.

42 Griffiths, *Henry VI*, p. 692.

43 Ibid., p. 695.

44 Storey, *The End of the House of Lancaster*, pp. 93–104; M. Jurkowski, C.L. Smith and D. Crook, *Lay Taxes in England and Wales, 1188–1688*, Kew: Public Record Office [hereafter PRO], 1998, pp. 104–8.

45 R.A. Griffiths, 'The King's Council and the First Protectorate of the Duke of York, 1450–1454', *English Historical Review*, 99, 1984, pp. 67–82; R. A. Griffiths, 'Local Rivalries and National Politics: The Percies, the Nevilles and the Duke of Exeter, 1452–1454', *Speculum*, 43, 1968, pp. 589–632; M.K. Jones, 'Somerset, York and the Wars of the Roses', *English Historical Review*, 104, 1989, pp. 285–307.

46 B.P. Wolffe, *Henry VI*, London: Eyre Methuen, 1981, pp. 311–12.

2 THE MAKING OF A KING

1 C.L. Scofield, *The Life and Reign of Edward the Fourth*, 2 vols, London: Longman, 1923, Vol. 1, p. 92; PRO, C49/54, no. 8.

2 M.A. Hicks, *'False, Fleeting, Perjur'd Clarence': George, duke of Clarence, 1449–1478*, 2nd, revised, edn, Bangor: Headstart History, 1992, p. 149.

3 *The Usurpation of Richard the Third*, ed. C.A.J. Armstrong, Gloucester: Alan Sutton, 1989, pp. 61–2; C.D. Ross, *Richard III*, London: Eyre Methuen, 1981, pp. 88–9.

4 M.K. Jones, *Bosworth 1485: Psychology of a Battle*, Stroud: Tempus, 2002, pp. 67–70; M.A. Hicks, *Edward V*, Stroud: Tempus, 2003, pp. 25–6. But nb that a heraldic MS of *c.* 1475 suggests that the king may have been baptised in the cathedral after all, Hicks, *Edward V*, p. 206.

5 R.A. Griffiths, *The Reign of King Henry VI*, London: Ernest Benn, 1981, p. 719.

6 R.A. Griffiths, 'The Sense of Dynasty in the Reign of Henry VI', in *Patronage, Pedigree and Power in Later Medieval England*, ed. C. Ross, Gloucester: Alan Sutton, 1979, pp. 13–36, at p. 23; Frederic Madden, 'Political Poems of the Reigns of Henry VI. and Edward IV.', *Archaeologia*, 29, 1842, pp. 318–47, at p. 332.

7 Charles Ross, *Edward IV*, London: Eyre Methuen, 1974, p. 7.

8 Ibid.

9 BL, Cotton Vespasian F.III, printed in *Original Letters illustrative of English History*, 1st series, ed. H. Ellis, 3 vols, London: Harding, Triphook and Lepard, 1824, Vol. 1, pp. 9–10.

10 Ross, *Edward IV*, pp. 8–9; *A Collection of Ordinances and Regulations for the Government of the Royal Household, Made in Divers Reigns*, London: Society of Antiquaries, 1790, pp. *27–*28; Hicks, *Edward V*, pp. 70–1; *The Household of Edward IV: The Black Book and the Ordinance of 1478*, ed. A.R. Myers, Manchester: University Press, 1959, pp. 126–7; The National Archives: PRO, C66/531, m. 3.

11 A.F. Sutton and L. Visser Fuchs, 'Choosing a Book in Late Fifteenth-century England and Burgundy', in *England and the Low Countries in the Late Middle Ages*, ed. C. Barron and N. Saul, Stroud: Alan Sutton, 1995, p. 75.

12 Ibid., pp. 80, 86; A.F. Sutton and L. Visser Fuchs, *Richard III's Books: Ideal and Reality in the Life of a Late Medieval Prince*, Stroud: Sutton, 1997, pp. 31–5.

13 Sutton and Visser Fuchs, 'Choosing a Book', p. 75.

14 *Philippe de Commynes: Mémoires*, ed. Joël Blanchard, 2 vols, Geneva: Droz, 2007, Vol. 1, p. 290.

15 Ross, *Edward IV*, p. 270.

16 M. Hicks, *Edward IV*, London: Arnold, 2004, pp. 11–14.

17 Hicks, *Edward IV*, pp. 17–18.

18 Griffiths, *Henry VI*, p. 703.

19 Ross, *Edward IV*, p. 14.

20 Ibid.

21 H. Kleineke, 'Lady Joan Dinham: A Fifteenth-Century West-Country Matriarch', in *Social Attitudes and Political Structures in the Fifteenth Century*, ed. T. Thornton, Stroud: Sutton, 2000, pp. 69–87, at pp. 75–7.

22 Scofield, *Edward the Fourth*, Vol. 1, pp. 44, 51.

23 *Paston Letters and Papers of the Fifteenth Century*, ed. N. Davis, R. Beadle and C. Richmond, 3 vols, Oxford: Oxford University Press, 2004–5, Vol. 1, No. 88.

24 Scofield, *Edward the Fourth*, Vol. 1, p. 62.

25 Ibid., pp. 64–5; Ross, *Edward IV*, p. 26.

26 *Recueil des Croniques et anchiennes Istories de la Grant Bretaigne, a present nomme Engleterre, par Jehan de Waurin, seigneur du Forestel*, ed. W. Hardy and E.L.C.P. Hardy, 5 vols, London: HMSO, 1864–91, Vol. 5, pp. 292–3.

27 *An English Chronicle*, ed. J.S. Davies, London: Camden Society old series 64, 1856, p. 93.

28 Madden, 'Political Poems', pp. 331–2.

29 Scofield, *Edward the Fourth*, Vol. 1, pp. 85–6.

30 Ross, *Edward IV*, p. 27.

31 Ibid.; Griffiths, *Henry VI*, pp. 864–5.

32 *Calendar of State Papers and Manuscripts existing in the Archives and Collections of Milan*, Vol. 1, 1385–1618, ed. A.B. Hinds, London: HMSO, 1912, p. 27.

33 *Recueil des Croniques*, Vol. 5, p. 305.

34 Ibid., p. 318.

35 Scofield, *Edward the Fourth*, Vol. 1, pp. 94–5.

36 Ibid., p. 105.

37 *Paston Letters*, ed. Davis, Beadle and Richmond, Vol. 2, no. 613.

38 *Calendar of State Papers Milan*, ed. Hinds, p. 38.

39 Scofield, *Edward the Fourth*, Vol. 1, pp. 116–17.

40 This is proven conclusively by the Shrewsbury borough accounts: Shropshire Record Office, Shrewsbury bailiffs' accts. 3365/899, f. 16. I am grateful for this reference to Dr Simon Payling. Ross, *Edward IV*, p. 31, following the 'Short English chronicle'; *Three Fifteenth Century Chronicles*, ed. J. Gairdner, London: Camden Society new series 28, 1880, p. 76, places him (apparently wrongly) at Gloucester.

41 *English Chronicle*, ed. Davies, p. 110 gives 3 Feb. for the battle and 2 Feb. for the portent.

42 Christopher Allmand, *Henry V*, London: Methuen, 1992, p. 91.

43 *English Chronicle*, ed. Davies, p. 110.

44 Scofield, *Edward the Fourth*, Vol. 1, p. 149, following William Worcester's annals; according to Gregory's chronicle the meeting took place at Burford: *Historical Collections of a Citizen of London in the Fifteenth Century*, ed. J. Gairdner, London: Camden Society new series 17, 1876, p. 215.

45 *Historical Collections*, ed. Gairdner, p. 215.

46 Griffiths, *Henry VI*, p. 874.

47 *Paston Letters*, ed. Davis, Beadle and Richmond, Vol. 1, no. 114.

48 *Calendar of State Papers Milan*, ed. Hinds, p. 39.

49 Madden, 'Political Poems', p. 345.

50 Scofield, *Edward the Fourth*, Vol. 1, p. 150.

3 THE ESTABLISHMENT OF EDWARD'S RULE, 1461–5

1 Charles Ross, *Edward IV*, London: Eyre Methuen, 1974, p. 10.

2 *Historical Collections of a Citizen of London in the Fifteenth Century*, ed. J. Gairdner, London: Camden Society new series 17, 1876, p. 215; C.L. Scofield, *The Life and Reign of Edward the Fourth*, 2 vols, London: Longman, 1923, Vol. 1, p. 149; Ross, *Edward IV*, p. 32.

3 *Calendar of State Papers and Manuscripts Existing in the Archives and Collections of Venice*, Vol. 1, 1202–1509, ed. R. Brown, London: HMSO, 1864, no. 374.

4 PRO, KB145/7/1.

5 R.A. Griffiths, *The Reign of King Henry VI*, London: Ernest Benn, 1981, pp. 874–5; *Calendar of State Papers Venice*, ed. Brown, no. 370.

6 *Calendar of State Papers Venice*, ed. Brown, no. 370.

7 Eight years later, one of Edward's companions on this ride, Humphrey, Lord Stafford, would ask in his will that restitution be made for the goods and money that had been unlawfully taken: *Somerset Medieval Wills 1383–1500*, ed. F.W. Weaver, London: Somerset Record Society, Vol. 16, 1901, pp. 196–201.

8 Scofield, *Edward the Fourth*, Vol. 1, p. 182.

9 Ibid.

10 PRO, C81/1488/3–4.

11 Ross, *Edward IV*, p. 43.

12 Ibid., p. 49.

13 Ibid., p. 51.

14 J. Hughes, *Arthurian Myths and Alchemy: the Kingship of Edward IV*, Stroud: Sutton, 2002, p. 193.

15 M.A. Hicks, 'Edward IV, the Duke of Somerset and Lancastrian Loyalism in the North', in M.A. Hicks, *Richard III and his Rivals: Magnates and their Motives in the War of the Roses*, London: Hambledon, 1991, pp. 149–63, esp. pp. 151–7.

16 Ross, *Edward IV*, pp. 50–1.

17 Ibid., p. 53.

18 M. Jurkowski, C.L. Smith and D. Crook, *Lay Taxes in England and Wales, 1188–1688*, Kew: PRO, 1998, pp. 109–10; Ross, *Edward IV*, p. 55.

19 Ross, *Edward IV*, pp. 60–1.

20 Scofield, *Edward the Fourth*, Vol. 1, p. 381.

21 *Calendar of State Papers Venice*, ed. Brown, nos 372, 374.

22 Ross, *Edward IV*, p. 63; *Anchiennes Croniques d'Engleterre par Jehan de Wavrin*, ed. Dupont, 3 vols, Paris: Jules Renouard, 1858–63, Vol. 3, p. 184.

23 Ross, *Edward IV*, p. 63.

24 On what follows, see above all J.G. Bellamy, 'Justice under the Yorkist Kings', *American Journal of Legal History*, 9, 1965, pp. 135–55.

25 *Paston Letters and Papers of the Fifteenth Century*, ed. N. Davis, R. Beadle and C. Richmond, 3 vols, Oxford: Oxford University Press, 2004–5, Vol. 1, no. 117.

26 Ibid., Vol. 2, no. 663.

27 Ibid., no. 684.

28 Ibid., Vol. 1, no. 333.

29 PRO, KB27/806, rex rot. 3d, and also see C.H. Williams, 'A Fifteenth-Century Law Suit', *Law Quarterly Review*, 40, 1924, pp. 354–64. The reference cited by Bellamy, 'Justice under the Yorkist Kings', p. 139, n. 22, is based on a misreading of the King's bench plea roll for Easter term: Edward did not sit in King's Bench in Easter term 1462, most of which he spent in the midlands.

30 Ross, *Edward IV*, p. 70.

31 On this subject see I. Rowney, 'Resources and Retaining in Yorkist England: William, Lord Hastings and the Honour of Tutbury', in *Property and Politics*, ed. A.J. Pollard, Gloucester: Alan Sutton, 1984, pp. 139–55; I. Rowney, 'The Hastings Affinity in Staffordshire and the Honour of Tutbury', *Bulletin of the Institute of Historical Research*, 57, 1984, pp. 35–45; Ross, *Edward IV*, p. 75.

32 Ross, *Edward IV*, p. 71.

33 D.B. Quinn, 'Edward IV and Exploration', *Mariner's Mirror*, 21, 1935, pp. 275–84; D. B. Quinn, 'The argument for the English Discovery of America between 1480 and 1494', *Geographical Journal*, 127, 1961, pp. 227–85.

34 An exclusive market place for certain goods. Since the reign of Edward III all English wool exports had to be directed through Calais, after the loss of Gascony the sole English possession on the European mainland. The merchants of the Calais staple (the staplers) formed a tightly knit community.

35 The Teutonic (or German) Hanse (or Hanseatic league) was a loose federation of the merchant communities of towns in the Holy Roman Empire and the Baltic region. In England the Hanse had its principal headquarters in the London 'Steelyard'.

36 *Historical Collections of a Citizen of London in the Fifteenth Century*, ed. J. Gairdner, London: Camden Society new series 17, 1876, p. 227.

37 Ross, *Edward IV*, pp. 377–8.

38 Ibid., pp. 69–72.

4 FOREIGN POLICY, THE KING'S MARRIAGE AND THE BREAK WITH WARWICK, 1461–8

1 H.E.L. Collins, *The Order of the Garter, 1348–1461*, Oxford: Oxford University Press, 2000, pp. 53–62, 156, 288–95, 300.

2 Ibid., pp. 160, 168–70, 173.

3 C.D. Ross, *Edward IV*, London: Eyre Methuen, 1974, p. 105.

4 Ibid., p. 56; C.L. Scofield, *The Life and Reign of Edward the Fourth*, 2 vols, London: Longman, 1923, Vol. 2, pp. 469–70.

5 R.A. Griffiths, 'The Sense of Dynasty in the Reign of Henry VI', in *Patronage, Pedigree and Power in Later Medieval England*, ed. C. Ross, Gloucester: Alan Sutton, 1979, pp. 13–36, at p. 23; P. Johnson, *Duke Richard of York*, Oxford: Clarendon Press, 1988, pp. 48–50.

6 Ross, *Edward IV*, p. 84.

7   Ibid., pp. 84–5; Scofield, *Edward the Fourth*, Vol. 1, pp. 211–12, 247.

8   Scofield, *Edward the Fourth*, Vol. 1, p. 307.

9   Ibid.

10 M. Smith, 'England and Spain 1483: A Bride for Edward of Middleham?', *The Ricardian*, 6, 1983, pp. 229–34, at pp. 229–30.

11 Scofield, *Edward the Fourth*, Vol. 1, p. 346.

12 *Polydore Vergil's English History*, ed. Henry Ellis, London: Camden Society old series 29, 1844, p. 117.

13 Ibid., p. 172.

14 *The Usurpation of Richard the Third*, ed. C.A.J. Armstrong, Gloucester: Alan Sutton, 1989, p. 67.

15 Peter Hammond, 'The Illegitimate Children of Edward IV', *Tant D'Emprises – So Many Undertakings: Essays in Honour of Anne F. Sutton*, ed. Livia Visser-Fuchs, *The Ricardian*, 13, 2003, pp. 229–33 at p. 229.

16 Ross, *Edward IV*, p. 316.

17 The purported pre-contract with Eleanor Butler would later assume considerable political importance when it was cited as invalidating the King's marriage to Elizabeth Wydeville and thus bastardising his children.

18 John Ashdown-Hill, 'The Elusive Mistress: Elizabeth Lucy and her Family', *The Ricardian*, 11, 1999, pp. 490–505.

19 Ibid., p. 498.

20 PRO, E101/411/15, f. 14v.

21 *Usurpation of Richard the Third*, ed. Armstrong, pp. 66–9.

22 PRO, E101/412/8.

23 Ross, *Edward IV*, pp. 316–17; Hammond, 'Illegitimate Children', pp. 229–33. Hammond's identification of two other bastard children is problematic. The evidence for Isabel Mylbery's paternity is inconclusive, while the identification of the wife of Henry Harman, the clerk of the Crown in the court of King's bench, as a daughter of Edward IV is based on a misreading of the Kent Visitation of 1574 – it was Henry VII who married Edward's daughter, not Harman.

24 *Polydore Vergil*, ed. Ellis, p. 117.

25 *Anchiennes Croniques d'Engleterre par Jehan de Wavrin*, ed. Dupont, 3 vols, Paris: Jules Renouard, 1858–63, Vol. 2, p. 326.

26 *Calendar of State Papers and Manuscripts Existing in the Archives and Collections of Venice*, Vol. 1, 1202–1509, ed. R. Brown, London: HMSO, 1864, no. 395.

27 Livia Visser-Fuchs, 'English Events in Caspar Weinreich's Danzig Chronicle, 1461–1495', *The Ricardian*, 7, 1986, pp. 310–20, at pp. 312–13. The translation is my own.

28 *Usurpation of Richard the Third*, ed. Armstrong, p. 61.

29 *Letters and Papers Illustrative of the Reigns of Richard III and Henry VII*, ed. J. Gairdner, 2 vols, London: Longman, 1861, Vol. 1, p. 32.

30 PRO, C81/848/3926.

31 *Calendar of State Papers Venice*, ed. Brown, no. 372.

32 *Usurpation of Richard the Third*, ed. Armstrong, pp. 61–3.

33 *Anchiennes Croniques*, ed. Dupont, Vol. 2, p. 326.

34 M.A. Hicks, *Warwick the Kingmaker*, Oxford: Blackwell, 1998, p. 258.

35 Ross, *Edward IV*, p. 93; *Letters and Papers illustrative of the Wars of the English in France during the Reign of Henry VI*, ed. J. Stephenson, Vol. 2, Pt. 2, p. [783].

36 Ross, *Edward IV*, p. 94.

37 M.A. Hicks, 'The Changing Role of the Wydevilles in Yorkist Politics to 1483', in *Patronage, Pedigree and Power in Later Medieval England*, ed. C.D. Ross, Gloucester: Alan Sutton, 1979, pp. 60–86, repr. in M.A. Hicks, *Richard III and his Rivals: Magnates and their Motives in the Wars of the Roses*, London: Hambledon, 1990, p. 216.

38 A.J. Pollard, 'Elizabeth Woodville and her Historians', in *Traditions and Transformations in Late Medieval England*, ed. D. Biggs, A.C. Reeves and S. Michalove, Leiden: Brill, 2001, pp. 145–58.

39 Hicks, 'Changing Role', p. 219.

40 Ross, *Edward IV*, pp. 110, 115.

41 Ibid., pp. 104–7.

42 Scofield, *Edward the Fourth*, Vol. 1, pp. 401–2.

43 *Usurpation of Richard the Third*, ed. Armstrong, p. 63.

44 Ross, *Edward IV*, pp. 116–17.

5 CRISIS, EXILE AND RETURN, 1468–71

1 A.F. Sutton, 'Sir Thomas Cook and his Troubles: An Investigation', *Guildhall Studies in London History*, 3, No. 2, Apr. 1978, pp. 85–108; M.A. Hicks, 'The Case of Sir Thomas Cook', in M.A. Hicks, *Richard III and his Rivals: Magnates and their Motives in the War of the Roses*, London: Hambledon, 1991, pp. 419–33; Ross, *Edward IV*, p. 120 (for Isle of Wight); M.L. Kekewich, 'The Lancastrian Court in Exile', in *The Lancastrian Court*, ed. J. Stratford, Donington: Shaun Tyas, 2003, pp. 95–110, at pp. 102, 107–8 (for Fortescue).

2 *Ingulph's Chronicle of the Abbey of Croyland*, ed. H.T. Riley, London: Henry Bohn, 1854, p. 439.

3   *The Plumpton Letters and Papers*, ed. Joan Kirby, Cambridge: Cambridge University Press, 1996, p. 40.

4   John Warkworth, *A Chronicle of the First Thirteen Years of the Reign of Edward IV (1461–74)*, ed. J.O. Halliwell, London: Camden Society old series 10, 1839, p. 6; Charles Ross, *Edward IV*, London: Eyre Methuen, 1974, p. 123.

5   Ross, *Edward IV*, pp. 127–8.

6   Warkworth, *Chronicle*, ed. Halliwell, pp. 47–51.

7   *The Paston Letters*, ed. J. Gairdner, 5 vols, repr. Gloucester: Alan Sutton, 1986, Vol. 5, no. 719.

8   Warkworth, *Chronicle*, ed. Halliwell, pp. 46–7.

9   C.L. Scofield, *The Life and Reign of Edward the Fourth*, 2 vols, London: Longman, 1923, Vol. 1, p. 497.

10 Scofield, *Edward the Fourth*, vol 1, p. 541; Warkworth, *Chronicle*, ed. Halliwell, p. 11.

11 Scofield, *Edward the Fourth*, Vol. 1, pp. 498–9.

12 Warkworth, *Chronicle*, ed. Halliwell, p. 47.

13 *Calendar of State Papers and Manuscripts Existing in the Archives and Collections of Milan*, Vol. 1, 1385–1618, ed. A.B. Hinds, London: HMSO, 1912, nos. 173–4; Hicks, *Warwick*, 277–8.

14 M.A. Hicks, *'False, Fleeting, Perjur'd Clarence': George, Duke of Clarence, 1449–1478*, 2nd, revised, edn, Bangor: Headstart History, 1992, p. 38.

15 *The Crowland Chronicle Continuations: 1459–1486*, ed. Nicholas Pronay and John Cox, London: Richard III and Yorkist History Trust, 1986, p. 13; *Calendar of State Papers Milan*, ed. Hinds, no. 177; Charles Ross, *Edward IV*, London: Eyre Methuen, 1974, p. 135.

16 *Paston Letters and Papers of the Fifteenth Century*, ed. N. Davis, R. Beadle and C. Richmond, 3 vols, Oxford: Oxford University Press, 2004–5, Vol. 1, no. 245.

17 Ross, *Edward IV*, p. 136.

18 *Paston Letters*, ed. Davis, Beadle and Richmond, Vol. 1, no. 245.

19 Ross, *Edward IV*, p. 136.

20 P. Fleming and M. Wood, *Gloucestershire's Forgotten Battle: Nibley Green 1470*, Stroud: Tempus, 2003, pp. 51–94; Ross, *Edward IV*, p. 134.

21 Ross, *Edward IV*, pp. 139–40.

22 M.A. Hicks, *Warwick the Kingmaker*, Oxford: Blackwell, 1998, p. 284; Ross, *Edward IV*, p. 138.

23 Hicks, *Warwick*, pp. 282–3.

24 'Chronicle of the Rebellion in Lincolnshire, in 1470', ed. J.G. Nichols, *Camden Miscellany I*, London: Camden Society, 1847, p. 6.

25 Ross, *Edward IV*, p. 149.

26 Customarily, traitors were executed by hanging, drawing and quartering.

27 Hicks, *Warwick*, p. 287.

28 *Calendar of State Papers Milan*, ed. Hinds, no. 191.

29 *Paston Letters*, ed. Davis, Beadle and Richmond, Vol. 1, no. 256.

30 Hicks, Warwick, p. 297.

31 P.W. Hammond, *The Battles of Barnet and Tewkesbury*, Gloucester: Alan Sutton, 1990, pp. 36–7; Scofield, *Edward the Fourth*, Vol. 1, p. 539; Ross, *Edward IV*, p. 153. Charles Ross corrected the date of Edward's departure (given by the chronicler Warkworth as 29 Sept.) on the basis of the King's Lynn records.

32 For what follows see Livia Visser-Fuchs, '"Il n'a pas lion ne lieppart, qui voeulle tenir de sa part": Edouard IV in Exile, October 1470 to March 1471', in *L'Angleterre et les pays Bourguignons: relations et comparaisons (XVe–XVIe s.)*, ed. J.-M. Cauchies, Neuchâtel: Centre Europeen d'Etudes Bourguignonnes, 1995, 91–106; Livia Visser-Fuchs, 'Richard in Holland, 1470–1', *The Ricardian*, 6, 1983, pp. 220–8; M. Vale, 'An Anglo-Burgundian Nobleman and Art Patron: Louis de Bruges, Lord of la Gruthuyse and earl of Winchester', in *England and the Low Countries in the Late Middle Ages*, ed. C. Barron and N. Saul, Stroud: Alan Sutton, 1995, pp. 113–31; R. Horrox, 'Preparation for Edward IV's Return from Exile', *The Ricardian*, 6, 1982, pp. 124–7.

33 Scofield, *Edward the Fourth*, Vol. 1, pp. 551, 562, 566.

34 PRO, KB9/1052, no. 2.

35 Scofield, *Edward the Fourth*, Vol. 1, pp. 546–7.

36 Hammond, *Barnet and Tewkesbury*, p. 56.

37 *The Historie of the Arrivall of King Edward IV A.D. 1471*, ed. J. Bruce, London: Camden Society old series 1, 1838, p. 2.

38 Ross, *Edward IV*, p. 165; *Royal Commission on Historical Manuscripts, 12th report (Rutland mss)*, Appendix, Pt. 4, London: HMSO, 1888, pp. 2–4.

39 *Arrivall of Edward IV*, ed. Bruce, p. 11; Ross, *Edward IV*, p. 165; *Anchiennes Croniques d'Engleterre par Jehan de Wavrin*, ed. L.M.E. Dupont, 3 vols, Paris: Jules Renouard, 1858–63, Vol. 3, p. 210.

40 *Arrivall of Edward IV*, ed. Bruce, p. 2. H. Kleineke, 'Gerhard von Wesel's Newsletter from England, 17 April 1471', *The Ricardian*, 16, 2006, pp. 66–83, at p. 79. Charles Ross interpreted von Wesel's list of prisoners as referring to the men arrested in the autumn of 1470 immediately after Henry VI's restoration: Ross, *Edward IV*, p. 155 and n. 1.

41 Hammond, *Barnet and Tewkesbury*, p. 76.

42 Hammond, *Barnet and Tewkesbury*, pp. 76–7.

43 *Arrivall of Edward IV*, ed. Bruce, p. 30; P.A. Haigh, *The Military Campaigns of the Wars of the Roses*, Stroud: Sutton, 1995, pp. 131–4.

44   Hammond, *Barnet and Tewkesbury*, pp. 100–2.

45   Hammond, *Barnet and Tewkesbury*, pp. 103–5.

46   Hammond, *Barnet and Tewkesbury*, p. 105.

47   Hammond, *Barnet and Tewkesbury*, pp. 106–11.

48   *Calendar of State Papers Milan*, ed. Hinds, no. 220.

49   *Calendar of Close Rolls, 1468–76*, London: HMSO, 1953, no. 858.

6   RE-ESTABLISHING THE REGIME, 1471–5

1   PRO, CP40/839, rot. 96d.

2   For Danby see Norman Doe, 'Danby, Sir Robert', *Oxford Dictionary of National Biography*, *sub nomine*.

3   D.E. Lowe, 'The council of the prince of Wales and the decline of the Herbert family during the second reign of Edward IV (1471–1483)', *Bulletin of the Board of Celtic Studies*, 27, 1977, pp. 278–97.

4   *The Crowland Chronicle Continuations: 1459–1486*, ed. Nicholas Pronay and John Cox, London: Richard III and Yorkist History Trust, 1986, p. 147.

5   *Calendar of State Papers and Manuscripts existing in the Archives and Collections of Milan*, Vol. 1, 1385–1618, ed. A.B. Hinds, London: HMSO, 1912, nos. 229–30.

6   C. Ross, *Edward IV*, London: Eyre Methuen, 1974, p. 191; John Warkworth, *A Chronicle of the First Thirteen Years of the Reign of Edward IV (1461–74)*, ed. J.O. Halliwell, London: Camden Society old series 10, 1839, p. 25.

7   *Paston Letters and Papers of the Fifteenth Century*, ed. N. Davis, R. Beadle and C. Richmond, 3 vols, Oxford: Oxford University Press, 2004–5, Vol. 1, no. 268.

8   Ross, *Edward IV*, p. 192; Warkworth, *Chronicle*, ed. Halliwell, pp. 26–7.

9   P.J. Begent and H. Chesshyre, *The Most Noble Order of the Garter, 650 Years*, London: Spink, 1999, p. 313.

10   An apanage is the economic provision made for a younger child of a ruler.

11   C.D. Ross, *Richard III*, London: Eyre Methuen, 1981, p. 10.

12   *Calendar of the Patent Rolls, 1467–77*, London: HMSO, 1900, p. 297.

13   Ross, *Edward IV*, p. 188.

14   J.R. Lander, 'Attainder and Forfeiture, 1453–1509', *Historical Journal*, 4, 1961, p. 130.

15   Ross, *Edward IV*, p. 190.

16   *Paston Letters*, ed. Davis, Beadle and Richmond, Vol. 1, no. 277.

17   Ibid., no. 281.

18   Ross, *Edward IV*, pp. 190–1.

19   *Calendar of State Papers Milan*, ed. Hinds, no. 231.

20   Ross, *Edward IV*, pp. 212–13.

21   Ibid., pp. 211–12.

22   Ibid., pp. 210–11.

23   *Crowland Chronicle Continuations*, ed. Pronay and Cox, p. 135.

24   *Calendar of State Papers Milan*, ed. Hinds, no. 313; *Philippe de Commynes: Mémoires*, ed. Joël Blanchard, 2 vols, Geneva: Droz, 2007, Vol. 1, pp. 287–8.

25   *Philippe de Commynes*, ed. Blanchard, Vol. 1, pp. 289–91.

26   Ibid., p. 291.

27   Ross, *Edward IV*, p. 233.

28   Ross, *Richard III*, pp. 34–5.

29   Ross, *Edward IV*, p. 234.

30   *Philippe de Commynes*, ed. Blanchard, Vol. 1, p. 295.

31   Ibid., p. 281.

32   *Calendar of State Papers Milan*, ed. Hinds, no. 308.

33   Ibid., no. 313.

34   M. Jurkowski, C.L. Smith and D. Crook, *Lay Taxes in England and Wales, 1188–1688*, Kew: PRO, 1998, pp. 117–18.

7   THE FINAL YEARS, 1475–83

1   *Calendar of State Papers and Manuscripts Existing in the Archives and Collections of Milan*, Vol. 1, 1385–1618, ed. A.B. Hinds, London: HMSO, 1912, no. 355.

2.   Ibid., no. 366.

3   B.D. Williams, 'The Foreign Policy of Edward IV, 1475–1483 and the Anglo-Breton Marriage Alliance of 1481', *The Ricardian*, 7, 1986, pp. 270–80.

4   C. Ross, *Edward IV*, London: Eyre Methuen, 1974, p. 283.

5   Ibid., p. 290.

6   *The Crowland Chronicle Continuations: 1459–1486*, ed. Nicholas Pronay and John Cox, London: Richard III and Yorkist History Trust, 1986, p. 151; *Polydore Vergil's English History*, ed. Henry Ellis, London: Camden Society old series 29, 1844, p. 171.

7   *Calendar of State Papers Milan*, ed. Hinds, no. 313.

8   C.L. Schofield, *The Life and Reign of Edward the Fourth*, 2 vols, London: Longman, 1923, Vol. 2, pp. 184–8.

9   M.A. Hicks, *'False, Fleeting, Perjur'd Clarence': George, Duke of Clarence, 1449–1478*, 2nd, revised, edn, Bangor: Headstart History, 1992, p. 153.

10   Ibid., p. 121.

11   Ibid., p. 123.

12   *Crowland Chronicle Continuations*, ed. Pronay and Cox, p. 147.

13   Hicks, *Clarence*, p. 129.

14   Ibid., pp. 135–6.

15   *Polydore Vergil's English History*, ed. Henry Ellis, London: Camden Society old series 29, 1844, p. 168.

16   C.D. Ross, *Richard III*, London: Eyre Methuen, 1981, pp. 25–6, 33–4.

8   EDWARDIAN GOVERNMENT

1   William Herbert, the young heir of Edward's early supporter who had died at Edgcote in 1469, was stripped of his father's earldom of Pembroke, which was instead settled on the young Prince of Wales, and compensated with the earldom of Huntingdon, made available by the elevation of Edward's stepson, Thomas Grey, to the marquessate of Dorset; William, Lord Berkeley, whose claim to a share of the Mowbray inheritance was overridden by the terms of the settlement of the dukedom of Norfolk on Edward's younger son was compensated with a newly created viscountcy of Berkeley in 1481.

2   Charles Ross, *Edward IV*, London: Eyre Methuen, 1974, pp. 191, 193.

3   *The Crowland Chronicle Continuations: 1459–1486*, ed. Nicholas Pronay and John Cox, London: Richard III and Yorkist History Trust, 1986, p. 139.

4   J.R. Lander, 'The Yorkist Council and Administration, 1461–85', in J. R. Lander, *Crown and Nobility, 1450–1509*, London: Edward Arnold, 1976, pp. 171–90; J. R. Lander, 'Council, Administration and Councillors, 1461–85', ibid., pp. 191–219; Ross, *Edward IV*, 308–10; J.L. Watts, 'Ideas, Principles and Politics', in *The Wars of the Roses*, ed. A.J. Pollard, London: Macmillan, 1995, pp. 110–33; J. L. Watts, 'The Policie in Christen Remes: Bishop Russell's Parliamentary Sermons of 1483–84', in *Authority and consent in Tudor England: Essays presented to C.S.L. Davies*, ed. G.W. Bernard and S.J. Gunn, Aldershot: Ashgate, 2002, pp. 33–60.

5   Hannes Kleineke, 'Richard III and the Court of Requests', *The Ricardian*, 17, 2007, 22–32, pp. 23–4.

6   *Calendar of State Papers and Manuscripts Existing in the Archives and Collections of Milan*, Vol. 1, 1385–1618, ed. A.B. Hinds, London: HMSO, 1912, no. 240.

7   A.D.K. Hawkyard, 'From Painted Chamber to St. Stephen's Chapel: The Meeting Places of the House of Commons at Westminster until 1603', in *Housing Parliament:*

Dublin, Edinburgh and Westminster, ed. Clyve Jones and Sean Kelsey, Edinburgh: University Press, 2002, 62–84, pp. 65–6.

8   *The Parliament Rolls of Medieval England*, ed. C. Given-Wilson et al. 16 vols, Woodbridge: Boydell Press, 2005, Vol. 13, p. 64.

9   Ibid., p. 257.

10   Ibid., p. 354.

11   C.L. Scofield, *The Life and Reign of Edward the Fourth*, 2 vols, London: Longman, 1923, Vol. 1, p. 246.

12   R.G. Davies, 'The Attendance of the Episcopate in English Parliaments, 1376–1461', *Proceedings of the American Philosophical Society*, 129, 1985, pp. 30–81.

13   PRO, C49/55/14, 55; 56/14, 39; 58/19, 30, 60; 60/3, 18, 25, 28; 61/21, 26; 64/44, 45, 52, 60, 79; 65/7, 30, 37, 45, 53.

14   *Paston Letters and Papers of the Fifteenth Century*, ed. N. Davis, R. Beadle and C. Richmond, 3 vols, Oxford: Oxford University Press, 2004–5, Vol. 1, no. 173.

15   M. McKisack, *The Parliamentary Representation of the English Boroughs during the Middle Ages*, Oxford: Clarendon Press, 1932, pp. 61–5.

16   *Paston Letters*, ed. Davis, Beadle and Richmond, Vol. 1, no. 172.

17   *Calendar of Close Rolls, 1461–8*, London: HMSO, 1949, p. 160; PRO, C81/1492/15; *The History of Parliament: The Commons 1386–1421*, ed. J.S. Roskell, Linda Clark and Carole Rawcliffe, 4 vols, Stroud: Alan Sutton, 1992, Vol. 1, p. 59.

18   Lucy Brown, 'Continuity and Change in the Parliamentary Justifications of the Fifteenth-century Usurpations', in *The Fifteenth Century VII: Conflicts, Consequences and the Crown in the Late Middle Ages*, ed. L. Clark, Woodbridge: Boydell, 2007, pp. 157–73, esp. pp. 161–9.

19   For what follows see M. Jurkowski, 'Parliamentary and Prerogative Taxation in the Reign of Edward IV', *Parliamentary History*, 18, 1999, pp. 271–90.

20   M. Jurkowski, C.L. Smith and D. Crook, *Lay Taxes in England and Wales, 1188–1688*, Kew: PRO, 1998, pp. 109–10.

21   Ibid., pp. 110–11.

22   Ibid., p. 110.

23   *Calendar of State Papers Milan*, ed. Hinds, No. 282.

24   Jurkowski, Smith and Crook, *Lay Taxes*, pp. 115–17.

25   Ibid., pp. 118–19.

9 EDWARD: MAN AND MONARCHY

1   *Philippe de Commynes: Mémoires*, ed. Joël Blanchard, 2 vols, Geneva: Droz, 2007, p. 290.

2   *The Usurpation of Richard the Third*, ed. C.A.J. Armstrong, Gloucester: Alan Sutton, 1989, pp. 65, 67.

3   *Polydore Vergil's English History*, ed. Henry Ellis, London: Camden Society old series 29, 1844, p. 172.

4   Sir Thomas More, 'History of King Richard III', in *Richard III: The Great Debate*, ed. Paul Kendall London: Folio Society, 1965, p. 32.

5   *Ingulph's Chronicle of the Abbey of Croyland*, ed. H.T. Riley, London: Henry Bohn, 1854, p. 445.

6   *English Historical Literature in the Fifteenth Century*, ed. C.L. Kingsford, Oxford: Clarendon Press, 1913, pp. 385–7.

7   *Usurpation of Richard the Third*, ed. Armstrong, p. 65.

8   *Polydore Vergil*, ed. Ellis, p. 172.

9   *Usurpation of Richard the Third*, ed. Armstrong, p. 67.

10 More, 'Richard III', p. 37.

11 *Calendar of the Patent Rolls, 1476–85*, London: HMSO, 1901, p. 371.

12 *The Great Chronicle of London*, ed. A.H. Thomas and I.D. Thornley, London, 1939, p. 233.

13 S.A. Mileson, 'The Importance of Parks in Fifteenth-Century Society', in *The Fifteenth Century V: Of Mice and Men: Image, Belief and Regulation in Late Medieval England*, ed. L. Clark, Woodbridge: Boydell, 2005, pp. 19–37, p. 53; John Warkworth, *A Chronicle of the First Thirteen Years of the Reign of King Edward the Fourth*, ed. J.O. Halliwell, London: Camden Society original series 10, 1839, pp. 24–5; R. Fabyan, *The New Chronicles of England and France*, ed. H. Ellis, London: F.C. & J. Rivington, 1811, p. 654; PRO, C81/836/3323; C81/850/4006–7; C81/878/5406–9; E28/90/37; E101/411/13, f. 28v; E101/412/2, f. 10v; E404/72/4/55; E404/77/2/36; PSO1/29/1520–23; PSO1/35/1828; PSO1/42/2200; PSO1/43/2201–2.

14 *Usurpation of Richard the Third*, ed. Armstrong, p. 67.

15 More, 'Richard III', p. 32.

16 *The Crowland Chronicle Continuations: 1459–1486*, ed. Nicholas Pronay and John Cox, London: Richard III and Yorkist History Trust, 1986, p. 153.

17 *English Historical Literature*, ed. Kingsford, p. 386.

18 *Crowland Chronicle Continuations*, ed. Pronay and Cox, p. 149.

19 Ibid., p. 125.

20 Ibid., p. 151.

21 Ross, *Edward IV*, p. 9.

22 Ibid., p. 273.

23 E.g. PRO, E101/412/2, f. 32v; C.L. Schofield, *The Life and Reign of Edward the Fourth*, 2 vols, London: Longman, 1923, Vol. 2, p. 299.

24 Ross, *Edward IV*, pp. 273–4.

25 PRO, C49/55, no. 35.

26 *The Historie of the Arrivall of King Edward IV A.D. 1471*, ed. J. Bruce, London: Camden Society old series 1, 1838, p. 13.

27 *Paston Letters and Papers of the Fifteenth Century*, ed. N. Davis, R. Beadle and C. Richmond, 3 vols, Oxford: Oxford University Press, 2004–5, Vol. 2, no. 760; *Ingulph's Chronicle*, ed. Riley, p. 445.

28 *Arrivall of Edward IV*, ed. Bruce, pp. 13–14.

29 A.F. Sutton, L. Visser-Fuchs and P.W. Hammond, *The Reburial of Richard, Duke of York, 21–30 July 1476*, London: Richard III Society, 1996, pp. 2–3.

30 *Calendar of Papal Letters, 1458–1471*, ed. J.A. Twemlow, London: HMSO, 1933, p. 623.

31 PRO, E101/411/15, f. 14; *Historical Collections of a Citizen of London in the Fifteenth Century*, ed. J. Gairdner, London: Camden Society new series 17, 1876, p. 203, where the episode is found under the year 1458–9; whereas Simon Walker, 'Ive, William', *Oxford Dictionary of National Biography*, *sub nomine*, ascribes Say's censorship to the 1460s, it is not clear on what grounds.

32 Ross, *Edward IV*, p. 275; Helen Marsh Jeffries, 'The Composer John Plummer and St. George's Chapel', in *St. George's Chapel Windsor in the Fourteenth Century*, ed. N.E. Saul, Woodbridge: Boydell and Brewer, 2005, pp. 135–49; and see also the literature cited there.

33 Ross, *Edward IV*, p. 275; Tim Tatton-Brown, 'The Constructional Sequence and Topography of the Chapel and College Buildings at St George's', in *St George's Chapel in the Late Middle Ages*, ed. Colin Richmond and Eileen Scarff, Windsor: Dean and Chapter of Windsor, 2001, pp. 5–6.

34 PRO, E101/496/17.

35 PRO, E405/80, rot. 31.

36 PRO E36/113, fol. 44; E405/66, rot. 3.

37 Ross, *Edward IV*, p. 272.

38 *Historical Collections*, ed. Gairdner, p. 215.

39 Ross, *Edward IV*, p. 55.

40 PRO, E159/253, rot. 25.

41 *Crowland Chronicle Continuations*, ed. Pronay and Cox, p. 139.

42 *Usurpation of Richard the Third*, ed. Armstrong, p. 65.

43   *Polydore Vergil*, ed. Ellis, p. 172.

44   *Usurpation of Richard the Third*, ed. Armstrong, p. 67.

45   M.A. Hicks, *Edward IV*, London: Arnold, 2004, pp. 36–7, 51–2; 'Financial Memoranda of the Reign of Edward V', ed. R. Horrox, in *Camden Miscellany XXIX*, London: Royal Historical Society, 1987, pp. 209–10.

46   On this point, see David Starkey, 'Henry VI's Old Blue Gown: the English Court under the Lancastrians and Yorkists', *Court Historian*, 4, 1999, pp. 1–28.

47   *The Travels of Leo of Rozmital through Germany, Flanders, England, France, Spain, Portugal and Italy, 1465–1467*, ed. M. Letts, Cambridge: Cambridge University Press, 1957, p. 47.

48   Ibid., p. 45.

49   *Crowland Chronicle Continuations*, ed. Pronay and Cox, p. 149.

50   Schofield, *Edward the Fourth*, Vol. 1, p. 273.

51   Ibid., pp. 376–7.

52   Ross, *Edward IV*, p. 95.

53   M.A. Hicks, *'False, Fleeting, Perjur'd Clarence': George, Duke of Clarence, 1449–1478*, 2nd, revised, edn, Bangor: Headstart History, 1992, p. 130.

54   *Paston Letters*, ed. Davis, Beadle and Richmond, Vol. 1, no. 236.

55   Ross, *Edward IV*, p. 354.

56   PRO, E101/412/8.

57   *Crowland Chronicle Continuations*, ed. Pronay and Cox, p. 149.

58   *Usurpation of Richard the Third*, ed. Armstrong, p. 65.

59   *Crowland Chronicle Continuations*, ed. Pronay and Cox, p. 153.

60   M.A. Hicks, 'King in Lords and Commons: Three Insights into Late-Fifteenth-Century Parliaments 1461–85', in *People, Places and Perspectives*, ed. K. Dockray and P. Fleming, Stroud: Nonsuch, 2005, pp. 131–53.

61   Ross, *Edward IV*, p. 71.

10   THE END OF THE REIGN

1   *Philippe de Commynes: Mémoires*, ed. Joël Blanchard, 2 vols, Geneva: Droz, 2007, Vol. 1, p. 290; M.K. Jones, '1477 – The Expedition that Never Was: Chivalric Expectation in Late Yorkist England', *The Ricardian*, 12, 2001, p. 278.

2   *The Usurpation of Richard the Third*, ed. C.A.J. Armstong, Gloucester: Alan Sutton, 1989, p. 59.

3   *Philippe de Commynes*, ed. Blanchard, Vol. 1, pp. 480, 507.

4   *Polydore Vergil's English History*, ed. Henry Ellis, London: Camden Society original
     series 29, 1844, p. 171.

5   *Usurpation of Richard III*, ed. Armstrong, p. 59.

6   *Philippe de Commynes*, ed. Blanchard, Vol. 1, p. 480.

7   *Polydore Vergil*, ed. Ellis, p. 172.

8   Dean and Canons of Windsor mss, XI.B.6, rot. 2; *The Crowland Chronicle
     Continuations: 1459–1486*, ed. Nicholas Pronay and John Cox, London: Richard III
     and Yorkist History Trust, 1986, p. 153.

9   *Usurpation of Richard III*, ed. Armstrong, p. 69.

10 A.F. Sutton and L. Visser-Fuchs with R.A. Griffiths, *The Royal Funerals of the House
     of York at Windsor*, London: Richard III Society, 2005, p. 12.

11 Ibid., pp. 14–45.

12 Ibid., p. 86.

13 Ibid., p. 91.

14 Much ink has been and continues to be spilt on this subject. A useful summary
     may be found in M.A. Hicks, *Edward V*, Stroud: Tempus, 2003, pp. 167–89.

15 Sutton, Visser-Fuchs and Griffiths, *Royal Funerals*, pp. 30, 66–74, 106.

16 Ibid., pp. 111–24.

11   CONCLUSION

1   T.S. Freeman, '"Ut Verus Christi Sequester": John Blacman and the Cult of Henry
     VI', in *The Fifteenth Century V: Of Mice and Men: Image, Belief and Regulation in Late
     Medieval England*, ed. L. Clark, Woodbridge: Boydell, 2005, pp. 127–42.

2   Charles Ross, *Edward IV*, London: Eyre Methuen, 1974, p. 419.

3   Both quotes taken from C. Richmond, 'What Cade Did Not', *TLS*, 11 February 2005,
     p. 24.

4   Christine Carpenter, *The Wars of the Roses: Politics and the Constitution in England c.
     1437–1509*, Cambridge: Cambridge University Press, 1997, p. 204.

Index

Strange Histories

The Trial of the Pig, the Walking Dead, and Other Matters of Fact from the Medieval and Renaissance Worlds

Darren Oldridge

Strange Histories presents a serious account of some of the most extraordinary occurrences of European and North American history and explains how they made sense to people living at the time.

Using case studies from the Middle Ages and the early modern period, this book provides fascinating insights into the world-view of a vanished age and shows how such occurrences fitted in quite naturally with the "common sense" of the time. Explanations of these phenomena, riveting and ultimately rational, encourage further reflection on what shapes our beliefs today.

What made reasonable, educated men and women behave in ways that seem utterly nonsensical to us today? This question and many more are answered in the fascinating book.

ISBN13: 978-0-415-28860-6 (hbk)
ISBN13: 978-0-415-40492-1 (pbk)

Available at all good bookshops
For ordering and further information please visit:
www.routledge.com

Medieval Worlds
A Sourcebook

Edited by Roberta Anderson and Dominic Bellenger

Medieval Worlds is a comprehensive sourcebook for the study of western Europe from the fifth to the fifteenth century. The era was one of immense diversity and openness to new ideas in areas ranging from technology to natural philosophy.

The texts collected in this volume present a wide range of documentation, including chronicles, legal and official state and church papers, biographies, poems and letters. Covering the whole of Europe, the range of texts offered illustrates the complexity as well as the unity of the medieval world. Subjects range from the diverse worlds of monasteries, the papacy, the crusades and women to the different roles of town and countryside.

Complete with introductions and full commentary, a glossary and guides to further reading, *Medieval Worlds* is an essential source for all students of medieval history.

ISBN13: 978-0-415-25308-6 (hbk)
ISBN13: 978-0-415-25309-3 (pbk)